Caspar Whitney

A Sporting Pilgrimage

Riding to hounds, golf, rowing, football, club and university athletics. Studies in English sport, past and present

Caspar Whitney

A Sporting Pilgrimage
Riding to hounds, golf, rowing, football, club and university athletics. Studies in English sport, past and present

ISBN/EAN: 9783337288716

Printed in Europe, USA, Canada, Australia, Japan

Cover: Foto ©Andreas Hilbeck / pixelio.de

More available books at **www.hansebooks.com**

A SPORTING PILGRIMAGE

Riding to Hounds, Golf, Rowing, Football, Club and University Athletics. Studies in English Sport, Past and Present. By CASPAR W. WHITNEY. *Illustrated.*

New York: HARPER & BROTHERS, *Publishers.*
MDCCCXCV.

Copyright, 1894, by HARPER & BROTHERS.

All rights reserved.

PREFACE

The games of our college days and sports of our manhood are too often viewed in the light of mere athletic spectacles, where victory is the sole desideratum. Those who give the subject a little serious consideration, however, recognize the lessons of the play-ground as having most lasting and most beneficial effects.

Sport makes manly boys and gentle men; quickens the judgment, puts pluck in the heart and strength in the body. As Whyte-Melville once wrote, it "rouses manly qualities of body and mind, excites intellectual faculties and muscular powers, braces the nervous system, and stimulates arm, heart, and brain to healthful effort. Few true sportsmen but are frank of nature, kindly and generous."

Until comparatively recent years, we of the United States have been too thoroughly occupied with the work of building up a great nation to give much thought to play. Now, however, that sport in America is fast developing, it is essential to an intelligent understanding of this development and its purpose, to turn for our precedents to the country which cradled nearly every game we have. Hence, to thoroughly understand the present condition and the object of modern games in the United

Copyright, 1894, by HARPER & BROTHERS.

All rights reserved.

PREFACE

The games of our college days and sports of our manhood are too often viewed in the light of mere athletic spectacles, where victory is the sole desideratum. Those who give the subject a little serious consideration, however, recognize the lessons of the play-ground as having most lasting and most beneficial effects.

Sport makes manly boys and gentle men; quickens the judgment, puts pluck in the heart and strength in the body. As Whyte-Melville once wrote, it "rouses manly qualities of body and mind, excites intellectual faculties and muscular powers, braces the nervous system, and stimulates arm, heart, and brain to healthful effort. Few true sportsmen but are frank of nature, kindly and generous."

Until comparatively recent years, we of the United States have been too thoroughly occupied with the work of building up a great nation to give much thought to play. Now, however, that sport in America is fast developing, it is essential to an intelligent understanding of this development and its purpose, to turn for our precedents to the country which cradled nearly every game we have. Hence, to thoroughly understand the present condition and the object of modern games in the United

States, it is necessary to study their past traditions and present systems in England. With such an object the pilgrimage here recorded was undertaken.

There has been no intention of presenting detailed descriptions or elaborate history: there are here in these pages only the impressions of a student of amateur sport, who is deeply grateful for the opportunity of spreading the doctrine of sport for sport's sake only.

CONTENTS

CHAP.		PAGE
I.	THE ENGLISH SPORTING SPIRIT	3
II.	RIDING TO HOUNDS—IN THE "SHIRES"	24
III.	RIDING TO HOUNDS—IN THE "PROVINCES"	71
IV.	UNIVERSITY SPORTSMANSHIP	90
V.	ROWING—AT OXFORD AND CAMBRIDGE	114
VI.	ROWING—ON THE THAMES	157
VII.	UNIVERSITY FOOTBALL	179
VIII.	CLUB FOOTBALL	203
IX.	UNIVERSITY ATHLETICS	220
X.	CLUB ATHLETICS	278
XI.	CLUBS	301
XII.	CYCLING	310
XIII.	CRICKET	320
XIV.	GOLF	331
XV.	A BIT OF HISTORY	363
XVI.	FIRST LESSONS	382

ILLUSTRATIONS

	PAGE
WHIPPING IN A STRAGGLER	*Frontispiece*
CALLING OFF THE HOUNDS	5
CUTTING OUT THE WORK	8
IN FULL CRY	11
A STIFF WALL	15
"'WARE HORSE"	19
SAILING ON THE ISIS AT OXFORD	22
ON THE EXMOORS—GOING TO COVERT	25
WITH THE DEVON AND SOMERSET STAG-HOUNDS—A MEET AT CLOUTSHAM	27
AN ORDINARY THORN-HEDGE AND DITCH	31
WATER DITCH AND HEDGE-TOPPED BANK IN THE QUORN COUNTRY	35
A THORN FENCE IN THE BELVOIR COUNTRY	37
THORN FENCE IN THE COTTESMORE COUNTRY	39
THE QUORN HOUNDS	43
QUORN KENNELS	45
DOUBLE DITCH AND FENCED BANK	47
DITCH AND "STAKED-AND-BOUND" FENCE	50
BELVOIR HOUNDS—DUKE OF RUTLAND'S	53
BELVOIR KENNELS	57
A MEET OF THE PYTCHLEY HOUNDS AT ALTHORP PARK, EARL SPENCER'S RESIDENCE	59
PYTCHLEY HOUNDS	63
THE PYTCHLEY KENNELS	65
EARL SPENCER'S STABLES	69
AN OLD-TIME PYTCHLEY "OXER"	73
COTTESMORE STABLES	75
COTTESMORE HOUNDS	77
COTTESMORE KENNELS	79
LORD RIBBESDALE, MASTER OF THE QUEEN'S BUCK-HOUNDS	80
THE CRICKETERS' INN, A FAVORITE MEET OF THE QUEEN'S STAG-HOUNDS, AND THE VEHICLE IN WHICH CARTED DEER ARE HAULED	81

ILLUSTRATIONS

	PAGE
DEVON AND SOMERSET STAG-HOUNDS	83
A KILL WITH THE DEVON AND SOMERSET STAG-HOUNDS	86
DUKE OF RUTLAND'S GAMBLER	87
AN ENGLISH BEAGLE	88
THE CHRIST CHURCH (OXFORD) BEAGLES	89
AN UNDERGRADUATE'S ROOM AT CAMBRIDGE	93
AN ENGLISH FOOTBALL PLAYER	96
A COLLEGE BARGE	99
PUTNEY BRIDGE, STARTING-POINT OF THE OXFORD-CAMBRIDGE BOAT-RACE	102
AN ORDINARY PUNT	103
AT OXFORD—LOOKING UP THE ISIS FROM FOLLY BRIDGE	105
AT CAMBRIDGE—LOOKING UP THE CAM	109
AT THE STARTING-POSTS OF A BUMPING RACE	115
"TUBBING"	120
THE ORIGINAL "TUB"	120
A COACHING "TUB"	121
A "CLINKER" FOUR-OAR	123
PROCESSION OF EIGHTS ON THE ISIS, OXFORD—SALUTING THE 'VARSITY	127
THE OXFORD COURSE	132
THE CAMBRIDGE COURSE	133
MR. LEHMANN COACHING OXFORD FROM HORSEBACK	135
OXFORD EIGHT-OARED BOAT—INTERIOR VIEW, LOOKING FORWARD, SHOWING POSITIONS OF SEATS AND FIXED ROWLOCKS	137
OXFORD UNIVERSITY BOAT-HOUSE	139
DIAGRAM OF BUMPING RACE	140
A "BUMP"	143
OXFORD TAKING OUT BOAT	147
RACING EIGHTS ON THE ISIS, OXFORD	149
THE BARRIER AT PUTNEY BRIDGE	153
COURSE OF OXFORD-CAMBRIDGE ANNUAL RACE FROM PUTNEY TO MORTLAKE	154
TRAINING QUARTERS OF THE OXFORD CREW AT PUTNEY	159
THE HENLEY COURSE—SCENE OF HENLEY REGATTA	162
TRAINING QUARTERS OF THE CAMBRIDGE CREW AT PUTNEY	165
LEANDER ROWING CLUB BOAT-HOUSE AT PUTNEY—USED BY CAMBRIDGE	167
LONDON ROWING CLUB BOAT-HOUSE AT PUTNEY—USED BY OXFORD	169
THE LONDON, LEANDER, AND THAMES ROWING CLUBS—LOOKING UP THE THAMES	171
RUGBY UNION SCRIMMAGE	181
THE ETON WALL GAME	183
A WINCHESTER "HOT"	187
"DRIBBLING" IN THE ASSOCIATION GAME	189
"PASSING"	193

ILLUSTRATIONS

	PAGE
PUTTING THE BALL IN PLAY FROM SIDE LINES IN RUGBY UNION	195
PUTTING THE BALL IN PLAY—RUGBY	197
"HEADING"	201
BLACKHEATH FOOTBALL GROUNDS AND CLUB-HOUSE	205
A BRADFORD CLUB FOOTBALL CROWD	209
YORK VS. ENGLAND	213
ASSOCIATION FOOTBALL FIELD	217
OXFORD ATHLETIC FIELD AND CLUB-HOUSE	223
CAMBRIDGE ATHLETIC AND CRICKET FIELD AND CLUB-HOUSE	227
QUEEN'S CLUB, LONDON—FOOTBALL AND ATHLETIC FIELD	233
DIAGRAM OF QUEEN'S CLUB GROUNDS	237
OXFORD RACQUET AND FIVES COURTS	239
TYPE OF ENGLISH HURDLE	241
THE WATER HAZARD ON THE RANELAGH GOLF LINKS	259
THE OXFORD TRACK ATHLETIC TEAM WHICH MET AND DEFEATED YALE	268–269
THE YALE TRACK ATHLETIC TEAM WHICH MET OXFORD	273
LONDON ATHLETIC CLUB GROUNDS, AT STAMFORD BRIDGE	279
QUEEN'S CLUB—RACQUET AND TENNIS COURTS	283
BRADFORD A. C. CLUB-HOUSE AND GROUNDS	287
BRADFORD CRICKET CREASE AND HOUSE	289
RICHMOND ATHLETIC FIELD AND CLUB-HOUSE	291
POLE VAULTING ON A MATTRESS AT BRADFORD	295
POLO-FIELD AND RACE-TRACK, RANELAGH CLUB	297
INTERIOR OF PRINCE'S CLUB	302
PRINCE'S CLUB-HOUSE	303
HAMPTON COURT, FROM GARDEN—SITE OF ONE OF THE OLDEST TENNIS-COURTS	305
THE SPORTS' CLUB	308
KENNINGTON OVAL	313
LORD'S—SHOWING PUBLIC STAND ON THE RIGHT	321
THE PAVILION AT LORD'S	325
OXFORD CRICKET-GROUND AND CLUB-HOUSE	327
ALMOST AS EXCITING AS SALMON FISHING	332
PLAN OF GOLFING COURSE, ST. ANDREWS	333
A VIEW OF THE ST. ANDREWS LINKS	335
"BUNKERED"	338
CLUB-HOUSE AND HOME HOLE, ST. ANDREWS	339
A LOST BALL	341
HOLE O' CROSS, HEATHERY HOLE, HIGH HOLE, AND THE RIVER EDEN, ST. ANDREWS	342
ROYAL NORTH DEVON CLUB-HOUSE AND FIRST TEEING-GROUND, WESTWARD HO	343
LOOKING TOWARDS THE SEA, WESTWARD HO	345

ILLUSTRATIONS

	PAGE
PLAN OF THE GOLFING COURSE OF THE ST. GEORGE'S GOLF CLUB	348
THE "SAHARA"	349
ST. GEORGE'S CLUB-HOUSE, SANDWICH	351
"WALKINSHAW'S GRAVE"	352
"HELL" BUNKER	353
THE "MAIDEN"	355
A VIEW OF HOYLAKE	357
ROYAL LIVERPOOL CLUB-HOUSE, HOYLAKE	359
A HOYLAKE PUTTING-GREEN	361
MODERN GOLF CLUBS	365
HOLDING CLUB—CORRECT POSITION	367
BACK VIEW—BEGINNING OF FULL SWING FOR DRIVING—INCORRECT POSITION	370
BACK VIEW—BEGINNING OF FULL SWING FOR DRIVING—CORRECT POSITION	371
FRONT VIEW—BEGINNING OF FULL SWING FOR DRIVING—INCORRECT POSITION	372
FRONT VIEW—BEGINNING OF FULL SWING FOR DRIVING—CORRECT POSITION	373
THE WAGGLE	383
FRONT VIEW—ENDING OF FULL SWING AFTER DRIVE—INCORRECT POSITION	384
FRONT VIEW—ENDING OF FULL SWING AFTER DRIVE—CORRECT POSITION	385
BACK VIEW—ENDING OF FULL SWING AFTER DRIVE—CORRECT POSITION	386
BACK VIEW—ENDING OF FULL SWING AFTER DRIVE—INCORRECT POSITION	387
FRONT VIEW OF FEET FOR DRIVING—CORRECT POSITION	388
FRONT VIEW OF FEET FOR DRIVING—INCORRECT POSITION	388
ADDRESSING BALL FOR DRIVE—CORRECT POSITION	389
CORRECT POSITION OF FEET IN HIGH LOFTING	389
FRONT VIEW—BEGINNING OF HIGH-LOFTING STROKE	390
FRONT VIEW—FINISH OF HIGH-LOFTING STROKE	391
FRONT VIEW—GETTING OUT OF A BUNKER	392
LOFTING A STIMIE	393
FRONT VIEW—BEGINNING OF THREE-QUARTER SWING	393
FRONT VIEW—ENDING OF THREE-QUARTER SWING	394
BEGINNING OF HALF IRON SHOT—CORRECT POSITION	395
ENDING OF HALF IRON SHOT—CORRECT POSITION	395
FRONT VIEW—PUTTING—CORRECT POSITION	396
FRONT VIEW—PUTTING—INCORRECT POSITION	396

A SPORTING PILGRIMAGE

I

THE ENGLISH SPORTING SPIRIT

I AM well aware I shall be exposing myself to a charge of triteness by proclaiming, what every one already knows, that the average Britisher is an athlete, the English nation an athletic one, and its subjects, both men and women, more universally and genuinely imbued with the spirit than those of any other race on earth. But one must journey to England, and watch the native at play on his own soil, study his traditions and systems, and marvel at the completeness with which every opportunity is developed, to fully appreciate the extraordinary interest and the widespread activity taken in every branch of sport.

When first I reached London, and struggled to keep comfortably warm by the feeble heat of the tiny grates that are indigenous to the country, I thought I had discovered whence arose this athletic predilection.

It seemed to me, as I sat at my writing-table wrapped in my steamer rug in a desperate and chilly endeavor to thaw out the Muse, that the Englishman must, in self-defence, seek exercise of some kind to keep his blood from congealing. At this writing, however, I confess my first impressions to have been libellous, and acknowledge the Englishman an athlete for the very good and simple reason that it is bred in the bone, and because he inhales a sporting atmosphere from the very day he is old enough to trundle a cricket ball on the village common.

It puzzles one to decide on what sport to write first or where to begin your studies of traditions, for here, indeed, is an embarrassment of riches. If you arrive in the hunting season you immediately decide that none can possibly have so great a following, a conclusion you straightway realize to have been hasty when you view the absorbing interest football excites; and later, when these give place to rowing and cricket, you are persuaded that each in its turn must be the national sport. And thus, if you will take my advice, you had best leave the question of the most popular game, for, indeed, every sport is the national one in its season; only painstaking and lengthy mathematical calculation could settle the matter definitely. I have been endeavoring, since ever the good ship *Ems* landed me at Southampton, to determine upon the particular game that might be called the national one, but up to date I have succeeded only in drawing forth criticism on my lack of discernment.

It is a nation of sport lovers, from "me lord" that follows the hounds, to the very costermonger racing his whippets — a survival, by-the-way, of the time of the Stuarts. Heretofore the particular sport of the more humble classes, whippet racing has been but lately raised to a more elevated plane. There is a movement to make the sport something beyond a struggle between costermongers' dogs down a lane of shouting spectators, with the masters standing at the finish for the encouragement of their respective entries, and the National Whippet Racing Club, recently organized under the presidency of Sir John Astley, intends inaugurating regular meetings which it is hoped may be made as fashionable as they now are popular.

The American sportsman marvels at this enormous general participation in all sport, just as he stares in won-

CALLING OFF THE HOUNDS

derment at the pheasants he may see feeding in fields as peacefully as barn fowls—and quite as indifferent to onlookers—or plentifully stocking the poulterers' shops in London; or, if he happens to hail from New York, as he is amazed at having violets for one penny (two cents) a bunch offered him along Piccadilly.

It seems as if every animal and every tree in Great Britain had some one to care for it, and every Englishman to move in an atmosphere of sport. Even the very drivers of the stages, that ramify London most conveniently, economically, and quickly, throw their whip with a sportsman's air, and handle the reins with a skill altogether superior to any similar class of jehus I have ever seen. And what a good type of horse they drive! Would that our own Fifth Avenue Stage Company could be induced to replace its present stock of tottering and spare-ribbed toilers with the stout, good-looking horses of the London 'bus.

It is hardly necessary to say that with every branch of sport filled to overflowing, the papers naturally cater to the public taste by giving unlimited space to each in season. You will find a column and a half of hunting meets, and an entire page of a daily sporting paper completely taken up with brief reports of football matches. The London papers teem with fixtures—swimming, football, athletics, lacrosse, hunting, steeple-chasing, horse-racing, boxing, racquets, lawn-tennis, single-stick, fencing, hockey, rabbit-coursing, water polo, ice and roller skating, dog shows, cattle shows, horse shows, even cat shows (with six hundred entries), to say nothing of fairs and other such provincial entertainment, with which we are somewhat familiar in our own country. The horse and dog shows are not confined to London; they are held in various sections of the country at different times throughout the year, but in winter the best producing shires (counties) of Great Britain send the pick of their horses to the hackney, shire, and hunter shows that are held successively at Islington. And the success of these shows seemed to me directly traceable to the wholesome competition between counties, which brings in touch so many workers for the common betterment.

The types of mankind I saw as participants and spectators furnished me the most interesting studies of my trip, for not only do "the people" have their own sports, but one finds them at all those of the gentry. If you go to a meeting of the stag or fox hounds you will see

CUTTING OUT THE WORK

—I was almost going to say hundreds—certainly scores of people on foot as keen for the sport as those on horseback. You will find them not only at the covert side, but following the chase, and I have counted them in at the death. This, I may add, is much more common in stag than in fox hunting, because the configuration of country in the former gives these enthusiasts on occasions a better opportunity of keeping up with the field. You will discover them, where opportunity affords, on the golf links watching the play, around the judging rings of the horse shows, as keenly observant of the awards as the master-horseman; you will see them at the university athletic sports, on the banks of the Isis and of the Cam, at Oxford and Cambridge, joining in the general enthusiasm of the boat-racing, while at Putney they will blacken the banks of the Thames in front of the club-houses of the two 'varsity crews, waiting for the boats to be launched, and stand for hours watching the practice. Needless to say you will find them in unlimited numbers at the football, and even at the cricket match, which draws a larger proportion of the gentry than probably any other of the English sports, except the Oxford and Cambridge boat-race on the Thames.

I think the character of spectators at the horse shows impressed me most strongly, because these are not the mere amusement-giving spectacles of a football match or boat-race, and require a certain love of the animal and an appreciation of its qualities, and I thought I could detect in this keen interest among all classes that which has given "little England" so honorable a place in horse-breeding.

It is after witnessing this general outpouring of all sorts and conditions of men that one begins to understand why Great Britain is so pre-eminently a sporting nation.

Moreover, this interest of the people is fostered by all English sportsmen; by the hunts, the universities, and by sporting clubs. Every opportunity is taken to encourage their attendance. You may even read in your London morning paper, while the Oxford and Cambridge crews are at Putney for their final work, the precise hour that each will take its daily practice on the Thames. There is no sport out-of-doors, so far as I have been able to discover, where the people are not welcome, and there are no spectators more enthusiastic in their support or more solicitous that the best man should win.

Maybe I can give no better illustration of this universal participation in sport than to say that in the town of Oxford, which has a population of about 50,000, there are sixteen football clubs, exclusive of the university teams, and that in Oxfordshire (*i.e.*, the town and county), with about as many inhabitants as New Haven, the site of Yale, there are upwards of one hundred teams that play the game regularly throughout the season. It is to be supposed, of course, that the interest about Oxford would be keener than elsewhere; but the illustration is a fair one, and a comparison with New Haven, which supports but very few teams outside of the university, quite in order. The number of football-players in England is legion. I have endeavored to form some accurate estimate of the total, but am unable to get results in time for publication here. However, I should say it would make a fair comparison with the players of the entire United States; though I should be much surprised to learn, as an English football enthusiast claimed to me, that there were quite as many, for the United States is a very large country, and the game has spread wonderfully and generally in the last two years. One reads, by-the-way, of no silly and ignorantly based objections (such as some of our

IN FULL CRY

papers printed last winter) to football in England, which is hardly explained by the play not being so hard or so "brutal" as ours, for the accidents in Association games are greatly in excess of what we have, but because the nation knows by long experience that it is good for the coming generation, and the "disturbing brother" dare not raise his voice.

Another illustration of the widespread popularity of athletics that extends to the very lowest social stratum, is furnished by the association of restaurant waiters in London, which, although hardly amateur, nevertheless emphasizes what I am endeavoring to tell the American public of the universal sporting spirit in England. Indeed, even the advertisement columns of the London press bespeak the breadth of this spirit, for one reads of some very curious matches, which the following, quoted *verbatim*, will go to prove:

"MR. FURNISS will sing a linnet against a linnet, one in the mouth, an home-and-home race, for £2 a side. A match can be made by calling at the Elephant and Castle, Orchard Street, Westminster, any evening after eight P.M."

It may be opportune to comment, in passing, on the exceedingly low entrance fee to all sporting entertainments in Great Britain. The popular charge at athletic, football, and cricket matches is a shilling (25 cents), with probably a sixpence (12 cents), or two shillings at most, to the reserved enclosure; at the horse shows a shilling gives you admission, and sixpence buys your catalogue.

There is something going on all the time, winter and summer. Those who cannot or care not to ride to hounds follow the harriers or the beagles or the otter-hounds on foot, of which there are a number of packs in the country, or attend the military tournaments in London, where they see the most skilful lemon-cutting, tent-pegging, fencing, single-stick play, bareback wrestling, and other feats common to such entertainments, while boxing and water polo and all known out-door games on land and water give ample field for the expansion of athletic tendencies. Even lacrosse, one of the very few American games that were not cradled in England, flourishes, I am sorry to say (sorry for our sportsmanship, though glad for the sake of a grand game), more than it does in the United States. There are several county teams, and a regularly instituted championship.

Baseball, too, is struggling for an existence. It may not be said to have actually attained favor in England, but there is a serious attempt to introduce it among the professional association foot-ball clubs in order to give players a summer game, and club managers an opportunity for reimbursement after the drain incidental to high-salaried cracks. Nothing tangible has developed, however, and the game seems to have done better among the amateurs, in the several districts where it has been attempted. Three or four years ago there was not an amateur club in all England, but in 1893 a dozen or more competed for senior and junior trophies, and immediately about London there is a sufficient number to have established a local-supremacy contest in the season just closed. Still, the game is not played by the best class, or, in most instances, by even a good class of athletes.

That the bicycle is quite as popular in England as in America may be supposed, and I might add that the amateur status of the racing men is even more questionable, if that be possible. As with us, the manufacturer's hireling has professionalized the sport from end to end of Great Britain, and driven *bona fide* amateurs out of active competition. The present state of affairs, indeed, is deplor-

A STIFF WALL

able, and the Cyclists' Union seems not only to be unable to improve it, but, worse to relate, has recently passed resolutions which emphasize its indifference to the situation.

Track athletes are countless, and although not quite such flagrant offenders against the ethics of amateur sport as the racing class of cyclists—chiefly because the Amateur Athletic Association has some very earnest workers, and does honestly strive to keep athletics clean—the general amateur status none the less is considerably below the standard of purity.

Book-makers at games are all too common, and " sharp " practices that go even so far as " roping," selling races, and running men " to order," are prevalent at nearly all the meetings. Outside of the universities and a very few clubs—so few as to be counted on the fingers of one hand —one may say there is no honesty (from an amateur point of view) in athletics in all of England. Certainly a disgraceful state of affairs in a nation of such sporting proclivities.

Although our own condition, outside of the colleges, is not all that we should like it to be, yet is there much to be thankful for that we have not reached such a depth of athletic degradation.

It is gratifying to record in this sweeping denunciation of English track athletics that the Scottish Amateur Athletic Association, in making strenuous efforts to cleanse its ranks, recently passed some rules to the point, among others " that the payment by clubs, to competitors, of travelling, hotel, and other expenses is strictly prohibited." I should explain that this expense question is one of the loop-holes for the escape of the dishonestly inclined. It will amuse American athletes to read that this Association has just reached the modern methods long in vogue with us by deciding that in broad jumping "any competitor touching the pit in front of the taking-off mark shall have such jump disallowed."

That cross-country running flourishes in England may be imagined when I say that at the Junior championships which I attended near London, although the rain came down in torrents throughout the entire afternoon, and the going was extremely heavy, upwards of 130 competitors finished out of 150 starters, and some 2000 spectators remained to the end. But, sad to relate, here, too, the amateur status is quite as reprehensible as in the track athletics.

I have already alluded to the great numbers that play football, and it is too bad to spoil the picture by adding that outside of the universities its ethical standard is only a very little above that of track athletics.

Professionalism infests the game literally from end to end of Great Britain. In Association football it is legalized, and regularly organized leagues like unto our professional baseball are maintained; but there are also innumerable clubs that, while posing as amateur, are really as far from being such as those who openly hire their players. Indeed, the professional taint so thoroughly permeates Association football wherever it is played, that outside of the universities few club teams are honestly amateur. Rugby Union has not fallen so far from grace, though the pro-amateur abounds and is increasing; but, thanks to the supervision of efficient officials, there yet remains plenty of genuine amateur Rugby football.

Of horse-racing and steeple-chasing I can only say now, before treating them at length another time, that both attract vast crowds, and the condition of the second, outside of the hunt clubs, provokes unceasing scandal.

I have not touched on sport with rod and gun, because

"'WARE HORSE!"

my visit to England was not in the season for me to have seen any of it. It is difficult for me, however, after moving in the atmosphere of this great sporting nation, to reconcile with other impressions the Englishman's pheasant and grouse driving, where hundreds of birds are slaughtered, and the size of the bag seems to be the chief attainment. The American sportsman, who declines to shoot a doe, and is satisfied when his bag is large enough to furnish a bird to his own table and to a few of his friends, finds it hard to bring himself in touch with this side of the British sportsman.

Probably it is a degree of refinement in sport we have not yet reached, nor, if I know the American sportsman (I ignore the few men who jack and hound deer), are we likely ever to develop it. It is undoubtedly true that a certain skill is required to bring down every rocketing pheasant that comes within reach of your gun, or every hard-going grouse on which you pull trigger; but sitting behind battues and having your game driven to you seems, from an American point of view, to savor more of "pot hunting" than sport.

This chapter would be incomplete were I not to comment on an exhibition of yacht models and of canoes and small sailing-craft I had the good-fortune to attend in London. I want particularly to mention it because it appears to offer a suggestion to American yacht and canoe men that is well worth considering. As I have elsewhere intimated, the great secret of the universal interest in all kinds of sport in England seems to me to be the publicity of it all; the opportunity every man so inclined has of being a spectator, if not a participant; the taking, as it were, of the public into their confidence by the sportsmen. Unquestionably it is true that if you wish to excite general attention, whether in sport or what

SAILING ON THE ISIS AT OXFORD
Showing Shape and Rigging of the Local Centre-boarder

not, the surest way of doing so is to give the people a look in, and one cannot realize just how many different kinds and classes may be interested until the experiment has been made.

Here at this show in London, for instance, to say nothing of the crowds of landsmen, I saw all classes of yachtsmen, from those owning a racing eighty-footer or a sea-going steam-yacht down to the very waterman that plies his trade on the Thames.

There seems to be no good reason why our yacht clubs— the New York, the Larchmont, the Eastern, the Seawanhaka-Corinthian, and canoe clubs, of which there are so many, should not unite in one general and certainly very instructive exhibition of models. Aside from the pleasure it would give yacht and canoe men, there can be no doubt of its creating a more universal yachting spirit among our people; and that, it appears to me, is worth trying for.

It will be hardly necessary to discuss English yacht lines, of which there were, at this show, models of about every type, for our international contests have made them rather familiar. Those of the cruising-canoes and small sailing-craft, however, are rather strange to us, the lines being much fuller and the construction much heavier—a style of craft made necessary by the open waters on which some of the sailing is done. The exhibition of racing-canoes was meagre, but the few shown proved that the English designers could study American models with profit, while the sail area was very much smaller, comparatively speaking, than what we are accustomed to see on our waters. The "Canadian" canoes on view were hardly up to the best products of that home of canoe men, and were more than likely built in England and dubbed Canadian for trade purposes.

The most interesting feature of the exhibition was a style of craft put down on the catalogue as a canoe-yawl. This is built for river and estuary sailing, and the one I particularly studied was about eighteen feet long by four and one-half feet beam—certainly a most stanch-looking little affair, but fitted with much less sail than it seemed it should be able to carry. These yawls are built also for sea-going purposes, and used considerably as tenders on sailing-yachts of over eighty tons, in which case they measure about twenty feet water-line length by five feet beam. Just at the time I am writing the Royal Canoe Club is busy considering a change of rules regarding the modelling and constructing of racing-canoes. The bulb keel has appeared, and there seems to be a general tendency, as with us, to keep from building mere racing-machines.

II

RIDING TO HOUNDS

IN THE "SHIRES"

In England, riding to hounds forms a component part of the sportsman's education. You need not go into the country to learn the lesson. You have only to walk about London for complete conviction, as hunting subjects greet you at every turning—in the daily and weekly press, on the walls of the hotels, and in the shop windows. Wherever you go in the country you find the same evidence. Farmers and cabbies, almost invariably to be seen in breeches and leggings, adorn their wives and sweethearts with sporting jewelry, and follow the runs of the local hunt enthusiastically, while even the time-honored cock of the weather-vane, that rules undisturbed in most countries, is, in rural England, superseded by Reynard.

It will give results somewhat interesting to cast up the number of men and women who during the season ride to hounds, though I do not pretend to absolutely authentic figures, but present merely a bit of rough calculation that will convey an idea of its popularity. There are about 168 packs of fox and 14 of stag hounds in England, 20 of fox and 5 of stag hounds in Ireland, and 10 of fox-hounds in Scotland, with kennels holding all the way from 12 to 80 couple each. The Meath (Ireland) hounds are out five days of the seven, but all the Leicestershire and the best "provincial" packs in England, the Tipperary, the Kildare (Ireland), the Duke of Buccleuch's, and the Earl of Eglinton's (Scotland) hunt four days.

A very large number, of course, meet three days, and a few packs of fox-hounds in less-favored districts and practically all the stag-hounds hunt only twice each week, so that three would probably be the fair average figure of weekly runs.

The average number of mounts at the meets is not so easily estimated; in the "shires" 500 is not unusual in

ON THE EXMOORS—GOING TO COVERT

the height of the season, rarely less than 300 are seen, and 200 is considered somewhat of a poor turning out. In the Meath country, the Leicestershire of Ireland, 300 would probably be a gala field and 200 the usual limit. With the Devon and Somerset stag-hounds, which stand first in quality of sport and second to none in quantity of following, the fields are of huge proportions, as the illustration of the Cloutsham meet will show. Your Devonshire host will smile compassionately as you wax eloquent over the big fields of 500 you have seen at the Quorn covert-side, and take you out the next day to a meet at the Quantocks, and show you, likely as not, half as many again, on foot and in saddle, awaiting the " Hark together! hark! and forrard away" of huntsman Anthony Huxtable as the noblest beast of chase breaks covert. But there is only one Exmoor and one pack of real stag-hunting hounds in England.

The Ward Union, in the Meath country, and her Majesty's, and Lord de Rothschild's are the most prominent of the other stag-hounds, and attract about equally in number of following, which would be that between the "shires" and the more popular provinces; in the best of the latter, 200 is not an infrequent field and 100 an average. While few meets in England fail to bring out 100 horsemen and women, there are packs in outlying and sparsely settled districts where not more than 50 may be seen at the covert-side. It seems as if 100 would be a fair number, but to be within bounds let us call 75 the average that hunt three times a week, or 225 at each covert-side, which, multiplied by the number of hunts (217), gives the very considerable figure of 48,825 that are following hounds every week of England's season of five months. Even taking 50 as the average number, which is greatly underestimated, I think, we yet have the very respectable total of 32,550, and this computation has ignored completely the Harriers, of which there are 108 packs in England alone, 27 in Ireland, and 3 in Scotland, with from 8 to 35 couple each, to say nothing of the 35 packs of beagles in England. To be sure, these do not have such a following as the fox and stag hounds, but nevertheless they swell the grand total, and give strength to the argument, often heard after a good day's run, that hunting has

WITH THE DEVON AND SOMERSET STAG-HOUNDS—A MEET AT CLOUTSHAM

Vickery Bros.

about as many active followers among the best class as football or cricket.

What shall we say now of a national sport after this showing? Riding to hounds would seem to demand some consideration in the calculation, these figures being unquestioned proof of its popularity, while the amount of capital expended annually in the chase is greater probably than that in all the other sports combined.

A few years ago the usual estimate for maintaining a thoroughly first-class pack was $2500 per year for every day hunted; then it went up to $3000, and now it will average very close to $3500, making an annual cost of $10,500 for three days a week's chase of the little red animal, while in the "shires" it will fall but very little short of $15,000, if, indeed, it will not in some instances run higher.

And all this a tribute to fashion! The sportsmen of the old régime were not so fastidious as to pink and tops, nor required such a retinue of servants. Hunting was the sole incentive, and they had fully as much sport and killed just about as many foxes, even if their hunts were not turned out in such elaborate fashion. Nowadays, however, the master who neglects to put the hunt afield in the best style fails in office quite as much as if he missed giving good sport. The huntsman, two whippers-in, and two second horsemen must all be turned out in pink and leathers, and the huntsman and first whip have two good horses a day; and it takes money, and plenty of it, to support a hunt on this scale. Then there is the servant who goes afoot to dig out the fox when he has gone to earth, and the eight to ten dollars to the gamekeepers for each find on their respective beats. Besides which horses and hounds have frequently to be conveyed by train to distant meets, while there are few hunts that are not obliged to hire coverts to save them from falling into the hands of shooting tenants, to say nothing of the care and expense of keeping them up once they are rented.

It is not very difficult to see where $10,000 to $15,000 per year goes when it is remembered that the basis of all this sport and fashion is the kennels and stables, with their 50 to 60 couple of hounds and 30 to 40 head of horses, that must be fed and receive the very best of care from the most capable and trustworthy attendants.

Then, too, there is the damage fund, which grows larger as cultivation extends, and that *bête noire* of the English hunting-field, the free lance, increases in numbers and impudence. Not that all free lances are wilfully destructive, but they are quite a number in that large class of men who, owning not an acre themselves, fail to realize that while no single individual may cause a very great amount of destruction, the combined efforts of a large field will make sufficient havoc to work serious injury to the farmer who, even with fortune smiling upon him, can barely make both ends meet.

The free-lance problem is an ever-vexing one in England, and, indeed, I think the English hunting season reveals more men who live at some one else's expense than may be found at any one time or place on this earth. These light-hearted souls flit from shire to shire, sometimes taking their own cattle, quite as often exacting a mount from the good-natured and well-provided friends with whom they invariably stop, and never by any chance put themselves down for a shilling on the hunt clubs' subscription-books. All sorts of schemes have been suggested to run this hunting parasite to earth, an elaborate system of badges among others, but he will probably continue his flight unmolested until masters introduce a sliding-scale subscription and insist that every man who

AN ORDINARY THORN-HEDGE AND DITCH

follows the hounds shall pay his mite towards their maintenance. At present a subscriber puts down his name for a lump sum whether he rides one day or the four, and the necessary feature seems to be a fee that will discriminate. It certainly is not fair that the man who has a couple or three hunters and turns out once or twice a week, should subscribe so much as the one with a stud of ten or a dozen, and who hunts every day of the six.

As a general thing, the sporting spirit of the Englishman makes him careful of injuring the farmer, and punctilious in paying for the damage he inflicts. And in this he is met more than half-way by the farmer himself, whose sportsmanship, indeed, has been severely tested by the droughts and poor crops of the past few seasons. In fact, I am quite sure that nowhere is the general sporting spirit of England so much in evidence as in the hunting field. The most democratic gathering in Great Britain may be seen at the covert-side, where nobility, untitled gentry, and labor often meet for a purpose common to all. Horseflesh maintains a more universal aristocracy, for, as a rule, the average is about the same, each country requiring a standard which all endeavor to reach, whether to be in the vogue, or for the more practical purpose of living with the hounds.

I think, however, the most surprising experience to the on-looking American at the covert-side is the number of people on foot he sees, not only at the throw-off, but throughout the run.

Only those thoroughly well acquainted with the country can hope to find "shanks' mare" a satisfactory mount, but these seem almost by instinct to know the direction in which the fox is running, and you are sure to find a fair percentage invariably up with the hounds when there happens to be a check, unless, of course, the run has been of that rapturous nature described as "a quick thing over a grass country, strongly enclosed, in a good place, and only half a dozen men with the hounds." And the most notable feature of this outpouring is that not all on foot are, as one might naturally suppose, the hale and hearty members of the country's youth; hale and hearty are they, to be sure, and of both sexes, but many there are walking in the long shadows of their life's sun.

The hunting-fields of England are by no means monopolized by the early lustiness of vigorous manhood; at every meet I attended I saw men in the "sear and yellow," who, while probably taking few of the jumps—a comment equally applicable to the majority of an English field—usually kept as close to the hounds as the average of much younger years.

Even the people—the tillers of the soil, the miners in the collieries, the workmen in the foundries, the artisans in the factories—are all thoroughly imbued with the spirit, and in districts where these industries flourish, and where hunting is carried on despite the encroachments of trade, begrimed laborers join in the chase as enthusiastically as the most faultlessly attired gentry in pink. Especially is this true of Nottinghamshire and Yorkshire, where, when a covert is drawn near by, the foundries are deserted until the last laggard has passed out of sight.

Fortunately, indeed, the configuration of the country permits these vast crowds with little hinderance to the sport. Luckily may it be said that practically every enclosure has an outlet, towards which the overwhelming rush that follows "gone away" furnishes one of the sights of English hunting.

While these tremendous fields are picturesque, and undoubted evidences of a far-reaching interest, they have drawbacks nevertheless; for once the crowd has crushed its way through the first gate, it becomes a huge cavalcade of point to point riders, that from the vantage of an undulating country may view the direction of the hounds, making short-cuts, which not infrequently head the fox, and justly enough kindle the wrath of the master and the few of the first flight.

As for the traps, their number is legion, for so surely as all roads lead to Rome, so surely do all roads in England lead to a covert-side, and they are filled to overflowing for at least three days of every hunting week. The number of women in the saddle at an English or Irish meet is considerable; but though the percentage who ride a straight line is very small, the work of that few is nothing short of astonishing. Their endurance is alto-

John Burton & Sons

WATER DITCH AND HEDGE-TOPPED BANK IN THE QUORN COUNTRY

gether remarkable: day after day they will be found at the covert-side, hacking probably ten miles to the meet, to hunt all day and then hack back again—keeping it up week in and week out of the season. The character of English and Irish jumping renders such constant going possible, whereas in America our timber fences make an eventual wreck of the healthiest woman, if she persist in following hounds every day they are out. The explanation is simple: the English horse takes the ditch, or thorn fence, in his stride with little checking; the American stops up short, bucks over the post and rails, and is off again with another jerk. The woman's back during this gymnastic performance gets severe wrenching and twisting.

In very few parts of Great Britain are the farmers not in touch and active sympathy with the hunts, and in the greater percentage of the provincial districts they are to be seen in the field on good cattle. As a rule, the farmer of England is not only a lover of good horse-flesh, but has always been a large and expert breeder. The times have not dealt kindly with him, however, of recent years, so that in the month of my visit, February, 1894, several consecutively bad seasons had compelled him to sell the pick of his stable, and left him in sore financial straits. Should the current year duplicate the drought of the last two, which put the price of hay up to fifty dollars a ton, and that of grain at a proportionately exalted figure, it is hard to say how he will withstand the additional drain on resources that have already dwindled to slenderest proportions.

Yet, notwithstanding these hard times, the sporting spirit of the English farmer rings true. And with good reason the farmer, the landlord, and the tradesman are friendly to hunting, since it employs the first, increases the rent-roll of the second, and fills the till of the third, to say nothing of the hundreds upon hundreds of servants that find good berths in the stables, kennels, and fields. Nay, more: it has helped build a number of towns in England, and Melton-Mowbray, Croft, Market-Harborough, Chipping-Norton, and Chelmsford owe a great deal of their present prosperity to the hunting, of which they have been made centres. The exact figures

A THORN FENCE IN THE BELVOIR COUNTRY

have slipped me, but I think it is something like $50,000 a season that the tradesmen of Melton-Mowbray derive directly from hunting, and while that does not very likely sound to Americans as a figure large enough to instance, it is nevertheless a goodly sum to be distributed among the handful of tradespeople in any small country village of 5000 to 6000 inhabitants like Melton-Mowbray.

Hunting does more for the farmer than, with exceptionally intelligent cases, he realizes, and one wonders almost as much at the impolicy of the ignorant brute who surrounds his field with barbed wire, as at the vicious knave that runs its all but invisible deadliness through the top of a thorn hedge.

And how many a gallant heart has been stilled by the deadly work of the invisible wire! England, and likewise America, for we too have our list of martyred sportsmen, needs a law to deal severely with these despicable creatures. The farmer that does not wish his land ridden over, and is not a churl, will surround it with stiff, honest fencing; or, if he does put up wire, advertise it by a top board. But as for running wire through a hedge! he might, so far as the peril run by the riders is concerned, conceal loaded mines about his premises, to be fired by unsuspecting sportsmen.

The farmer of American hunting districts does not owe so much to the sport as does the Englishman, and, while it is criminal enough in both to surround their enclosures with concealed wire, the latter adds downright baseless ingratitude to his knavery when he lays traps in the hunting man's path.

But the farmer in England who is inimical to the hunt is the exception; as a rule, he is a stanch supporter (indeed, he is the mainstay of some hunts), raises horses (to be sure, with an eye to future and personal aggrandizement or he would not be mortal), takes the puppies out to walk, and is a helpful and sympathetic member of the hunting district.

The clubs appreciate the pleasure, as well as the value, of the present happy relations existing between themselves and the farmers, and members are carefully and continuously cautioned against doing unnecessary injury, and damage is conscientiously paid for to the very last penny,

THORN FENCE IN THE COTTESMORE COUNTRY

which, while being surely the only fair and politic course, nevertheless shows that the spirit of the hunting set towards the farmers over whose land they ride is not one of studied arrogance.

As a consequence, the coverts are well kept up (most of them are artificially stocked, though it is not acknowledged above a whisper in England), foxes preserved, keepers handsomely rewarded on a find, and a general harmony maintained towards the end of good sport.

And the history of fox-hunting—who will say how far it goes back? Horse, hound, and horn seem ever to have been sporting emblems of England's gentry, even of royalty; for did we not learn with our first lessons in history that Alfred the Great and several of his successors were ardent in the chase of stag and boar? And yet English literature is particularly and regretably devoid of the picturesque and reminiscent side of hunting, of which surely there must have been material without end.

The earliest manuscript, dating from the beginning of the fourteenth century, and which is in the Cotton Library of the British Museum, fails to light up this side of the sport, and these first days of hunting remain dark ages indeed, since, but for the exceptionally stray and more or less unauthentic bits here and there, we know comparatively little of it up to the middle of the eighteenth century.

Historians differ on the exact date hounds were entered solely to fox, varying between 1730 and 1750; but, at any rate, it is definitely known that not until the beginning of the eighteenth century did fox-hunting proper become a pastime, and that Mr. Meynell, the father of the modern sport, lived in 1782.

Previous to 1750, most of the sport was furnished by joining in one common pack for the day's chase the several kennels of the country gentlemen, nearly every one of whom always kept a few couple of hounds. These were invariably trencher-fed—that is, running loose and picking up food where best they might, like any other dog; but they made astonishingly good running in many instances, and some of the best hunts in England to-day are descendants of just such progenitors.

Women seem to have taken to the hunting-field from the beginning; in fact, are mentioned in the earliest manuscripts, and as riding astride, though Queen Elizabeth, who was very fond of the chase, rode sideways.

Strutt, the sporting historian, tells of an effort made by the hunting women of those days to have the "wearing of breeches" generally recognized as conventional form, if for no other reason, because, in case of accident, "decency was the better preserved"; but critics were as bigoted then as now, and protested that woman should either guard against accidents in a manner more consist-

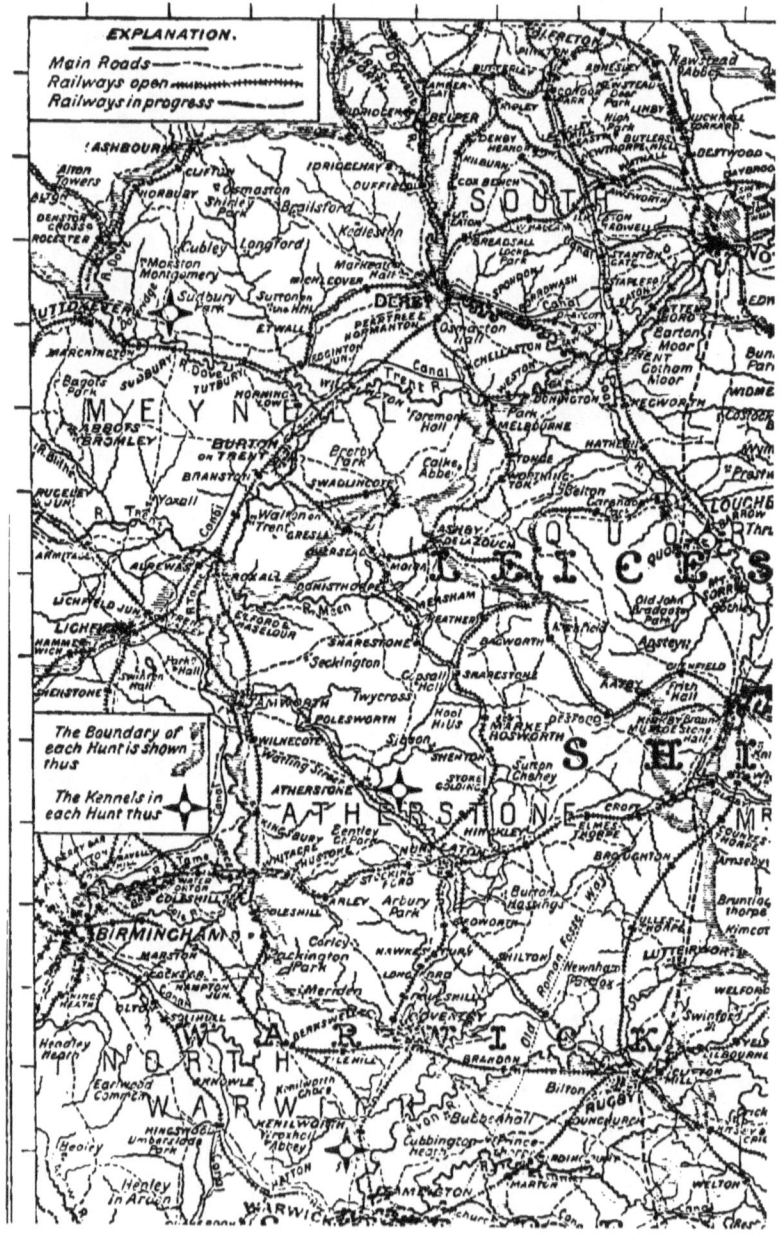

ent with the delicacy of the sex, or refrain from such dangerous recreations. Previous to visiting England, I was led to believe that all women who followed hounds in Devonshire and Somersetshire rode astride, and was prepared to see quite a cavalcade of Amazons in that country. I saw only one, however—an excellent horsewoman she was, too—but heard of several others. In fact, I found a very general feeling among thinking and reasoning people that riding astride was far and away the safer and more hygienic, and certain to become recognized as such at no distant time.

The era of fox-hunting as it is to-day, with its fast and furious riding, elaborate turning out, expensive kennels, and fashionable atmosphere, dawned with the opening of the nineteenth century; though that neither horse nor hound went the pace they do to-day is not to be doubted. Oxers and bull-finchers were probably more frequently met—the first of which was flown, and the latter scrambled through—but they knew not the staked-and-bound obstacles that now obtain.

All hunting England is divided into two parts—the "shires," which furnish the poetry, and the "provinces," which provide the prose of riding to hounds. It is a rather confusing division to the uninitiated, as all England is divided into shires (counties), and somewhat, too, into shire hunting, although not strictly so, since frequently it is the case that the country of one hunt may extend into two, and, in some instances of peculiar configuration, into even more counties. However, all England is certainly divided into shires, which are again as surely apportioned among the hunts.

Leicestershire, Rutlandshire, and a part of Northamptonshire comprise the "shires," so called; to speak of hunting in which means you have been following the hounds of the Quorn, Pytchley, Belvoir, Cottesmore, or Mr. Fernies. With the country so thoroughly and oftentimes intricately subdivided, it causes no little wonderment that there are not more conflicts between hunts, and yet they are so rare as to create surprise and unmitigated censure when they occur.

I have said that the "shires" furnished the poetry of English hunting, but I do not wish to imply that the prose of the provinces is heavy and uninteresting, or that the provincial soul is utterly without the poetry of hunting.

While the sportsman who has the good luck and very necessary length of purse to follow the hounds in High Leicestershire may shrug his shoulders at the sport in the provinces, he must not by any means persuade you that the shires comprise all that there is of good sport in England. There is only occasionally the pace, never, with a few exceptions, the style of turning out that characterizes the fashionable and highly-scented grass countries; but, nevertheless, for sport pure and simple, for hunting as distinguished from steeple-chasing, there are many provincial packs that will give you the rarest sport to be had in all Great Britain.

Americans that visit England for hunting are apt to confine their experiences to the shires, which, being more or less intolerant of the outside hunting world, are sure to give incorrect impressions to those who do not seek farther. Certain sets of Englishmen who hunt with the fashionable packs grow to the belief that the poor devil of a fellow who is not astride a three-hundred-guinea hunter, and does not have an occasional twenty-minute steeple-chase after a straight-going fox, knows nothing whatever of the sport of fox-hunting. But the average sportsman, and the average is high in England, knows better; his heart has beat as fast, like enough, watching the small gorse coverts shaking under the researches of a dozen or twenty couple of hounds, and his pride grown just as great in the one-hundred-guinea hunter, whose strength of quarters and intelligence have lifted him out of the heavy plough, and carried him safely across many a hidden drain.

This fact is always to be considered: that in the provinces there is, as a general rule, more actual hunting, the foxes are as plentiful and strong, the jumping yields as great a variety, and the hounds in many instances quite as good, with the advantage of smaller fields, that give them more room to work and permit of closer supervision by the huntsman.

THE QUORN HOUNDS

Your horse need not be a high-priced racer, but he must be a thorough hunter, with plenty of blood and bone and local training.

Generally speaking, the shires are less broken up than the provinces, and carry a higher scent, which explain the greater pace, and the coverts, fewer in number, permit those sustained bursts that have spread the fame of Leicestershire; the hounds are of the best, the horses the highest type of the racing hunter, and expense is of no consequence. In this country of fashion and extravagant expenditure you have, to begin with, a tremendous field where there is always an abundance of jealous riding, which is, however, not so much a condition of country as of human nature, and obtains everywhere in proportion to the number brought into competition. Only the exceptional few that may be in the first flight live with the hounds in one of those twenty-minute bursts over the high-scented grass; not that the jumps are so much more difficult than elsewhere, but the pace is faster and the average of good cross-country riders is ridiculously small compared with the average of fine horse-flesh. The stampede for the gate at the throw-off delays and straggles the field, but once through, it thunders on to the next, where it leaves a score or more, the number diminishing rapidly by the time half a dozen fields have been covered, until, at the end of the fifteen or twenty minutes' burst, probably, of the several hundred that started out so gallantly, only a handful will be up at the first check.

It is a blessed thing for English hunting that every field does have a gate as an outlet for this great mass of riders, otherwise there would be little sport for anybody, or, if they improved in cross-country performance, it would be an exasperating task for the huntsmen to keep the hounds at work with their noses down.

In the provinces they ride to hunt, and sport alone is the primary object; in the fashionable countries the great majority hunt to ride, turning out chiefly because it is the thing to do, and sport gives the vogue a dash of exhilarating color.

It is a fact, as "Brooksby" has said, and Brooksby knows whereof he speaks — which every one will admit

QUORN KENNELS

who reads his *Hunting Countries of Great Britain*, the best published work on the subject—that in all of England you want a good horse—one that has been schooled in the country, has bone and blood, can jump, and, in most instances, go the pace; but in the shires you want a superlatively good mount. Nowhere else in the world will be found such a collection of superior horse-flesh — such big-boned, blue-blooded hunters, that represent anywhere from one to five thousand dollars. Two hundred guineas (*i.e.*, $1000) is considered in High Leicestershire rather a moderate price, and probably three to four hundred would be a nearer average of the cost of the hunters at, for instance, the Quorn covert-side, while several that had cost 1000 guineas were pointed out to me, and I had the pleasure of running my hand down the steel-like legs of one in Lord Lonsdale's stud for which had been paid 2000 guineas ($10,000). Rather a tidy sum to give for one's hunter.

Nowhere, either, are to be found such kennels or hunts turned out in so elaborate and finished a fashion, with servants, sometimes to the number of half a dozen, superbly mounted, and all in pink and leathers.

The Leicestershire hunter must have speed, exceptional jumping qualifications, and endurance. He must have been schooled to the country, otherwise the best rider and the finest-bred horse in the world will come to grief. He must be the superlative animal that is demanded, not only to combat his way in the crowd, but to cover the country; for he will be called on to negotiate a "bottom," fly an "oxer," and alight unerringly on the bank of a double, to pop over the awaiting ditch on the landing side. He must be tractable and intelligent, and in the sharp bursts of twenty to thirty minutes over the high-scented grass and furrow and ridge of the shires he must be a racer, if his rider would be with the hounds.

We of America are prone to fancy our hunting country stiffer than the Englishman's, and point to the timber of Long Island to bear us witness; but there is so great a dissimilarity between the two that comparison can scarcely be made. They differ totally in that the jumping of one is all open, while with the other it is practically all hidden. It is not that the average jumps in England are so high or so stout so much as it is in the concealment of their true nature. It is easy enough to pop over a bank with a hedge on top of it, but when that bank and hedge have a ditch on the take-off side, and in mid-air you get the first intimation of a yawning drain on the landing side also, you begin to appreciate some of the difficulties that make staying with the hounds no boy's play. When you have dropped into a "bottom," with its rotten and overhanging bank, and stayed there long enough to see the last of a straggling field go past you, you realize that all hunting in Leicestershire is not smooth going over velvety turf; and when you come, finally, to the terrific "oxers" and the staked-and-bound hedges, with timber on both sides, that are to be found in the Pytchley country, you conclude there is just

DOUBLE DITCH AND FENCED BANK

as stiff jumping in England as the tallest and stoutest post-and-rails of the Meadow Brook country afford. Comparatively speaking, it is a simple matter to ride up to timber and buck over it, or, if the way is clear, to take it in your stride, for you see precisely where you are going to land. In most of our country we have clear going and unobstructed view for every jump we make; but in nearly all of England you never know what awaits you, and rarely can you see where you are going to land. You need faith and nerve and a superior hunter for such going; but when you have all three, and the fox is running straight, then indeed are you blind to all danger, aglow with that rapturous excitement for which —to quote Whyte Melville—many are content to live, and even, in a few sad cases, to die.

There are undoubtedly hunters in America just as well bred and quite as clever, that would perform with equal satisfaction if schooled to the country. Indeed, there is no reason why we should not have as good, since we buy in same market—Ireland; but the average in Leicestershire is, of course, much higher than in America, first, because of the infinitely larger number of men that ride to hounds, and, second, because the country demands more of the horse. Outside of the "shires," with a few famous exceptions, our hunters are of quite as good, and in many cases of superior, breeding.

It would be naturally supposed that an American-bred horse could hardly be worked successfully over such a country as Leicestershire, and yet Mr. Foxhall Keene has at Melton-Mowbray, in Nimrod, one of a stud of ten as fine hunters as money can buy, a product of American breeding, that, without claiming to be a superlative animal, compares favorably with the best cross-country performers in the "shires."

As for the riding, I do not hesitate to say that, in proportion to the size of the fields, one sees better form in America than in England. In the first place, of the several hundred at the covert-side, probably ten per cent. make a pretence at going straight, and with this in daily evidence, the constant attendance of so great a number of second horses, so many of which were never by any chance called into service, afforded me no end of quiet amusement.

Those who go straight, however, are the hardest riding and cleverest horsemen in the world, though even these do not excel the pick of our cross-country performers, for in the shires I always observed Mr. Keene with the very first of the first flight, while in the Meath country the two Eustis brothers—William C. and George P.—showed to equal advantage.

As a matter of fact, with all the difficulties of the English hunting country, the man who, at the throw-off, picks out his own line and rides it has no trouble whatever in keeping with the hounds ; but it is essential to know the country, and absolutely necessary to have a horse schooled to it.

Melton-Mowbray, known as the "hunting metropolis" of England, which might with equal truth be called the hunting centre of the world, is in Leicestershire, one hundred miles from London. Within a radius of about twenty miles are the kennels of the Quorn, Pytchley, Belvoir, Cottesmore, four of the greatest packs in England, and these, together with Mr. Fernies', furnish hunting for every day of the week, Sunday excepted, from beginning to ending of the season. But Melton-Mowbray is a little world of itself, and a very fashionable one at that, and you must not go there unless you have a long purse and a superlative hunter, and, if you would be in the first flight, a good heart. The Pytchley are a bit far off to hunt with regularly, but the best meets of all the others are close, and, as a usual thing, the kill is near at home. One rarely has to hack more than eight or ten miles to the covert-side, and even this is a part of the day's pleasure, for more beautiful country would be hard to find. It is a country, too, which seems almost to exist for the fox, both gentry and farmers alike having been reared from childhood to care for and respect the knowing little beast.

DITCH AND "STAKED-AND-BOUND" FENCE

First of the subscription packs of Leicestershire— first, indeed, of all subscription packs of Great Britain— is the Quorn.

A meet of the Quorn hunt is a sight for the gods. Whether it be advertised for one of the handsome old residences with which the country abounds, or for a park, or cross-roads, the scene differs only in its setting. And it is picturesque in the extreme, with the hounds as a central figure, the master, huntsmen, first and second whips, and second horsemen, all in pink, forming an inner circle, surrounded by hundreds of horsemen and women, the roads leading from all directions blocked to a gorging point with traps of every description, while on all sides the fields stretch away in their velvety beauty, cross-sectioned by the national fence of thorn.

But it is at the covert-side, on a Quorn Friday, say, where the heart of the sportsman thrills as he notes the perfect discipline of the tremendous field, and delights in the largest number of superbly mounted horsemen he has ever seen anywhere. As the pack gives tongue (and what music ravishes the ear of the sportsman like the tuneful cry of the hounds!), every ear strains to catch the sound of " Gone away !" every eye to see the gathering of reins, the settling of hats, the evident sympathy between horse and rider, each impatient to be away with the first of that mad rush which follows the signal.

The Quorn pack is supported by Melton-Mowbray, though I dare say the master, Lord Lonsdale, who has been showing some of the best sport the hunt has ever had, must draw on his own very comfortable bank account at the end of the season to make ends meet. No hunt is turned out so elaborately, nor are the servants of any so grandly mounted from its stable of thirty, though the master's fad of hogging the hunters' manes is a disfigurement to such good cattle. They have some of the best country in Leicestershire and some of the stiffest, though it is not so broken up as the Cottesmore and the Belvoir, and furnishes great stretches of running that makes the pace at times the very fastest.

The fifty-five couple of hounds, divided into a dog and bitch pack, and used alternately, as is the case generally in the shires, are a thoroughly workmanlike lot, which, while lacking the Belvoir symmetry in coloring and high breeding, are very fast, and under huntsman Tom Firr, who has no superior in England, well qualified to lead the hardest-riding hunt of the hardest-riding country in the world.

The Belvoir, a private pack of the Duke of Rutland's, is not only the oldest in England—its books dating from 1756—but certainly the most beautiful to watch at the covert-side. One must go into the kennels and have the pack brought up for his inspection, as Frank Gillard, the huntsman, was kind enough to do for me, to fully appreciate the big bone and straight legs and the beautiful evenness in coloring of these hounds, every one of them with the Belvoir tan head and black saddle-mark on groundwork of purest white.

It always amazes a layman that any huntsman can distinguish his hounds apart; but to stand by the Belvoir, in which you cannot for your life pick one from the other, so alike are they, and see Gillard draw them out by name one after the other, while they scan you quizzically through beautiful and intelligent eyes, is an experience worth going a long way for. Gillard is a notable kennel man, and has shown an extraordinary knowledge of hounds and great skill and judgment in keeping the quality of this pack up to the standard that has made its reputation world-wide.

There are fifty-eight and a half couple, averaging, like all in Leicestershire, from twenty-two to twenty-four inches in height, and from these over one hundred puppies are every year sent out to walk, only the pick of them being retained. The present duke is rather advanced in years, and is never seen afield, though his deceased predecessor was a thorough-going sportsman, and quite as much interested in Gillard's work with the hounds as the huntsman himself.

The Belvoir district is a thoroughly good one from end

BELVOIR HOUNDS—DUKE OF RUTLAND'S

John Burton & Sons

to end, with a great variety of country, including wide stretches of grazing land, heavy plough—for the farmers till their soil to the utmost depths—and all kinds of fencing, some of it pretty stiff, as enclosures are guarded by the strongest of staked-and-bound fences, made doubly formidable by ditches that are wide and deep, to say nothing of the post and rails used to repair hedges and the stone walls to be found in some parts.

Saturday is to the Belvoir what Friday is to the Quorn, and on favored occasions one may enjoy one of those sharp bursts of twenty to thirty minutes for which the Belvoir hounds are famous, and to live with which requires the fastest of horse-flesh. As a usual thing the country is amply stocked with foxes, but the hunt is not mounted so well as the Quorn, and as a rule does not give such good sport as Lord Lonsdale's pack. There are more checks, and it is only occasionally that the hounds have an opportunity of showing the great pace of which they are capable.

Many hunting-men consider that in all of Leicestershire the best sport is to be had in the sparsely settled Cottesmore country, where coverts run from small gorse to big woodlands, and extended pastures that hold a good scent give hard and fast runs. There is jumping enough of every kind, including stone walls, blackthorn hedges, and wide drains, and one requires an enduring as well as a fast horse, for it is well broken up in some parts. The kennels and stables, in which are fifty-five couple of hounds and thirty-eight horses, are probably the most costly in England, and the master, Mr. W. Baird, and huntsman, George Gillson, never fail to furnish good sport.

Few are so old as, and no subscription pack is more famous than the Pytchley, which takes its name from the ancient Elizabethan mansion, Pytchley Hall, where, in the days of Lord Althorp, the hunt club used to meet. It is the Quorn's great rival, and every year six riders from each meet in a time-honored steeple-chase over four and a half miles; this year the Quorn, on whose team, by-the-way, were two Americans, Mr. Foxhall Keene and Mr. Elliott Zborowski, won by 43 to 21 points. It is the only hunt in Leicestershire with a distinctive uniform, its pink coat bearing the white collar which every one has learned to associate with this famous old club. The time-honored club-initialled brass buttons of the pink coat content the other hunts of the fashionable shires.

Some of the stiffest jumping in England is to be found in the Pytchley country, and the biggest "oxers" around Market-Harborough, and the staked-and-bound hedges, with timber on both sides, are altogether too stiff to be ridden straight. What there is of the country in Northamptonshire is largely plough, and some of it is heavy enough to check the rush of the typical shire field. Generally speaking, however, Pytchley is less hilly and trying to horses than is High Leicestershire, though they do not have the long runs, because of the frequently occurring villages that keep Reynard from going straight.

There is a plenty of foxes. The farmers are stanch supporters of the master, Earl Spencer, whose beautiful place, Althorp Park, provides the most picturesque site of any hunt stables and kennels in England. No hounds are better handled than these fifty-five couple by William Goodall, the huntsman, and, next to the Quorn, the servants are the best mounted, drawing on a stud of thirty-two hunters.

Compared with these first packs of England, the Meath fox-hounds of Ireland are juvenile, for, although they have been an institution many years, it was not until recent times that they began to be classed among the cele-

BELVOIR KENNELS

John Burton & Sons

brated hunts, though having always furnished first-rate sport. Indeed, their present prominence goes back no longer than five years ago, when, under the mastership of Mr. Jack Trotter, they were plunged first into fame and afterwards into debt, the latter coming very near eclipsing the former. Mr. John Watson, the present master, who hunts his own fifty-five couple of hounds, succeeded Mr. Trotter, and has managed to repair the fortunes of the Meath, until it is now on very nearly as sound footing as ever it was, and the sport of the past two seasons has not been excelled anywhere in the kingdom. Certainly no hunt is more favored by nature, for the Meath country is a never-ending picture of the most beautiful shades of green, emphasized here and there by woodland, while the climate, tender yet invigorating, makes you impatient of in-door confinement. You have only to catch a glimpse of Ireland to appreciate the appropriateness of its sobriquet—Emerald Isle.

And what jolly good sportsmen and what grand horses they breed in Ireland! The wit and whole-soul fellowship of the one is as proverbial as the magnificent cross-country qualities of the other.

This Irish horse long ago evinced an excellence in the hunting-field that made its reputation and stamped its progeny. But it must not be supposed that the mere fact of being bred in Ireland is a guarantee of an exceptionally or even thoroughly good mount. The demand for hunters of late years has naturally greatly increased the number of breeders as well as dealers, and a large class of an indifferent type has been put on the market. There are unquestionably more of the very highest type of hunters bred in Ireland to-day than ever, but the inferior class has likewise increased, probably at a greater ratio. You must be a judge of horse-flesh, or buy through a dealer or breeder whose judgment and honesty can be relied upon, if you would secure one of that rare sort—the weight-carrying hunter with plenty of quality. There are quite as many blanks as prizes. However, the general spirit among the sportsmen of Ireland is none the less towards maintaining the standard of the Irish hunter, since, as one of them told me, no mare is retained after she has outlived her usefulness, for once the hunting days are over they are either "shot and boiled up as feed for the hounds, or sent over to Germany."

In England, also, the efforts of horsemen are being directed towards the betterment of the hunter, and the show I saw in London last spring attested the success of the movement. The Hunters' Improvement Society has turned its attention to the development of good honest animals that have bone and blood and fair pace, and the exhibits in the yearling and two-year-old classes, as the result of the departure, were good enough to please every sportsman with an eye for raising the national type. Nor is the horse the only one of the hunting-field receiving attention, for the hound shows have done a great deal to the same end, so much so I wonder the example has not been followed in America, where we need some such elevating power at work.

A MEET OF THE PYTCHLEY HOUNDS AT ALTHORP PARK, EARL SPENCER'S RESIDENCE.

The Meath hunt is turned out nearly if not quite as elaborately as those of the shires; both whips and one of the second horsemen are in pink, and, in fact, pink appeared to be more generally worn by the field than was the case at any meet I attended in England, Leicestershire included. Certainly the riding impressed me as averaging higher, and more women rode the line. Altogether, the atmosphere seemed to be more sport-laden in the Meath country than any other outside that of the Devon and Somerset stag-hounds. They have a variety of jumping, from wide open drains to stone walls, but the greatest share of obstacles is banks, quite as often without thorn hedges as with them, and with a drain on one side or the other, and frequently on both. Some of these banks are very high, guarded by wide, deep ditches, which are suggestively called "gripes," and sometimes their banks are sloping and boggy, and oftentimes topped by a blackthorn hedge eight feet high, and very stout, as the face and clothing of those who crash through it bear witness. That these deep, wide drains are formidable traps to the unwary may be judged from the existence of a guild known as "wreckers," whose vocation is farming, and avocation, on hunting days, dragging, by aid of tackle and ropes, and for a consideration, the hapless out of the drains. Foxes are fairly plentiful, and there is probably less artificial stocking of coverts than in any of the large hunts.

An English friend told me, when I first arrived on the other side, that not to see Devonshire and Somersetshire was not to have seen hunting England, and I heartily agreed with him after I had made the trip. There is something about this part of England that wins you instantly, if you have a particle of that sentiment which Nature in her untrammelled and romantic beauty arouses.

It is thoroughly unique in its picturesque wildness, for though the downs stretch away in limitless acreage, and the coombs are deep and winding, yet there is no harshness in the scene, Nature seeming to have touched all with a refining hand —carpeting the downs with blooming heather, and lightening the darkest coombs with brightest flowers. When I add that this is the home of the noblest beast of chase, and of the most thorough-going sportsmen in the world, I think I have given sufficient reason for endorsing my friend's opinion. There are many parts of Great Britain where they chase the stag, but none outside of this country where they hunt it.

Stag-hunting has existed ever since the chase became the earliest sport of civilized man, but in its present form not in England until the reign of Queen Elizabeth.

The Devon and Somerset stag-hounds were one of the most famous as well as oldest packs in Great Britain, with an unbroken history from 1598 down to 1825, when they were sold for some unaccountable reason, and not until a couple of years later was the nucleus of the present pack purchased.

On the history of the modern pack, which has had its bright and dark days, it is not my purpose to dwell, but merest comment on these hounds would be singularly incomplete without reference to Mr. Fenwick Bisset, who revived and carried on the hunt in its best days, and to Lord Ebrington and Mr. Basset, who continued the good work, and especially to the latter for improving the hounds and maintaining the old traditions, beloved alike by hunt members and farmers. It was under the generous and sportsmanlike mastership of these men, too, which has endeared their memory to every sportsman in the Devon and Somerset country, that the late Arthur Heal, that past-master in the art of stag-hunting, gave the royal sport which made him an ideal to all subsequent huntsmen. He was connected with the hunt for thirty years, eighteen of which he carried the horn, and under him served as first whip Anthony Huxtable, the present huntsman, who is making a worthy successor to his altogether remarkable preceptor. Lucky it is indeed he received the training of such a school, for the present master lacks the qualities which were most conspicuously possessed by his predecessors. Nor do misfortunes come singly, for poor Miles, one of the best "harborers" the hunt ever had, and

PYTCHLEY HOUNDS

W. H. Grove

whom I helped to a bite of luncheon and a wee bit of Scotch afterwards, but a few short weeks ago, has since gone over to the majority; he was a faithful servant, and will be a severe loss to the club. The harborer, next to the huntsman, is the most necessary personage to the success of the hunt; indeed, I am not sure that he is not the most essential, for it is his skill and never-flagging perseverance that locate the stag which furnishes the sport of the day. It is he who in the misty dawn scours the country, and in the dim, uncertain light bends low over the slot-imprinted turf to read whether hind or stag has passed on into the covert beyond, and it is his craft which assures him finally, after a careful circle of the wood, that the quarry is surely located. Misjudgment on his part would almost invariably mean a day's sport spoiled. But Miles closed his career with as clean a record as ever harborer had.

Once the stag is marked, the responsibilities of the harborer end, and those of the huntsman begin. On the morning of the meet he kennels his hounds near by, and drawing out a few couple of the most tried and largest, called "tufters," puts them into the covert. It would not do to turn in the entire pack, lest they should run riot over the several scents that are likely as not to obtain, for on the ability of the "tufters" to rouse and separate the stag from the herd largely depends the success of the day. Nor are skill of the tufters in the covert, and size and bone of the pack generally—some of them standing as high as twenty-six inches, and all over twenty-four, for the work demands the stoutest of hounds, well put together, especially as to shoulders and feet, to stand the wear and tear of the broken country—the sole requisites of stag-hounds. They must possess that rare intelligence which enables them to follow a cold scent when the stag "soils" (takes to water), or "runs to herd" (starts up another deer while he settles in its lair), and to distinguish between the scent of hind and stag, old and young. No hunting-field calls for such superior qualifications in huntsman and whipper-in as stag-hunting in Devon and Somerset. The former must live with his hounds in a country interlaced with deep coombs (ravines), requiring oftentimes the hardest riding and best judgment; while the whip, whose duties in fox-hunting comprise preventing riot among hounds, verifying

THE PYTCHLEY KENNELS

halloos, and general utility work for the huntsman, in stag-hunting has the more important one of keeping a careful watch that the right deer is being chased.

Sluggish indeed must be the blood of the man who can sit his horse indifferent to the restrained but none the less joyous excitement that sweeps around the Devon and Somerset covert-side. Sometimes there are long hours of waiting while the "tufters" patiently work out their line; sometimes a sudden outburst of hound music makes the hearts of men and horses beat wildly, only to suffer the keener disappointment, as the "ware hind" of the whip tells the tufters are on the wrong line. But weariness of waiting is forgotten when at last a crash of music from the covert tells that the stag has been moved, and a transport of ecstasy thrills the field into restiveness as he breaks covert, and "brow, bay, and tray" show him to be a "warrantable" deer.

Instantly the whole field is in a commotion, every one tingling with impatience to be off on the trail of the noble quarry. But none is permitted to follow. The tufters are stopped until the remainder of the pack can be brought up and laid on. And then away it is indeed! sometimes straightaway to the sea, over the downs of purple heather, galloping downhill and uphill, for the endurance of the red-deer passeth all understanding (the one on my day with these hounds made a run of nearly eighteen miles before she went over the cliffs of the Bristol Channel), in and out the steep and narrow coombs, that are apt soon to get to the bottom of your horse, and where the longest way around—for a mile or two on a comparative level saves you a scramble into the depths of the ravine and the climb out again—is oftentimes the straightest way across. There are no fences to be jumped in this country, but it takes a strong mount and a stout heart and a considerable knowledge of the deer's habits and of the country to be up with the hounds when the stag comes at last to bay, almost invariably in water, for he knows the advantage of standing firmly on his legs, while the hounds must swim to the attack. And there with lowered head and unflinching eye he meets their onslaught, dying, like the gentleman that he is, fighting to the last.

There is none of the elaboration in turning out the Devon and Somerset stag-hounds that characterizes the shires and other fashionable countries. You put on pink or not as you feel inclined, and generally you do not, for only a comparatively few make a pretence of "doing the proper thing." Every one goes out for sport, whether the pursuit be after the stag, from August to October, or the hind, from late autumn to early spring. It is hunting from the word "go." Fifteen or even twenty miles to the covertside is hardly considered, and your mount must be a thoroughly good one, with plenty of endurance, for here he is both hack and hunter, and second horses in Devonshire are not brought out for ornament.

Compared with the royal sport of the Exmoors, stag-hunting as it obtains elsewhere in Great Britain is as insipid as water after wine. Of all the hunts that follow the carted stag, none probably furnishes so good an imitation of the genuine article as the Ward Union in Ireland, near the Meath fox-hounds, and it is one of the very few of its kind that attract sportsmen. As a usual thing it gives pretty good sport, for the configuration of the country is such that the deer nine times out of ten has a clear run, and is never viewed until it pleases him to stop. It is a subscription hunt, the consolidation of former garrison and civil packs, hunted by a committee of which that whole-souled and straight-going sportsman Percy Maynard, Esq., is executive, with huntsman Jim Brindley, son and successor of the famous Charles Brindley, who gave such good sport that on his death a monument was erected to his memory. There is a herd of about twenty deer in the paddock, and the kennels contain thirty-five couple of hounds, all of whose teeth, by-the-way, are filed down that they may not mangle the deer when it is caught.

Of carted stag-hunting in England, Lord de Rothschild's pack is the largest, and probably turned out in the best form, though Essex, Kent, and Surrey all furnish equal opportunities for a cross-country ride under more or less fashionable auspices. But I hurry by these that I may come to Her Majesty's pack, not that it is more sport-giving, but because it has been in the public eye almost continuously by reason of being cited, in the bill introduced into Parliament for the suppression of the pursuit of carted deer, as a terrible example of cruelty.

EARL SPENCER'S STABLES

First of all, let me assuage the fears of compassionate Americans as to the cruelty of this diversion; I cannot call it sport. Most of us, and I know I was of the number, have pictured the deer in the paddocks trembling at the approach of man, shivering with fear in the dark van as it is driven to the meet, bewildered at the uncarting, and, after a half-hopeful, fully terrorized flight, finally brought to a last desperate stand by fierce hounds that seek its life-blood. This is the hysterical pen-picture familiar to most readers of the press, but the facts do not support it. The deer, despite the fact that its antlers are sawed off, neither trembles at man's approach nor permits the hounds to worry him; indeed, they are frequently on very comfortable terms of intimacy. As for the terrors of uncarting and sight of the crowd, none of the deer I saw gave evidence of being so stricken, and one at least walked about looking at the crowd until some one "shooed" it off. A meet of the Queen's buck-hounds is quite, from a sporting point of view, the most ridiculous performance I have ever attended, and though the fields do have a sprinkling of sportsmen who follow for social reasons of varying degrees of pressure, the great majority turn out because it is one of the events of the locality, and very likely because the master and the hunt servants are the only ones in England that embellish their livery with gold-lace.

III

RIDING TO HOUNDS

IN THE "PROVINCES"

To comment on every pack of fox-hounds in provincial-hunting England would alone fill a volume. It is obviously hopeless, therefore, to touch on them all in a single chapter; nor would so elaborate a treatment be either instructive or interesting, since a certain amount of repetition would be inevitable. I have chosen the more important packs, and those that convey a comprehensive idea of the many different hunting countries of England.

Of all packs in the provinces the "blue hounds," as the Duke of Beaufort's in Gloucestershire are called, stand easily first. Indeed, it seems a misnomer to call this a provincial hunt, for few, even in the shires, have better horse-flesh, and none are turned out more elaborately. Badminton, as the hunt is known, dates 1728 (the present duke assuming the mastership in 1853), and is maintained in royal style in a country where a run of thirty miles may be had, and which is thoroughly hunted and preserved from early autumn to late spring.

And a charming country it is, with fences that are all negotiable, notwithstanding some of them are stone walls, and a sport-giving huntsman is the Marquis of Worcester, who is always with his hounds when required, although, curiously enough, he does not jump a fence. All the expenses of the hunt are assumed by the duke, whose popularity is attested by his tenants walking the fifty to sixty couple of puppies sent out annually, and the club uniform —blue coat with buff facing—may be worn only on his personal invitation.

A strong and clever horse is wanted here, for, while he need not fly fences in his stride, he must be jumping constantly.

The Cotswold differs from the duke's country in having severe hills that test both horse and hound to the utmost, though paltry hedges and loosely-made stone walls constitute the fencing. The country carries a good scent, and, with the hounds taking the walls in their stride, it requires an exceptional horse to live with them. The coverts are small; foxes are plentiful and strong and ready to go, and invariably set a line for the hills.

Yorkshire, it seems to me, should come next in our consideration, for, though pretty thoroughly claimed by farmer and artisan, the sporting inhabitants of this, England's largest county, do not propose that it shall be given over to cultivation entirely, and hunting is carried on in first-class style. The plough makes the scent cold, to be sure, but that does not deter your true Yorkshireman, who goes afield with the greater zest, because the true working qualities of his hounds, that come from the best blood of England, are more strongly brought out. The Yorkshire farmer, keen and well posted, is as true a sportsman as the best, and breeds a horse that is sought wherever he is sent to market. Indeed, high-class horses and hounds are a product of the county, though, in common with the farmers of all England, times have been very bad the last few years, and the type of to-day is inferior to that of a couple of years ago.

The Holderness pack, dating 1764, has the largest country of any hunt in England, and differs from most plough

AN OLD-TIME PYTCHLEY "OXER"

in not being cold-scented. The enclosures are large, and the chief obstacles wide, open drains, a few of them that may be negotiated only by wading. In fact, the ditches all over Yorkshire are wide and deep, but they are kept clean, and are safe jumping because of their firm banks.

Badsworth, once the pick of Yorkshire, is an old country with an enviable sporting history, but coal and iron interests have encroached upon it to such an extent in the last five years that it hunts now under greatest difficulty. Despite these disadvantages, however, it keeps up a high-class establishment, with large kennels, and a stable of over one hundred horses.

Bramham Moor is another old pack, dating back one hundred years, and one of the best blooded in England. It is not a good scenting country, and its great number of coverts make the work of the hounds exceedingly difficult and the runs slow. While there are the usual Yorkshire characteristics—low fences and ordinary ditches, with here and there a stone wall—in some quarters the fences are stiff, and conceal a wide drain which you " wot not of" until in mid-air. You want a good horse here, as, indeed, you do in all parts of Yorkshire, where hunting is not for the gallery, and the fields are out for business.

One of the most noted packs of this shire, and originally a part of the famous Raby country, is the Hurworth, which to this day, with the Zetlands and the Bedale, wear the black collar of the Raby hunt. And yet another that deserves a passing glance is the Sinnington, if for no other reason than because it dates 1668, and is the best trencher-fed pack in England, maintaining a remarkable consistency of form for hounds that are walked at out-quarters.

Lincolnshire, though not fashionable, is a thoroughly sporting country, which will always live in the memory of those that ride to hounds as the home of Assheton Smith and the Squire. It has been called, too, the home of the fox-hound, and it has four famous and liberally managed packs—Brocklesby, Burton, Blankney, and Fitzwilliam. The first and last (known as the Milton blood) have, like the Belvoir, furnished the blood for many another in England. Foxes are strong and plentiful, the country is well preserved, and though the fences, as a rule, are fairly easy, when stiff they are honest, and demand a good horse without calling for the extravagance of the shires. In the Fitzwilliam country, where the hounds have been one hundred and ten years in the family from whom it takes its name, the distances are long, coverts strong and widely separated, and hounds go sometimes thirty miles from the kennels, for, once disturbed, foxes travel a distance.

The Warwickshire goes back a century, and has some good grass land that is little inferior to Leicestershire, though in the north it is devoted largely to wheat. The banks, with ditch on one side only, do not often have a hedge, and although a good hunter is required, the country is negotiable all over.

The Meynell, formerly owned by he who is called the father of the modern chase, and willed to the country on his death, has kennel books dating back to 1818, and occupies the greater part of Derbyshire worth hunting. Derbyshire, largely devoted to dairy farming, is cut up into miles upon miles of small fields, with trimmed hedges,

COTTESMORE STABLES

neither staked nor bound, and seldom accompanied by a formidable ditch. Small enclosures, however, make a deal of jumping. but the hounds, unable to get away from the field, are stopped more often than the horses, and sport correspondingly suffers. It is a country little visited by outsiders, and the fields are not crowded, which is fortunate, since if they were their character would permit no sport at all. The coverts are artificial and small, but well preserved.

Of the packs in North Hamptonshire probably the Heythrop, South Oxfordshire, and Old Berkshire are the most notable. One can always count on a good run with these hounds; in wet weather across wolds and stone walls, and in dry weather through grassy vales that diverge in many directions. The stone walls are not formidable, can be flown by hounds, which not infrequently run away from the field, and there are no ditches to watch out for. The vales are narrow and sound—though heavy in wet weather —and the fences are the staked-and-bound variety, but of not too stiff a character. There are abundant foxes throughout, and, the fields not being large, hounds have a better chance and riders good sport. As a usual thing the fences may be taken on the fly, though there are a few banks with the thorn hedge and ditch on both sides that require two jumps, and some where the width of a double ditch and the strength of fence set the rider hunting for a weak spot. This is the country, too, of legendary lore, for here is pointed out Wayland Smith's cave, where lived the traditional invisible smithy, who would shoe your horse for sixpence on condition you put down the money and went away until the job was completed. The farmers take an active interest in the hunting, and small coverts, good foxes, and limited fields all combine to make good sport.

Nottinghamshire, with plenty of foxes, lies north of the fashionable shires, and is rather famous in having been the nursery of many names notable in the hunting-field. It is the dividing line between the large area of plough and grass, and, though little visited, none of its packs languish, being strongly supported by the residents of the county and by the city of Nottingham, which is of itself a thriving centre.

In fact, fox-hunting is extremely popular in this shire,

and turns out the largest fields of any provincial hunt. Working-men flock to the covert-side in embarrassing numbers, and, should the chase go in their immediate vicinity, the sound of the horn tempts them from the loam and mould which form so prominent a feature in the county's prosperity.

The hounds are good, but the ground does not hold so strong a scent as grass, and there is at once, therefore, a general falling off in pace; but hounds always carry a line, even though it be a slow one, and throwing up in the middle of a field, commonly seen in the shires, never occurs in this or other of the great plough districts. The high-class horse of the shires is not necessary, but one needs a thoroughly good and stout hunter, for the hills are stiff and the woods dense.

John Burton & Sons

COTTESMORE HOUNDS

That hunting should be attempted in Kent, the "Garden of England," is yet another instance of the strong sporting spirit of the Englishman, for drowsy Kent is not a good scenting country, with its cold, ploughed upland and large woodland, so dense a hound can scarcely crawl through, while one must frequently ride half a mile to advance a quarter of that distance. Such land as is not claimed by the heavy woodlands is completely taken up by hop and fruit gardens or by corn, where flints are plentifully scattered through the light plough. In such a country it may be supposed that only a strong, sensible horse and a hound that knows its business thoroughly are at all serviceable.

Hampshire is a country that, formerly all naked, hilly land, has been gradually reclaimed by cultivation, and where the chalky soil, which comes to the surface here and there, makes brilliant bursts unknown, and watching the hounds with their noses down the chief occupation of the day. It may not be exciting, but none deny it a good school for the hound and rider; though I acknowledge, before being challenged, that the average man goes out for sport, and not to be schooled.

Nevertheless, Hampshire is a thoroughly sporting country, with good packs and excellent hunting, and fields that, although small, are invariably composed of sportsmen who learn their business, if they never knew it before.

South Berkshire is probably the crack pack of this county, with handsome kennels and sixty couple of hounds and well-mounted servants, all turned out in good style. There is some pretty wild country in this shire, with a lot of heather, which, with its many devious paths that tempt the fox, are very trying to the hounds, and hunting in every meaning of the term is necessary, for the line must be picked out and the scent sought.

COTTESMORE KENNELS

John Burton & Sons

Generally speaking, there are no long bursts, and the frequency of the woods, and the density of coverts, tempt the fox to hang to them as long as possible, or, if driven out, to make for another.

The Tedworth kennels will always be celebrated in hunting annals, since they were originally built by Assheton Smith, who earned the reputation, and lived up to it, of being the hardest riding man in England.

Here, when he had outlived the pace of the "shires," he came in his sporting old age to follow the hounds over an easier, but equally sport-giving country, and here at sixty he rode and built up this pack, making two famous runs in a single day when he had turned eighty.

These hounds, presented by Mr. Smith's widow to the country in 1858, were far-famed for their height, which, according to trustworthy authorities, averaged twenty-six inches! veritable stag-hounds. The present pack does not show such proportions.

The downs of this country furnish the few opportunities in the shire for a good burst, and here is the place for those who hunt to ride, for there are no fences, and the small and widely separated coverts permit the fox to neither dwell in peace nor, when fatigued, rest in safety.

One's mind turns rather to stag than fox hunting at the mention of Devonshire and Somersetshire, and yet there is some excellent sport furnished by several packs.

In this country, where, as a rule, fences are wanting or unnegotiable, there is no danger of hounds being ridden over, and their work is most interesting and instructive.

The frequent lanes, with their hard, scentless roads, are a great hinderance to their work; but one learns here, where neither is hampered, the habits and endurance of the wild fox and the intelligence of the hounds. To watch the latter puzzle out a line that at first baffled is a treat not soon to be forgotten, and nowhere, really, can one have more genuine fox-hunting than in this most sporting section of England, where the scent is strong and foxes are plentiful.

LORD RIBBESDALE, MASTER OF THE QUEEN'S BUCK-HOUNDS

You can get a good run almost anywhere in Essex, notwithstanding there is altogether too much plough, though of a very good sort that holds a fair scent and is not too heavy for the horse.

The fences are easy—the ordinary bank and ditch, though sometimes the latter are pretty wide—the coverts small, and the hedges low. It is not a very popular country, resident gentry are few, and the chief support comes from the farmers, who do their duty freely and thoroughly.

Herefordshire is not a country that one would choose for the most enjoyable hunting, as it is thoroughly and miscellaneously cultivated—all sorts of gardens, corn-

THE CRICKETERS' INN, A FAVORITE MEET OF THE QUEEN'S STAG-HOUNDS, AND THE VEHICLE IN WHICH CARTED DEER ARE HAULED

fields, etc., filling the landscape in endless profusion—and the going is heavy, and the scent is not very strong. The jumping is chiefly over thorn hedges not very high, but exceedingly ragged; and sometimes a blind ditch makes it hazardous, while the "dingle," which corresponds to the Leicestershire "bottom," cannot often be negotiated, except where the ground is sound and the banks not too steep and clinging. Notwithstanding, the hunt is maintained in first-class style, its pack dates back sixty years, and the kennels are very handsome.

One of the most popular and favored countries, and one of the oldest and best packs in all of England, is the Waddon Chase near London, site of the Vale of Aylesbury, which, with its turf that is "sounder, fairer, and sweeter" than all others of England—Belvoir, Blackmore, Berkshire, or White Horse included—makes possible brilliant performances of a blood-stirring quality.

The fencing of the vale is stiff, but none too stiff for a good man and a good horse; and there are double ditches with hedged banks, and the best brook-jumping in England. The fields do not reach the swollen proportions of Leicestershire, and while you need not have a steeple-chaser you want a hunter that will jump and stay, and he cannot have too much quality.

Cheshire is a sporting and a pleasant riding country to be sure, for you are always on grass—there are no timber and no staked and laid fences; enclosures are small, fenced with thorn that are easily flown; fields not too large; and the hounds always going well. There is no point riding in Cheshire; the fox goes where he will unviewed until he yields his brush, and you are probably in the air more than anywhere else, except in the stone country of Gloucestershire.

Sussex is a beautiful country, but not a good fox-hunting one, for it is thickly wooded, hilly, extensively cultivated, and the deep soil makes very heavy going. You are constantly jumping; posts and rails are numerous, and a steady man and horse is necessary, for here, if anywhere, one must look before one leaps.

Worcestershire is a country given over largely to agriculture, and filled with small fields that require a great deal of jumping, for no sooner are you out of one than you are into another; but the fences are not stiff, which

DEVON AND SOMERSET STAG HOUNDS

Vickery Bros.

is a blessing when the hounds are running fast and the thorn hedges not bound.

There is a frequency and strength of the post-and-rails that fill the gaps of the hedges, and a deepness of plough, together with the ditch and occasional stone wall awaiting you as a surprise, which make this country, with its fair-sized coverts and strong foxes, by no means an easy one.

Norfolk is chiefly a shooting county, scantily populated, with double ditches and big banks, and small ditches and thorn fences.

Surrey is blessed with good packs, but damned by bad country. It does not advertise its meets, and its fields are small. Plough enclosures, separated by straggling fences that are frequently built on banks, constitute the going, though there is stiff clay in some parts, and hedged banks with a ditch on one and sometimes on both sides. The old Surrey pack is said to date back to 1750, but the building up of the London suburbs has so narrowed its limits in the last few years that the quality of sport has fallen below the standard of by-gone days.

Burstow is one of the best-supported hunts near London, whose popularity on Saturdays gives rather large fields. The enclosures are small, and the fences almost entirely bank and ditch with the thorn hedge, and sometimes a blind drain awaiting the unknowing.

Dorsetshire is a sporting country consisting mostly of chalky downs, and vales that are devoted to dairy farming. The jumps are all hedged bank and ditch, sometimes with a drop, and the enclosures in the vales are small and call for constant jumping. Blackmore Vale, the pick of this shire and the boast of the western counties, is a succession of vales, where the fences are rather stiffish, with closely grown hedge on banks that are five to six feet high.

Shropshire is not a very tempting nor a popular country, but nevertheless it furnishes much good hunting, despite the predominance of plough and the ditches that are unkempt, trappy, and deep.

South Durham, in this shire, instances how much in England is made out of a little, for though it is only thirteen miles square, of well-ploughed land, it is well provided with foxes and furnishes a good bit of sport. North Durham, at the very doors of the collieries, has plenty of foxes, and stone walls often too big to jump.

A KILL WITH THE DEVON AND SOMERSET STAG-HOUNDS

From a painting by Basil Nightingale
DUKE OF RUTLAND'S GAMBLER
A Belvoir Champion Fox hound

Staffordshire has more ragged hedges and uncleaned ditches than probably any other country in England. Some parts are like Cheshire, with its dairy farms and small enclosures and fair hedge-and-ditch fences; but its sport is gradually being curtailed by the industries of coal and iron, and the great mass of coverts it formerly had have disappeared, leaving but a copse here and there. It is not very much of a scenting country in the southern part, though North Staffordshire carries a scent almost everywhere.

Monmouthshire is hilly though ridable, with some grass and small fences. That it is a sporting country may be judged when it is commonly said one may "shoot a grouse, a partridge, or woodcock, kill a salmon, and be at the death of a fox all in one day." There are some tremendous hills, which call for the best staying qualities of horse and hound.

The Duke of Grafton's hounds, turned out in good shape and liberally managed, have some of the best parts of the Bicester, Warwickshire, and Pytchley countries, with every kind of going from light plough to strong grass, and small artificial coverts to heavy woods. Fences are merely hedge and ditch, but may be found in every variety from very easy to the wellnigh unnegotiable.

Hills & Saunders
AN ENGLISH BEAGLE

Oakley is one of the most favorably known of all the hunts, and has been in existence sixty years, its pack coming from the blood of the Belvoir, from which it takes its consistent symmetry. It is what might be called a sweet country, with its gentle rolling surface of tillage, divided by easy thorn fences and ditches that are sometimes in doubles.

Reviewing now the scenes of my pilgrimage, it seems,

indeed, as though all England had been laid out by the Creator for the hunting which is given its people to enjoy under the greatest possible advantages. The Englishman loves country life, enjoys his horses and his hounds, revels in the fresh air, and regards the beautiful landscape of green fields and trimly cut hedges with a pardonable pride in his bucolic skill. There is no home, be it ever so humble, whose owner does not strive to add his bit of coloring to this bower of tender rural beauty, with its soft, invigorating atmosphere and its flower-bestrewn highways.

Hills & Saunders

THE CHRIST CHURCH (OXFORD) BEAGLES

IV

UNIVERSITY SPORTSMANSHIP

There is a time-honored saw that tells us "Englishmen take their pleasures sadly"; but my studies at the English universities have inclined me to the opinion that, as touching comparative university athletics, we Americans take our sport and ourselves too seriously. One does not find at Oxford nor Cambridge that all-absorbing interest which makes the outcome of the football match uppermost in every athletically inclined American undergraduate's thoughts. Though you will see the English student body at the game, rarely is it represented at practice, except in straggling numbers of enthusiasts. If you talk with the average man at Oxford or Cambridge on the team-work and its prospects, he will evince interest, to be sure, but it is lukewarm compared with the spirit with which a Harvard, Yale, or Princeton undergraduate will discuss his eleven, and grow eloquent over the brilliant rushes of the half-back, or sorrowfully deprecate the slowness with which an end rusher gets down the field under a kick. The English university man will deal with generalities, and "fancies they are doing well enough"; he seldom criticises. Whereas the American is not satisfied with "well enough," is more particular in comment, and certainly more searching in his inquiry.

Tradition and years of experience, and, too, possibly, the less nervous, active disposition of the native Englishman, have persuaded him that, after all, the winning or losing of a football match will neither lengthen nor shorten his earthly career. He is human enough to wish to win, to use his best endeavors to that end, and to rejoice in his victory, but he is not going to lose any sleep over it. Too much store is not set on the mere winning, the cardinal principle being to do something athletic, and to do it to the best of your ability. And it does seem the more sensible way, and the best way of doing the greatest good to the largest number.

If you happen at the games of any one college of Oxford or Cambridge, you are immediately impressed by the manifest indifference of the contestants as to whose name goes up as winner on the announcing black-board, or what time is recorded against it. The idea appears to be—and, indeed, it is the proper one—an afternoon's sport first, and winning and records afterwards. The sports are carried on and tea served in the reading-room of the club simultaneously, and apparently one gives as much pleasure as the other.

I do not by any means wish to convey the impression that the English university athlete goes into his race, or his football game, or his boat, indifferent as to whether he wins or not. Quite the contrary; he is keen enough, and runs himself to a standstill against his opponent, or pulls his oar through until he drops (he would not be Anglo-Saxon if he did not); but in his inter-college games the mere winning does not become so much to him as the sport of it all and the general development it portends, while for the inter-university contests the serious side remains in the background until he is on the scratch with his rival.

And all this, too, where the percentage of those not actively engaged in some branch of sport is infinitely small, and where almost every man you meet is on his college torpid, eight, eleven, or fifteen.

On coming in touch with this spirit for the first time it impresses the American university man strangely, though none the less pleasantly. In defence of his own college at home, he immediately consoles himself with the mental reservation that the Englishmen do not attain so high a form in their athletics as do we—and it is true. But what if they do not? They certainly attain a good standard of skill, and by a system and spirit that give the most benefit to the greatest number. After all, that is the real value of athletics in our universities; and when one has been an eye-witness of their football matches, their rowing races, and their athletic sports generally, one realizes that the Oxford and Cambridge spirit is the more healthful and the more wearing.

English university athletes do not give the same careful attention to preparation for contests that we do; special trainers are not employed, the men themselves acting in that capacity; and while they may not reach the degree of perfection attained by our university teams, at the same time they do get "fit" enough to have made a table of rowing times which we have not yet equalled, to have recently defeated a picked team of Yale athletes in track and field sports, and to have compiled athletic records that compare favorably with the best performances of our superlatively trained athletes.

And the outcome of a contest is not taken so seriously. The sight, familiar to us, of members of a defeated football eleven throwing themselves prostrate on the ground in the agony of bitter disappointment would indeed make Englishmen stare in wonderment.

Now I would not feel myself an American—and first and last I am always that—if I did not confess my love of that enthusiasm, that whole-heartedness, which characterizes our athletes, and makes them feel that for the time

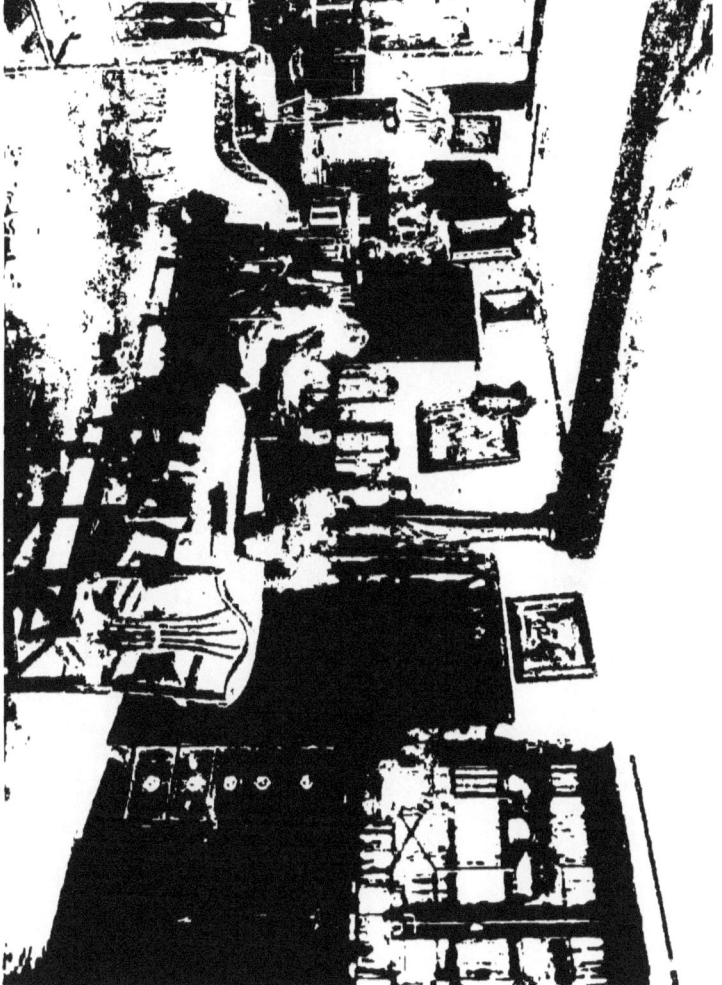

AN UNDERGRADUATE'S ROOM AT CAMBRIDGE

being there is nothing in the wide world so important as an honest triumph over their rivals. My heart invariably goes out to the boy down on the field who, in his hour of defeat, is not ashamed of a few tears, and I always want to make my way to him and grasp his hand and tell him I know he will win next time. Those tears come from the heart, and that boy will make the man who, later, grits his teeth and cuts his way through difficulties in this hurly-burly world. I would not have our athletes different. I believe that to whatsoever one turns his attention, whether as boy, to the sport of his college days, or as man, to the serious side of life's work afterwards, his success is the more likely if he throws his whole heart into it; and one cannot risk so much without experiencing corresponding emotion over the result.

It is by no means in this respect that I should wish our university athletes, and the traditions that inculcate this spirit, changed. There are no lessons here for us to learn from our English cousins. But it is in the lesser preparation, and in the "business," if I may use the word—and I hope I shall be correctly interpreted—that leads up to and surrounds our athletic contests, that the Englishman sets a good example. Particularly would I like to see its softening influences at work on the hard commercial atmosphere that envelops our big football matches, in diminishing the amount of money we annually expend fitting teams for contests, in moderating the speculative eye we have for large gate-receipts, and on the mystery that unnecessarily surrounds so much of the 'varsity crew's work as ignores the undergraduate, and would leave him out of touch with it altogether but for his superabundant enthusiasm and loyalty that surmount all obstacles. Here, I think, we can indeed learn a much-needed lesson, nor can we learn it too quickly.

It will surprise American university men to learn that it costs about $2300 to maintain the Oxford University Rugby Union football team during the season, less than $1500 for the Association team, and in the neighborhood of $3000 for the track athletic teams, while the crew trains and buys its shells and oars at an annual expenditure of from $2500 to $3000. No just comparison can be made between the English university football teams and our own 'varsity elevens, for neither the Rugby Union nor the Association approaches our game either in skill or demand on the players' physical endurance. It would be utterly impossible to fit our football players on the slight training done by the Englishmen, whose season of preparation is very much shorter, and whose game is simplicity itself compared with ours. But in rowing we stand on more equal basis, and the comparison of figures is interesting. Harvard and Yale spend from $9000 to $11,000 per year on their crews, of which the 'varsity eights probably represent from $6000 to $7000; which includes, among other things, shells that cost $500 to $600, oars $125, train-

AN ENGLISH FOOTBALL PLAYER

ing-table $1200 to $1500, and New London expenses about $1200. The maintenance of an American university football eleven figures between $14,000 and $16,000, a baseball nine about $8000 to $10,000 (Harvard last year spent $18,000), and a track athletic team about $5000.

Training-tables, as we have them, are unknown at either Oxford or Cambridge. Football teams do not change their usual course of living until about two weeks before the inter-university match, when they dine together in the common hall, and on food more or less especially prepared for them. College crews—that is, the torpids and the eights—during the short training period are breakfasted together by members of the college to which they belong, and dine as usual in the common hall and at their own individual expense. The 'varsity crew has about six weeks of training; during the three weeks at the university each member of the eight in turn daily entertains the other seven at a breakfast and dinner, while the three weeks at Putney, making the final preparations for their race, are spent in quarters at a regular training-table, and the expenses paid by their respective university boat clubs.

With the track athletic men there is even less pretence at training. They are not dined together even so much as the torpids, and receive very little attention until the 'varsity teams, that meet in dual competition annually on the Queen's Club Grounds in London, are chosen, when they usually have a week or ten days of training on the university grounds, and about the same length of time at Brighton, where they have the sea air as a tonic to their daily practice. They have no trainer, and the care-taker of the grounds acts as starter and general factotum. He may or may not have any particular knowledge of one sport or another (judging from the average form I saw in shot-putting, hammer-throwing, jumping, and hurdling, I should say he usually had not), except that which he has picked up from year to year by constant association with the athletes.

I am sure that throughout my study of English university athletics nothing made a greater impression upon me than the sportsmanlike feeling which exists, and is perfectly apparent to whosoever cares to look, between Oxford and Cambridge crews and teams. Whatever one crew does at Putney the other may see—if it likes. There is no attempt at stealing away, no substitutes sent out to watch and report. Each is on the Thames to perfect its work, and the other is at liberty to "size it up" as much as it may wish. It is quite common for one crew to follow in its steam-launch the rowing of the other. Indeed, the Cambridge captain, Mr. C. T. Fogg-Elliot, only a few days before the race this year, when asked if he had any objections, replied: "Not a bit. Follow all you like, and say what you please." And he meant it.

While at Putney members of the Oxford crew will occasionally dine at the Cambridge training-table, and the latter return the courtesy in kind. The men do not eye one another askance, and there is none of the embarrassment that attends the annual Harvard-Yale visitation when the crews are in quarters at New London. I had the pleasure of being a guest at a dinner given in London by the Sports Club to the Oxford and Cambridge Association football teams on the night of their annual match at Queen's, and although Cambridge had won a victory that every one—before the match—had given Oxford, and although every Oxford graduate and undergraduate was cocksure of winning, I could not, at the tables, distinguish the victors from the losers. And yet again, at the University Boat Race Dinner on the night of the day

A COLLEGE BARGE

H. W. Taunt & Co.

Oxford rowed easily away from Cambridge, was I the happy witness of that same thoroughly sportsmanlike spirit that makes no distinction between conquered and conqueror. I shall never forget those experiences of mine, sitting at the table with the athletes who but a few hours before had been engaged in a most earnest struggle to outdo the other. More than anything else in all my trip it brought home a vivid illustration of the charm and wholesomeness of sport for sport's sake only, of the *mens sana in corpore sano*.

The first step in the right direction was taken in America the winter of '92–'93, when Colonel Henry L. Higginson dined the Harvard and Yale elevens in Boston, and perpetuated the following year in New York by Judge Henry E. Howland's entertainment of the elevens from the same two universities. May the spirit thus begun develop until it has reached the farthermost corners of the United States, and the day arrive when Harvard and Yale will dine in harmony on the night of their annual boat-race, as do Oxford and Cambridge.

I cannot refrain from recounting another incident to yet further accentuate this sportsmanlike spirit and perfect willingness that all London, or the whole world, should see the crews at practice, if it cared to make the journey to Putney. The first morning I went to Putney, Mr. Lehmann, one of the two Oxford coaches, whom I had met, was detained in town, and did not turn up; therefore I asked a boatman to point out to me the other coach, Mr. McLean, and, approaching the latter, asked if the crew was going out, and when. With recollections of New London experiences I expected to have a well-bred, non-committal English stare turned full upon me. Judge, then, my surprise when Mr. McLean informed me, with as much consideration as though I were the most honored

PUTNEY BRIDGE, STARTING-POINT OF THE OXFORD-CAMBRIDGE BOAT-RACE.

old "blue," that the crew was going out in about half an hour, but only for a short paddle, and that if I wanted to see it at work I had better come that afternoon, when the men would launch their boat at "quarter before three."

And he knew me at that time only as one of the several hundred interested spectators standing on the river-bank waiting for the crew to bring out its boat! Fancy asking a Yale or Harvard coach at what hour the crew would come out, and the best place to see it at work! Perhaps a stranger would be told all about it!—per—haps!

It is to be expected that with such a spirit permeating the athletic system the question of eligibility would rarely, if ever, be raised. Each university assumes it is meeting sportsmen and gentlemen, and they have been carried through many years of competition with scarcely a scandal. No entry is ever challenged, and a departure from custom or tradition is regarded, both in and out of the university, as an acknowledgment of weakness. For instance, there happened to be in this ('94) year's Cambridge shell a man who, in the spirit of the law, was not eligible. Although he had not pulled a 'varsity oar four years—the limit, it is tacitly understood, a man may represent his university, without there being a positive ruling to that effect—his being in the boat was unusual, but accepted without protest by Oxford as a confession by Cambridge of their sore need; and that was the end of it.

There is no limit of years a man may row on his college eight in the summer regattas, though four is the stipulated time on a 'varsity, football, cricket, and athletic team, and it bespeaks the sportsmanship of the undergraduate body that this, in our eyes, lax ruling is so seldom taken advantage of. There are no meetings every now and again to consider this one's or that one's eligibility; names of men not really *bona fide* undergraduates

AN ORDINARY PUNT
Racing punt has the ends decked over and is much narrower

are rarely offered for candidacy, and captains neither seek nor encourage them. It is simply a tradition that the colleges and universities shall be represented by athletes from the student body, and no one thinks of asking why, or attempts to evade the prerogatives of custom. If a college puts on a man not strictly in keeping with the spirit of the unwritten law, it places that college in an undesirable light before all the others. As a university man said to me when I asked him point-blank what there was to prevent a captain or college or even university from putting on crack men who were not eligible, "There is nothing to prevent, but the university would not like it, and it would be bad form, you know." I need hardly add that there are no efforts made by either university to induce good football players or oarsmen to forsake one for the other; even the recruiting among preparatory schools—Eton, Harrow, and the others—is *nil*, and matriculating to play on an eleven or row in the boat would be somewhat of a novelty. If men ever do return to play football or cricket or to row (as, for example, like the Cambridge oarsman cited before), no disguise is attempted.

Men who attain the distinction given by making the 'varsity crews and teams are called "blues" at the English universities. A significance derived from the fact that only such as they are entitled to wear the 'varsity color, which with Oxford is dark blue, and with Cambridge light blue. The substitutes, or second-string men, are known in track athletics only as half-blues, and not entitled to the full blue caps, shirts, or coats.

The athletic costumes are highly pleasing in their modesty. The track athletes do not wear inappropriate and indecent rowing-shirts, but add to them quarter-sleeves; while the oarsmen do not strip to the buff, as our college oarsmen do. Respectable costumes appear not to handicap their performances. Oxford and Cambridge have a pretty custom of sporting their colors in the annual eight-oared race by means of a tiny flag (about six inches square) flown from a correspondingly diminutive staff in the bow of the boat, where all may see it.

The manner of meeting the athletic expenses of the

AT OXFORD—LOOKING UP THE ISIS FROM FOLLY BRIDGE. College barges on left; tow path where men run with the boats on right; University boat house in distance

H. W. Taunt & Co.

university is entirely in accord with the spirit that gives all sport in the English universities such wholesome life. It is fairly well known, I doubt not; but, for the few to whom it may be news, let me say that Oxford University is composed of twenty colleges and three halls (colleges of lesser importance); Cambridge of eighteen colleges. Each college has its own athletic association. At some, rowing, football, cricket, track, and all athletic interests are amalgamated and have a common treasury, to which each contributes and on which all draw. In other colleges, though the number is comparatively small, every athletic organization has a distinct treasury. But, whether united or divided, the system of supply is the same.

Every man when he "goes up" (they "go up" when they matriculate, and "go down" when they graduate in English universities) lends his support to whichever of his college athletic interests he is predisposed; if he rows, in addition to his own college club he joins the university boat club, and pays a certain small sum, representing his initiation fee and dues. From this fund, annually recruited, each college maintains its several football, cricket, athletic teams, and crews.

For the support of the university teams and crews each college is assessed *per capita*, giving according to the number of its athletic undergraduates, besides which it pays entrance fees to the university boat club for each crew in the summer regatta. In other words, every athlete in the English university pays his contribution towards the maintenance of the university sport. If he runs, the prizes are a silver medal for first and second, both medals being alike in value; and if he rows, the trophies are flags or well-chosen but inexpensive cups or medals.

Contributions from the undergraduates are not necessary in our universities, or at least have not been during the last few years, because of the increased drawing properties of football and baseball, whose large receipts have not only supported these teams and the crews, but aided in furnishing American universities with the finest and most completely equipped athletic fields and buildings in the world.

And this brings us to the question of gate receipts, where again we may with profit carefully study the example set us by the Englishmen. Nearly all the football games played at Oxford are free to the public, the only occasion on which a charge is made being when the visiting team happens to be one of the numerous semi-professional combinations with which Great Britain is filled to overflowing, and that have an eye to the gate. At Cambridge the same is practically true, only a little more so, for the university owns no enclosed football ground, nor, indeed, an athletic field, strange to relate—and, by-the-way, is endeavoring just now to raise enough money to purchase one. In the meantime all athletic meetings are held on an enclosed field which is rented from the cricket club. Near this is an open common large enough for twenty football fields, on which most of the football matches are played. A few of the colleges of Cambridge have private cricket grounds, and some even a football field, but these are not free to the university.

Apropos of the large number of men that go in for one kind or another of sport, one Saturday while at Cambridge I counted one lacrosse, one hockey, and four football matches being played simultaneously on the big common, while the university track athletic sports were being decided on Fenner's field, near by, and down on the river I found six eights at work.

AT CAMBRIDGE.—LOOKING UP THE CAM
Boat-houses on left; tow path where men run with the boats on right

Oxford is much more favored in the matter of athletic fields. First of all it has an immense tract of land open to the sight-seeing public called "The Parks" (I counted one cricket and nine football fields marked out, and there is room for as many more), on which all university football and cricket matches are played. Then there is a University Athletic Association field, a recent acquisition, and a handsome club-house, with dressing-rooms, and a reading-room up-stairs, where during meetings the very charming and thoroughly English custom of serving tea is observed. This field is devoted entirely to track athletics, and an admission fee charged, to go towards paying for the club-house. Besides this, several of the colleges have cricket and football fields of their own, and lawn-tennis courts are scattered over the university precincts. Oxford and Cambridge never meet on one another's grounds. There are no home-and-home games. Their two football matches, Rugby Union and Association, and their track athletic contests, are decided on the Queen's Club ground in London; their cricket match at Lords, also in London; their boat-race, as everybody knows, of course, on the Thames, from Putney to Mortlake.

In every instance where there is an entrance fee the general admission is usually a shilling, with possibly a sixpence or another shilling for any particularly reserved place. At athletic games and football matches on both university grounds, and at Queen's Club, it is a shilling, with a sixpence for a programme, though at the annual Oxford-Cambridge track athletic meeting at Queen's, which equals cricket in quality of spectators, five shillings is charged for some seats.

At the 'varsity cricket-match at Lords, where the largest and most generally fashionable concourse of spectators may be seen, and which lasts for three days, the daily popular admission will be one shilling, while a guinea ($5.25) gives a reserved seat in the public stand for the three days of the match. The universities get a third, I believe, of the gate receipts of the contest at Queen's and Lords. There are also club pavilions, open only to members.

The particularly pleasing side of these small entrance fees is the retention of the low figure at which they were originally placed, notwithstanding the greatly increased popularity of the sports.

It is not necessary for me to remind American university men of the very distinct difference between this estimable plan of the Englishman and our enterprising watchfulness over the gate receipts. There was a day, within the memory of us all, when the charges to our games were comparatively small, but, as football and baseball grew in popular favor, the admission fees increased proportionately, until now, if we are fortunate enough to get them at first hands, it costs two dollars and a half for a ticket to a Harvard-Yale-Princeton football match, two dollars to have a seat at the Intercollegiate championships, and one dollar and a half to see a game of baseball.

My mission in Great Britain, however, was to make a study of English amateur sport, and not to write dissertations on the questionable policy of exalted charges at our own university games; but I cannot resist drawing comparisons, nor from reiterating what I have so often said, that we are doing college sport a great injury by making it so much of a business venture — a charge to which we lend color by giving the revenue of our games such important consideration. It is a harm probably we all do not appreciate just at the present day, but there is no question that, in the course of a year or so, if present methods are continued, the time must come when we will realize that we could have done college amateur sport a much better service, and put our teams into the field just as fit, and won quite as many victories, on treasuries considerably less corpulent than those that obtain to-day at Harvard, Yale, and Princeton. Money, money, money, seems to be the cry, and it will be the curse, if indeed not the downfall, of honest university sport. I hope I shall live to see fifty cents the limit of admission to our great football games, one dollar purchase the best reserved seat, and the match decided either on college grounds or removed from large cities, where the mass that has no special interest in the outcome of the sport gathers to give it the coloring of a mere holiday spectacle.

V

ROWING

AT OXFORD AND CAMBRIDGE

ALL things have had a beginning, but one must go back to the monks, whose cloister game had so close a connection with the origin of our present court-tennis, if one desires to reach the beginning of sport at Oxford and Cambridge on either land or water. There seems always, in fact, to have been sport of one kind or another at the English universities—a trite remark, by-the-way, since the same might be said with equal truth of any institution of Anglo-Saxon foundation. To what the very first English undergraduates turned their athletic attention has not been given posterity, but the earliest sport, so far as I could get any definite tracing, seems to have been fox-hunting. Although of a necessity riding to hounds must have been limited to those that could afford such comparatively expensive sport, yet it appears to have had quite a following. To be sure it never became common to the student body, as the various branches of athletics are to-day, but alumni reminiscences in personal diaries dating well back to the beginning of the present century indicate that it flourished enthusiastically among a certain percentage of undergraduates. Naturally fox-hunting begat a certain amount of steeple-chasing, to which in turn is accredited, many years later—about 1850—the organization of the first cross-country run on foot. History records

AT THE STARTING-POSTS OF A BUMPING RACE

H. W. Taunt & Co.

that an unsatisfactory day's sport over the hurdles, because of poor mounts, led to an indignation meeting of the riders, and the suggestion of a cross-country run, which came off a few days later, to the immortalization of the very leg-weary but plucky boys that covered the course.

Throughout the history of sport at both Oxford and Cambridge a considerable element of horsemen is found down to the present day. While neither of the universities has an organized hunt, the undergraduates of each have ample opportunity of riding to hounds with the several good packs in the immediate vicinity, Oxford being probably a little more favored in this particular, though more men at Cambridge keep horses—a fact which the nearness of Newmarket very likely explains.

The only hunting done from the universities is after the Christ Church, Oxford, and Trinity College, Cambridge, beagle packs, which have regular runs, sometimes after rabbit, frequently over a drag, and always followed afoot. Both also play polo, and annually decide an inter-university match, which sometimes shows pretty good form, but more often does not. Then, too, Oxford perpetuates the memory of its early steeple-chasing days by holding a meeting every year a few miles outside the university precincts, which, although not recognized by the faculty, nevertheless flourishes, and is one of the most interesting sporting fixtures of the year.

First in importance and in the affections of all English university men is boating, which, although appearing always to have been in vogue, has no authentic records earlier than 1822, and those from the private diary of a 'varsity oar. Even what one reads of this period alludes to rowing as something that had been going on time out of mind, and there is no way, consequently, of knowing when it actually began, unless one went back to the introduction of pleasure-boats in England. There is, I have been told, somewhere an ancient pamphlet, though I could not put my hand on it, that tells of rowing at Oxford in 1815, but even this would not reach the beginning, for Eton, England's renowned public school, is said to have preceded both Oxford and Cambridge. By-the-way, the term "public school" has a different significance in England from what we understand in America. Eton, Harrow, Winchester, Westminster, Charterhouse, the famous preparatory schools for the universities, are called public schools, though they are no more public in our applied interpretation of the word—*i.e.*, free tuition—than are our Exeter, Andover, St. Paul's, and Lawrenceville, to which they correspond. Such as we call public (free) schools are in England known as board schools, from being governed by supervisory boards.

Of the Eton rowing one can only say that it existed before any history on the subject, in print to-day, was written, and next to Eton was Oxford, and, following it, Cambridge. Which was the first of the Oxford University colleges to put on a boat seems equally indefinite, for the records of this university, particularly of the early years before the forties, are singularly incomplete and vague, and in most instances gathered from private diaries. Christ Church, Brasenose (invariably written and spoken of as B. N. C.), Jesus, Exeter, Queen's, and Balliol appear to have been the first on the river, and tradition has it that the great rivalry of those very early days was between the B. N. C. and Jesus boats.

The Brasenose boat-club record covers a few of the early years between '30 and '37, but gives very little information other than the number and names of the boats that were on the river, and contains nothing tangible of the earlier history.

As everybody knows, the first Oxford and Cambridge University race was in 1829, the second not until 1836, and another not until 1839. The intermediate years furnish interest chiefly from the increase of college crews on the river and the growing boating spirit.

The date of the first bumping race is quite beyond the historian's ken, but from the nature of the rivers at both Oxford and Cambridge it is highly probable it must have been the very earliest of college boat racing. The story handed down of the origin of these races at Oxford tells of undergraduates who, having gone picnicking upon the Isis above the locks, and remaining until the eleventh hour, raced back to get home betimes. No one has anything to say how the choice of turn at the locks was settled on the first occasion, but it is simple to understand that, after several of these excursions, the boats took precedence according to their prowess, and that their place— or position, as it is called—on the river soon became, as it is to-day, a survival of the fittest. Their method of getting out of the lock was as expeditious as unique: the stroke went forward, and, shoving against the side of the lock, ran down the gunwale of the boat until he reached his seat, when he dropped into it and set to work. So soon as one boat got out another followed as quickly as possible, and then the next and the next, until all were racing for home and dear life.

The transition from this primitive, if effective, system to the present bumping races seems simple, for there could not have been many of these early aquatic sprees before it became apparent that the narrowness of the river would not permit an overtaking boat to pass the one it was rowing down without danger of collision.

Thus it came about naturally that, instead of attempting to pass one another, that crew was considered to have

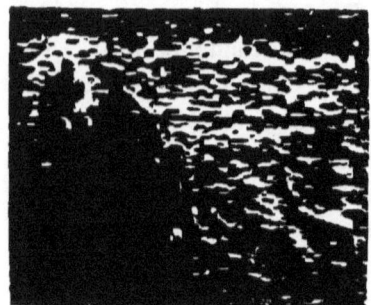

"TUBBING"   H. W. Taunt & Co.

shown its superior speed which succeeded in overtaking and bumping a leading boat, and therefore took the bumped boat's turn in getting out of the lock on the next junketing trip up the Isis. The rule in force to-day on both university rivers, that one boat may not pass another on penalty of fine, owes its existence to the experiences of those days.

As may be supposed, the boats that figured in these early contests were of the kind called in England clinker built and known to us as lapstreaks, which Harvard and Yale used in their first races, and which are used to-day at Oxford and Cambridge for "tubbing."

Although rowing was first taken up at Oxford, Cambridge seems to have been much more advanced in the organization of its boating interests and in the completeness of its early records. The University Boat Club at Cambridge, indeed, was formed in 1827, but it would be extraneous to the subject in hand to go into an unimportant detail, therefore I shall confine myself to only such history as marks eras in the English university boating progress.

Among some old books at Oxford I unearthed a few

THE ORIGINAL "TUB"   H. W. Taunt & Co.

A COACHING "TUB"

H. W. Taunt & Co.

records that seemed to me to be of interest to all students (whether English or American) of early university rowing.

In 1837, Christ Church, Corpus Christi, Exeter, Balliol, Queen's, St. John's, and Wadham had boats on the river, and a curious foot-note to the statement says they "rowed without gang-board [whatever that may mean!], and started with a whole stroke instead of a half one as before." In this year, too, although there was no Oxford-Cambridge University race, Queen's College, as head of the river at Oxford, and St. John's, as occupying a similar position at Cambridge, raced 2¼ miles on the Thames, the former winning in 14 minutes and 10 seconds.

I could not discover the precise year the torpids began rowing, but frequent references are made to them as being on the river in 1836.

In 1838 the strokes of all the rowing colleges at Oxford

met to consider a challenge from Cambridge to row in London; but at this time, as there was no university boat club at Oxford, and no 'varsity crew, Oxford in reply proposed to row their first boat on the river against that of Cambridge, an offer the latter declined on the plea of their first boat's crew, St. John's, not being in good condition. The outcome of this challenge, however, was the formation that same year of the Oxford University Boat Club, "to have a crew continually practising for the defence of the university, and also funds to pay the expense of any race."

The following year they launched their first 'varsity boat and christened it the *Isis*, a description of which somewhat recalls the *Oneida* and *Shawmut*, the famous first racing-boats of Harvard and Yale. It was 51 feet 6 inches long, "colored white inside, with dark-blue gunwale inside and out, oars up to neck painted white, with dark-blue blades." Cambridge this same year had a boat 49 feet 6 inches in length, pulled by a crew averaging 11 stone 5 pounds (159 pounds). In the early days of English university boating, watermen –*i.e.*, professional boatmen or employés of the various college boat clubs—frequently rowed under college colors. Cambridge however, in 1839, passed a rule that its boat "should be manned by gentlemen steerers, and the crew to be undergraduates or those passed at the last examinations." Oxford followed by a similar rule prohibiting such mixing of amateur and professional elements, so that the early forties witnessed the entire abandonment of the practice.

College crews at this time could not have been confined to their own students, judging by some personal diaries which record as not an unusual thing Brasenose men rowing in an Exeter boat, or Queen's men having a seat in a Corpus Christi boat. But in 1842 Balliol inaugurated a

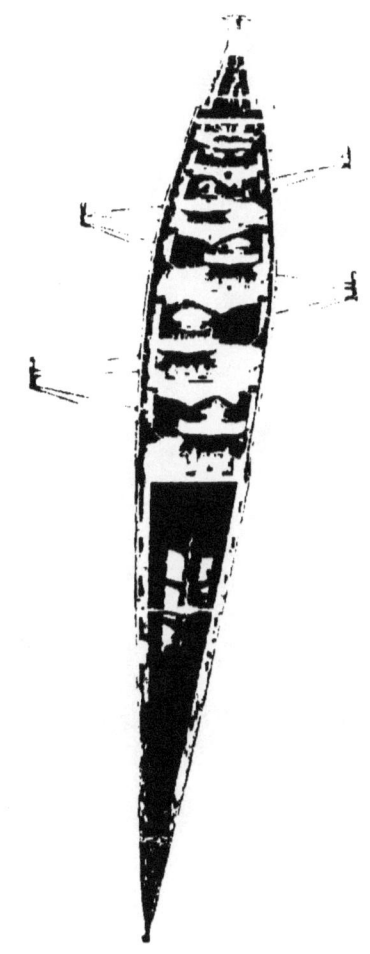

A "CLINKER" FOUR-OAR
Showing position of seats that obtains in all English racing-boats

system, now general, by forming a boat club, and restricting the crew to the undergraduates of its own college. They signalized this departure by launching a new boat, christened *St. Catharine*, quite the most ornate in English university boating history. It was built of oak, 52 feet long, " black and gold, with a red streak outside, oars varnished half-way down, blades black, with red ring between black and varnish, dolphins on blades, and college arms on the rudder."

It may be assumed that at this period the rowing spirit of the universities was increasing materially every year, 'varsity crews created more enthusiasm, and so numerous did candidates become for the torpids and eights as to create a rule at Oxford in 1842 allowing colleges to put on two eights, provided they had also one torpid on the river; a rule, by-the-way, that has been since rescinded, as each college is permitted now to put on but one eight, although it may have as many torpids as it can muster.

It must not be supposed that rowing was progressing in these years without hinderance. It would be curious indeed if it had been without set-backs, for the early history of no sport shows it to have been entirely clear of obstacles, either in England or America.

The greatest difficulty with which English college boating-men had to contend seems to have been an evident disinclination of university authorities to either recognize their sport or restrain their active opposition.

I found in some musty old books a fiat that had been pronounced against "playing of marbles on the steps of the Bodleian" (the famous library building of Oxford), and "bowling of a hoop down High Street," the winding and picturesque thoroughfare of Oxford; yet again these faculty prerogatives were exercised, and touched the boating-men more closely. for in 1837 the Christ Church crew, when head of the river, was taken off, because rowing was not "gentlemanly amusement." But this opposition could have been only short-lived, for there is nothing to show that the sport was actually retarded, and it is obvious the undergraduate enthusiasm was not diminished by these strictures, for in 1858 Oxford had fourteen eights on the river, and as there are to-day only about twenty, it is evident the boating spirit was pretty keen at that time.

Turning now for a running glance at our own university boating history by way of comparison, we find that while Oxford in 1858 had fourteen boats on the river, Harvard and Yale had rowed but two races, and at each rowing was in its infancy. The Yale Boat Club, indeed, which has the honor of being, in point of age, the second rowing club in America (the Detroit Boat Club, organized in 1839, being the first), was formed in 1843, as every American college man knows, and the Harvard Boat Club in 1846. From 1860 to 1864, when there were no races between Harvard and Yale, and the sport was having a particularly hard struggle for existence, Oxford was putting twenty-seven crews on the Isis annually—sixteen eights and eleven torpids. Oxford and Cambridge had their first boat-race in 1829; Harvard and Yale in 1852. It became a regular annual fixture with the former from 1856, with the latter from 1876. Oxford and Cambridge first used wooden outriggers in 1846; Yale introduced them in 1855. In 1857 the English crews rowed in boats without keel as they do to-day, and in the same year Harvard built a six-oared shell, the first one in America, 40 feet long (made short in order to turn a stake easily), of white pine, and fitted with iron outriggers. English universities used sliding seats for the first time in 1873; Yale in 1870. The English university best time is 18 minutes

PROCESSION OF EIGHTS ON THE ISIS, OXFORD—SALUTING THE 'VARSITY

H. W. Taunt & Co.

47 seconds, made last year (1893) by Oxford in the race against Cambridge from Putney to Mortlake, a distance of four and a quarter miles, with a strong tide and wind in their favor, or, to quote from the records of the race, "an easterly wind on the back of a flood tide"; the American university best time is 20 minutes and 10 seconds, made by Yale against Harvard in 1888 over the four-mile course on the Thames at New London, with a fair tide. It is not possible to draw comparisons between the best times made by the Oxford and Yale crews, for the course from Putney to Mortlake is a fast one, much more so than that of our own Thames, and in 1893 it was especially favoring. Indeed, the tides of the English Thames will average between four and six miles an hour, and it is a recorded fact that of late years they run up and out much quicker than formerly, owing to natural forces at work on the embankment and channel; therefore the crews of these days have much more favoring conditions, so far as pace of tide is concerned, than those of four or five years ago. On the American Thames the tides on race-day will, on an average, run from one to two miles an hour.

Dropping history and coming down to the present, I believe I can give the clearest impression of the system and conditions of boat-racing at the English universities by telling how the crews are made up, what races they have, their training, etc. It may be understood that what I say applies to both Oxford and Cambridge, except one or the other is mentioned particularly, though, generally speaking, Oxford is cited, from the fact of its crews standing pre-eminent in university racing.

By all odds the boating interest is the greatest one at both of the universities. I have heard it said by casual observers that football attracts larger crowds and creates more general interest, but my careful investigations during a visit at each university have not borne out such assertions, and I believe I am right in saying that rowing appeals more generally to the undergraduates than any other single sport, not even excepting cricket. Nor are there more individual men actually playing football than rowing, taking the 'varsity, the college eights, and torpids into consideration. It is true that some of the men who row on the torpids are also on the eights, and that the 'varsity is necessarily recruited from the college eights; but that diminishes the total number of individual contestants very little; and, as a matter of fact, the same may be said also of cricket and football, for of those who play on their college elevens and fifteens a certain percentage are chosen for the 'varsity teams. Nor do I hesitate in my statement as touching the drawing power of boating when I consider the Oxford-Cambridge, Rugby Union, and Association football matches played at Queen's in London, or the cricket match decided at Lords. Of the two, cricket draws by far the greater numbers, and, as I have said in an earlier chapter, certainly attracts a larger proportion of fashion than football (which we, with our Springfield and Thanksgiving-day games, can hardly understand); but neither of them, nor even both together, furnish the great mass of spectators that on the day of the Oxford-Cambridge boat-race blacken the banks of the Thames, and the Putney, Hammersmith, and Barnes bridges which span the course from Putney to Mortlake. While the difference in attendance is not so greatly in favor of rowing at the college regattas at Oxford and Cambridge, the banks of the Isis and the Cam during the torpid races in February and the eights' week in May—to say nothing of the other innumerable racing events throughout the year, ending with the trial eights in December, from which the 'varsity candidates are chosen—are lined with a host of spectators, largely in excess of the number to be found at the corresponding purely college matches at cricket and football.

The boating spirit is keen indeed, and the strongest part of it, to my way of thinking, is its interest for every undergraduate in the university. It is a non-athletic man indeed (of whom there are extremely few) who does not take the liveliest concern in his college torpids or eights, or in some one of the numerous aquatic events that are going on throughout the season. Nor is his interest merely a perfunctory one; it may not be so vigorously exploited as that to which we are accustomed at our football and baseball games, but you will find him down on the banks, and even, maybe, if he is particularly keen, running with his college boat.

It is unquestionably this especial spirit that has done more than anything else to raise the standard of English university rowing skill to its present plane, and it is one of the best lessons we in America can learn.

I deny that the English undergraduate is as much more athletic in his tendencies than the American undergraduate as the greater number of rowing-men at Oxford and Cambridge and the keener rowing spirit would indicate. While it is unquestionably true, as I have already written, that the English nation, and of course the English university men, are more generally inclined towards sport than are we, yet the paucity in numbers of our rowing-men may not be traced to the want of athletic inclination at our universities.

In the matter of water and of general rowing facilities, there is no comparison. The Oxford and Cambridge courses are to those of Harvard and Yale, or any other of the American university courses of which I know anything, as the (about) fifty-foot creek at Princeton is to the

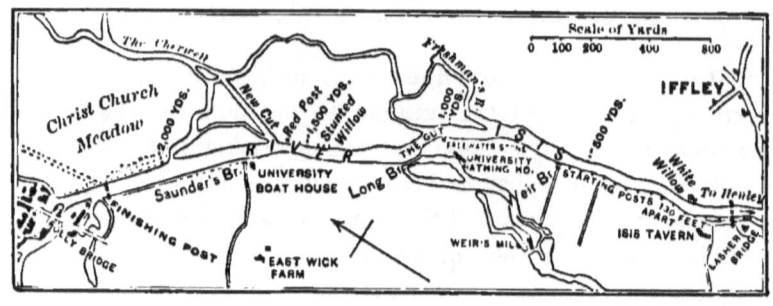

THE OXFORD COURSE
Iffley to college barges, 1¼ mile.   Lashers to finish, 1¼ mile.

Charles River on which Harvard rows. The Isis at Oxford will average about as wide as two shell-lengths. The Cam at Cambridge is narrower, so much so that two eights can pass in safety only by each paddling very slowly. There are some parts of it where they cannot do even that. If, therefore, these English universities have developed such a healthful and far-reaching rowing spirit, and turned out so many crews, it is not because they have been favored by exceptional racing water. The very necessity of the bumping races, in vogue at both, bespeaks the difficulties with which they have had to contend. Neither can it be attributed to the greater quantity of material. I know it is the popular American idea that both Oxford and Cambridge have between 4000 and 5000 students each, but the facts are that the former has something like 2400, and the latter about 2800. On our side Harvard has 3100 students; Yale, 2400; Princeton, 1200; Pennsylvania, 2500; Columbia, 1600; Michigan, 2800; Cornell, 1800.

The reason for this great rowing spirit at Oxford and Cambridge may be found in the encouragement given the undergraduates. Every man is taken into the confidence of his university boating doings. He is made to feel that he is part and parcel—as in very fact he is—of the general machinery that builds up the 'varsity, and he is given a daily opportunity of watching the crew which is to uphold the aquatic honor of his *alma mater*.

If he have any latent boating spirit in him, the natural result is that he will be found a candidate for his college torpids, or, if not physically fitted for rowing, on the banks running with them, or at least on the college barge lending their efforts the encouragement of his presence.

Each college at Oxford has a barge moored to the right bank of the Isis, which is dressing-room, reading-room, and grand-stand in one, it being taken to Henley during the races there. The narrower river at Cambridge does not permit of barges.

Neither is the undergraduate, nor indeed the sport-loving public of England at

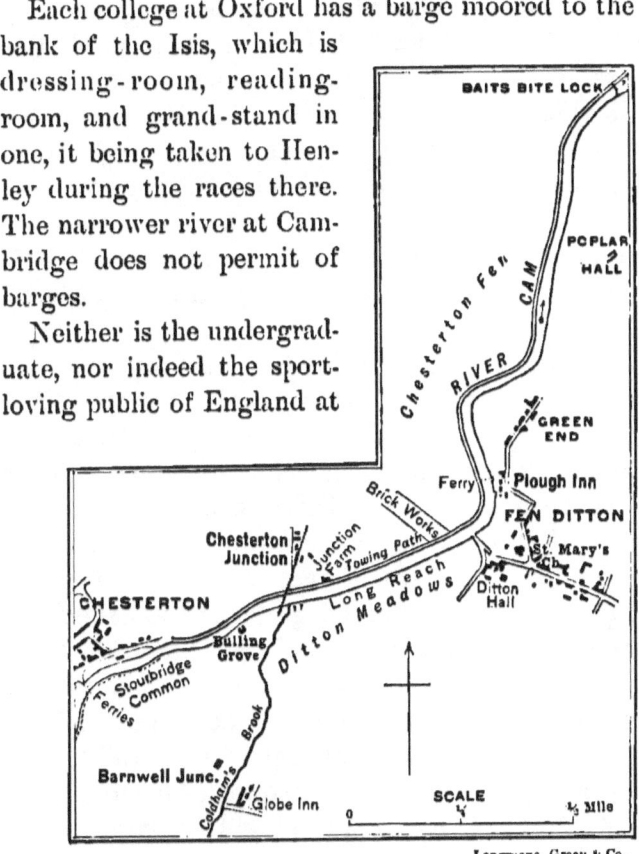

THE CAMBRIDGE COURSE
1¾ mile

large, deprived of the opportunity of watching the 'varsity crews when they have discontinued training on the college courses, and gone to Putney for the three weeks of final preparation for their great race.

Bearing in mind the secretive methods of his own 'varsity crews at New London, it takes an American college man completely off his bearing to witness the absolute indifference of Oxford and Cambridge to either private or public supervision of their practice on the Thames.

Nor is it attempted in the slightest degree to evade this publicity. On the contrary, the crews seem to appreciate the general interest taken in their work, and tacitly invite the public to come and enjoy it. The London daily newspapers publish the time in which each 'varsity rows the course, and regularly print the hour at which the men will go out on the river, morning and afternoon, and in consequence the banks are covered by all kinds of interested spectators.

Still further, this same feeling is carried into the very life of the oarsmen. The crews mingle at Putney in a thoroughly delightful manner, exchanging social amenities at quarters, and on occasion following one another about the river in the coaching launch. There are no spying substitutes sent out to return with tales that neither demoralize the form of the watched nor improve that of the watcher; no stationing of "heelers" along the banks to catch the time of the rival eight; no subterfuges of any kind to trick the opponent or mystify alumni.

This year—and it is not the first time on record, I am told—Mr. R. C. Lehmann, although a Cambridge oarsman, joined Mr. D. H. McLean, who rowed his four years on the Oxford 'varsity, in coaching the Oxford crew. Probably it will give a clearer conception to the American college man of just how the reverse of secretive is the boating atmosphere at Oxford and Cambridge to say that, through the courtesy of Messrs. McLean and Lehmann, the HARPER's WEEKLY photographer was without hesitation permitted to take a view of the Oxford shell in which their crew defeated Cambridge last year and this. It was photographed to show the arrangement of seats, which differ from ours in being placed at the sides of the

MR. LEHMANN COACHING OXFORD FROM HORSEBACK

boat, instead of one behind another, as is the case with us. The Oxford and Cambridge boat-houses on the Thames stand side by side, and for all one sees to the contrary they might be the crews of a single university preparing to meet a common rival. It is certainly a most pleasing picture of the true spirit of sportmanship.

Surely no one will say, who is at all conversant with

university rowing, that this spirit has militated one iota against their form or the English university record table.

It is easy to understand after visiting Oxford and Cambridge how such a rowing spirit is bred in the undergraduate, and why at the English universities so large a proportion of the student body is actively engaged in boating.

It is not necessary to point out to American college men the dissimilar methods in vogue with us, where the candidates for class crews and the 'varsity almost steal away to their work, wellnigh unannounced, and certainly unattended. We all know that, with the exception of the Freshmen, the class crews receive but indifferent coaching and a paltry amount of encouragement from the undergraduate body through their long period of training. It is true that of late years the Freshmen have received much better coaching than previously, and that their practice creates more general interest, which is good, and due entirely, of course, to the annual inter-university Freshmen races at New London, but the actual number of those that follow their work to the day of the race is, still, none the less small; no smaller, however, than the number of undergraduates who watch the work of the 'varsity day by day. While the crew candidates are in the tank the limited vantage-ground for observation gives good reason for a small attendance of student spectators, which does not account for the fact that when the 'varsity has begun work on the river, practically none but the coaches follow it. Sometimes, possibly, occasional enthusiasts will stroll along the banks and endeavor to catch a glimpse of the crew, but they are few and scattered. It is true, to be sure, that at Harvard, Yale, Cornell, and Pennsylvania the rowing courses do not offer the same facilities for the undergraduates to follow as the narrow rivers at Oxford and Cambridge; but the difference is that the English university crews could get away from the students and do not, while the American college crews can get away and do. The more complete explanation is to be found in the unfortunate fact that not only does the university boat club fail to invite their attendance, but puts itself distinctly on record as not wishing it.

W. H. Grove.

OXFORD EIGHT-OARED BOAT — INTERIOR VIEW, LOOKING FORWARD, SHOWING POSITIONS OF SEATS AND FIXED ROWLOCKS

The shell is cedar, 61 ft. 10 in. long; 23 in. wide; depth—amidships, 9 in.; forward, 6½ in.; aft, 5½ in. Fitted with 24-inch slides, stopped to 15 in. Oars, 12 ft. 5 in. long, with 3 ft. 9 in. leverage.

That the undergraduates and that university men generally would be more than pleased to follow the work of the crews throughout their training season is evidenced beyond question by their tremendous outpouring on the day of the annual race at New London.

It is a twofold folly of us to ignore undergraduate interest in the 'varsity crew. I am sure it is answerable for the pronounced lack of rowing spirit in our American universities. The shiftless excuse that the 'varsity does not wish its form "given away" to the undergraduate is both absurd and harmful. If the undergraduate were capable of criticising, it ought to be regarded as an encouraging sign of a growing boating spirit; but unfortunately the average student of the present day is hardly up to it. Glaring faults he may detect, but scarcely any others that would not be immediately apparent to the veriest landsman.

What we need in American universities is greater interest in and more attention given our class crews, and the undergraduate encouraged to watch the 'varsity as often and in as large numbers as he likes.

I have always been of the opinion—and now, after my studies of English university systems and observation of their excellent results, I am convinced—that the secretive methods which prevail in the management of our university crews, and our tendency to make big gates at football and baseball games, are two of the most reprehensible and menacing features of American university sport.

The English boating year begins in October with the practice of the preliminary college crews and 'varsity trials, and continues, with only short intermissions at Christmas and Easter, straight through to the summer eights. In February the torpid races are held. In May the college eights contest for "position" on the river.

OXFORD UNIVERSITY BOAT-HOUSE

In midsummer there are singles, pairs, fours, and scratch matches without number, to say nothing of canoe, punt, sail-boat, and tub races, and various other aquatic sports, including the Naumachia, a mimic sea-battle which is exceedingly mirth-provoking for spectators, and furnishes a great deal of fun to men in tubs and clinkers.

The torpids (called Lents at Cambridge, because coming in that term) correspond to our Freshmen crews only so much as it is the first boat in which the university oarsman makes his début, from which, if he proves himself worthy, he develops into a candidate for his college eight.

Strictly speaking, there are no crews at Oxford or Cambridge that exactly resemble our Freshmen eights. There is no division of classes at English universities as with us; first-year men are called Freshmen, but thereafter are alluded to as second or third year men, though sometimes spoken of in the second year as Seniors, and Very Seniors in the third year. Moreover, torpids are not restricted to first-year men; they are simply the first—the awkward squad, so to speak—of the series of races at Oxford and Cambridge, and may be composed of men of any standing.

Each college is allowed to put on as many torpid eights as it likes—at least, there is no rule limiting the number—though only B. N. C., Christ Church, and one or two others have ever had as many as three torpids on in the same year. They have usually been divided into two divisions for their races, but this year there were so many second torpids that it was found necessary to add a third division. The boats are clinker-built, with fixed seats, and these and all others used in bumping races have a rubber ball about two inches in diameter fixed on the extreme point of the bow, to provide against possibility of injury to the cockswain when the bump is made.

The story of the bumping race is so picturesquely told by Richard Harding Davis in *Our English Cousins* that I shall not supplement his spirited pen-picture by any halting tale of mine, but confine myself rather to the technical side, and advise a careful study of the accompanying chart,

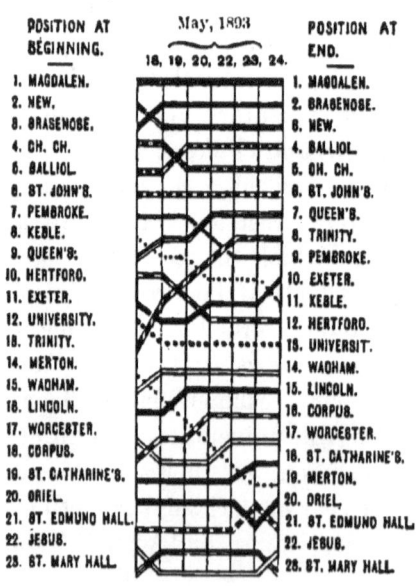

which shows the position of the college eights at the beginning of their races, May, 1893, and at the finish. The system applies equally to eights' and to torpids' racing.

Taking this chart, then, as a guide, and assuming the boats to be at the starting-posts awaiting the signal-gun, No. 1 would be nearest the finishing-line, about one mile away, and No. 23 would be at the extreme end, the farthest from the finishing-line, which would be about 1¼ mile. The boats are placed about 130 feet apart, and held in position by men on the bank with long poles, and to whom the cockswain gives aid by holding to a rope which is attached to the bank and known as the " bung," from its having a bit of wood at the end that floats it when cast off. The boats are started simultaneously on gun signal, and are instantly off, each trying to catch and bump the one in front of it, and when successful both stop rowing and pull into the side of the bank to give the others steerageway. Take Nos. 1, 2, 3, 4, 5, by way of example: If No. 3 bumped No. 2, then in the next day's rowing No. 3 would be 2d, and No. 2 would have dropped down one place. If in the next day No. 4 bumped No. 3, then No. 3 would have gone down another place. The racing is continued for a week, and as only one place can be gained in a day, it is easily seen that the progression towards the head of the river is rather slow, even if a bump is made at every opportunity. Where there are divisions a sandwich boat always exists ; that is, suppose 1, 2, 3, 4, 5 constituted one division, and 7, 8, 9, 10 a second. That would leave No. 6 the sandwich boat, and in the unfortunate position of having to row oftener than the others, for it must not only race at the bottom of the first division, but at the head of the second, and stay there until it bumps the last boat in the first division, when it assumes that place, and that which was the last boat of the first division becomes the sandwich boat, where it sticks until it regains the lost place or is bumped by the first boat in the second division, when it gets out of the sandwich, but goes down a place.

It is unnecessary to add that the first division of the torpids stands higher than the second, and consists of the boats that have, in the previous year's racing, gained the highest places on the river. The first and second torpids of any particular college correspond, perhaps, to our first and second Freshmen crews, but with the differences I have explained.

The form of the torpids, as might be expected, is not very good, but this year ('94) it was said to have been below the average.

The coaching devolves upon the captain or some member of their college eight, and their training amounts to very little. There is no pretence at gymnasium-work; indeed, I may say none is done by any of the English university oarsmen, neither university owning a gymnasium, though each has the use of rather ancient affairs. No gymnasium-work is done because, primarily, it is not believed in, and the climate permits of out-door exercise all the year round. They believe the best way of learning how to row and developing the muscles and lungs needed for rowing is by putting candidates into boats on the water, and thus while our oarsmen are snowed up, and obliged to resort to pulley-weights and tanks, the English college man is acquiring form on the river—better, of course, than all the pulleys ever manufactured. There is very little in-door work of any description except at racquets and fives at either Oxford or Cambridge, and only desultory attempts at fencing, boxing, and singlestick, and no wrestling. Nor is there any regular routine of exercise aside from work on the river, except running,

A "BUMP"

College barges on the left; men running with the boats on right bank

H. W. Taunt & Co.

when the condition of the men requires it. They have no training-table, and, as I have said in another chapter, there is no trainer either for crews or teams in an English university. Training is understood to be simple and wholesome diet, regular habits, and, of course, practice, though there is none of the hard, continuous work that is enforced upon our crews and athletic teams. Whether breakfasting and dining in their own rooms or on invitation, the crew-men are restricted to training diet, while their luncheon (which may be eaten anywhere) must be taken at a fixed hour, confined to cold meat, a glass of water or beer, bread, and a simple pudding or jelly. Extremest punctuality is observed in hours of rising, eating, and retiring.

When in training it is customary for them to breakfast together as guests of some member of the crew or of their particular college, and to dine together at their own expense, and every man who rows joins the University Boat Club, and pays £3 10s. ($17.50) initiation fee.

Although interest in the torpids and their races is great, that which is evinced in the practice of the eights (called Mays at Cambridge, because coming in that term) and in their regatta in May is naturally much keener, because, as representatives of their colleges, they race for supremacy on the river, and "eights week" is the most attractive one of the season at either of the universities.

There is very little more training; like the torpids, they are invited out to breakfast by the different men of the college or the crew, and at times, when the interest is very keen, they are even dined.

At the proper time a paper is posted at the porter's lodge of each college for the names of those who wish to subscribe themselves as hosts, and it is another instance of the boating spirit to say that the list includes practically every member of the college who can afford the entertainment.

They are coached by an old 'varsity oar who happens to be a member of their college, or, in the event of none being available, by a 'varsity oar of some other college, and during the eights' practice season the tow-paths along both the Isis and the Cam are filled with coaches on horseback, and I have seen one on a bicycle. A 'varsity coach at an English university, until he goes up with the crew to Putney, where the final touches are given, does not have the luxury of a steam-launch. The bumping races of the eights are conducted on the same system as those of the torpids, the only difference being that they are started 160 feet apart instead of 130 feet, and that they use regulation racing-shells.

Of the races in midsummer, that include the singles, pair oars, scratch eights, etc., it is only necessary to say that some extremely good rowing is to be seen, and that they are thorough sporting events. The colleges hold closed regattas of scratch events, for which there is no previous training, and for crews that are not chosen until the day of racing. The strokes are appointed by the college captain, but the balance of the crews are drawn from a hat into which the names of all entries are placed. Thus a scratch of four may be made up from as many different colleges as there are oars in the boat, while a pair may have, for instance, one Brasenose man and the other from Balliol.

The most important event of the year, so far as touching university representation, is the trial eights, which takes place the first week in December. During the racing of the torpids the captain of each college eight has his eyes open for suitable candidates, and in "eights week" the president of the University Boat Club and

OXFORD TAKING OUT BOAT

the coaches are looking for likely material for the 'varsity crew. After the summer regattas sixteen of the best men are chosen and made into two crews, and these race to decide which shall be picked as the nucleus of the 'varsity boat, the substitute or substitutes being chosen (though not necessarily) from the unsuccessful eight. The Cambridge trials are rowed over the Adelaide course at Ely, on the Ouse, about three miles against a slow stream. The Oxford trials race with the stream about two miles, at Moulsford-on-Thames. The former take about nineteen minutes, and the latter little over ten, and both row in heavy-built clinker boats on sliding seats. From this time the 'varsity crew may be considered as being in existence, though it does not begin work before January 10th, nor go into serious training until about six weeks preceding the inter-university race on the Thames.

Once they have gone into training their regular coaching begins, and they breakfast and dine together every day on the invitation and at the expense of one member of the crew, each in his turn, which continues until they go down to Putney, where they live in quarters, and have a regular training-table at the expense of the University Boat Club.

The manner of electing the 'varsity crew president (captain) differs at the two universities. At Oxford the captains of the college crews only are the electors, each college of the university thereby having but one vote. At Cambridge the captains of all the college crews—*i.e.*, torpids and eights—form the electing committee. Thus one college may have more votes than another, and old Cambridge men have questioned the advisability of a system that permits the representation of Trinity (which has four times as many undergraduates as any other college at Cambridge), while more promising material in other and smaller colleges is ignored. The Cambridge boat, in fact, seems to stand in need of more unity and less Trinity.

It may readily be seen from what I have written that neither Oxford nor Cambridge experiences anything like the difficulty of Harvard and Yale in turning out a 'varsity boat. Really there is no comparison whatsoever in the making up of eights at the English and American universities, since oarsmen come to their coaches ready-made, while we are obliged to build a new crew and develop untried men nearly every year. Only in the event of men making the 'varsity in their second or third college year do we get veteran material. Nevertheless, while our difficulty is infinitely greater, it could be much simplified if we patterned after the Englishmen in building up a boating spirit—creating more interest and rivalry in class crews, and not shutting out the undergraduate from all chance of keeping in touch with the 'varsity.

Of the form of Oxford—and I particularize because

RACING EIGHTS ON THE ISIS, OXFORD

certainly this year its crew rowed better than that of Cambridge — I should say that the first impression made is of its power and pace-making quality, although I could not discover that they covered their "spaces" more than we do. The men get a tremendous reach, their leg-work is a very strong feature, they get their backs into the stroke more than any crew I have ever seen, swing well back, farther than does Yale, bring their hands well in and several inches higher on the chest than we do, get away quickly, and do not hang an instant on the catch. Their recover is easy, but the time of slide is uniform, whereas the well-known Yale recover starts like lightning and slows down just on the catch; consequently, I noticed that the Oxford boat, although travelling very smoothly, kicked astern more than the Yale shell.

Oxford, sliding up to within about $1\frac{1}{2}$ inches of the rowlock, gets a stroke of about $10\frac{1}{2}$ feet, and does the major portion of work before the pin, well backed up by a steady (not a jerky) drive with the legs; the power is put on immediately the oars enter the water, and is kept on to the end. Yale slides about 3 inches astern of the rowlock, and gets a stroke of about $8\frac{1}{2}$ to 9 feet; their leg-work is good, but does not give the idea of such continuous power; their recover seems to me smoother and better for the pace of the shell than Oxford's. In blade-work and general watermanship Oxford is unexcelled. Their body-work, however, impresses one accustomed to watching Yale eights as being poor; there is a screwing of bodies that gives the crew an awkward, unfinished appearance, increased undoubtedly by the position of the seats, and I was somewhat surprised in following directly astern to note that, even in rough water, the boat travelled on a remarkably even keel. If they rowed in a shell such as ours—*i.e.*, with the seats directly back one of the other, longer outriggers, and swivel rowlocks—I am of the opinion they would find it impossible, with the present comparative indifference to the body, to keep the boat on so even a keel as they do with their present style of seats, their shorter outriggers, and fixed rowlocks. If the men in a Yale boat worked their bodies in a similar manner to what I saw in England, they would not get on much pace. The Englishmen sit higher in their shell than we do, and the boat is invariably cedar, built on a different plan from that followed by our builders. We construct the frame first and build over it, whereas the Englishmen make the cedar shell in sections on moulds, and fit the framework in afterwards. The result is that they turn out a boat that is absolutely smooth on its bottom, while in an American-built boat you can cast your eye along the keel and see the ribs at regular intervals; but the latter is lighter, and one made this year for Harvard by Davy was used in preference to an imported Rough.

While I was at Putney last March ('94) I timed the Oxford eight—8 minutes $31\frac{1}{4}$ seconds for 2 miles and 250 yards, at a stroke averaging 34 to 36 a minute, and with a strong tide and wind in their favor; 21 minutes and 49 seconds over the course of $4\frac{1}{4}$ miles, with a fair tide, rather roughish water, and no wind in their favor, rowing from 32 to 36 strokes; and 2 miles and 4 furlongs in 12 minutes and 32 seconds in rough water. The number of strokes to the minute in practice ranges, as with us, from 32 to 36, which in racing is raised, as occasion requires, from 34 to 37–8. A 40-to-the-minute stroke has yet to make its appearance in English university rowing, except for racing starts. Whether their form or ours puts the greater pace on the boat can only be decided, however, by a race, which we should have had this September on the Thames, from Putney to Mortlake, if Harvard and Yale

THE BARRIER AT PUTNEY BRIDGE
To keep clear the Oxford Cambridge Course

had acted on Oxford's suggestion, and in the spring of 1894 sent a joint challenge pending the result of the New London race, June 28th.

Which reminds me, by-the-bye: I learned in England that the man who masqueraded in New York during the winter of '92–'93 as a brother of Mr. Guy Nickalls, the famous Oxford sculler, and as a representative of the Oxford Boat Club, was an impostor, and his statement that the English crew would come to America and row us provided we paid its expenses pure fiction. The English university man is too good a sportsman to even dream of such a proposition. His crew will pay its own way when it comes to America—which will probably never be until we have rowed it on the Thames—and it will give ours a royal welcome when it goes to England.

The Oxford-Cambridge race is the most important and popular event of the English boating year, but it is entirely lacking in the gay and picturesque setting of our own Harvard-Yale race. The location of the English course does not furnish the scenic effects or provide the opportunities for gala accompaniment that the American course does. New London is two and a half hours from New York and Boston by the fastest trains, a favored yachting rendezvous, and an altogether charming resort; Putney, on the other hand, is a district of London, not over six miles from Charing Cross, and the great mass of people which throng the banks of the Thames and fill the bridges that span it come and go within two hours. There is no observation train decorated in college colors to follow the race from start to finish, filled with cheering partisans of the rival crews; no steamboats that, loaded to the gunwale with enthusiastic spectators, anchor along the course; no yachts covered from stem to stern with fluttering bunting, to make a highly colored lane for the last half-mile of the four; no booming cannon to salute the victors; and none of the hotel life that gives boat-race week in America an enjoyable social coloring.

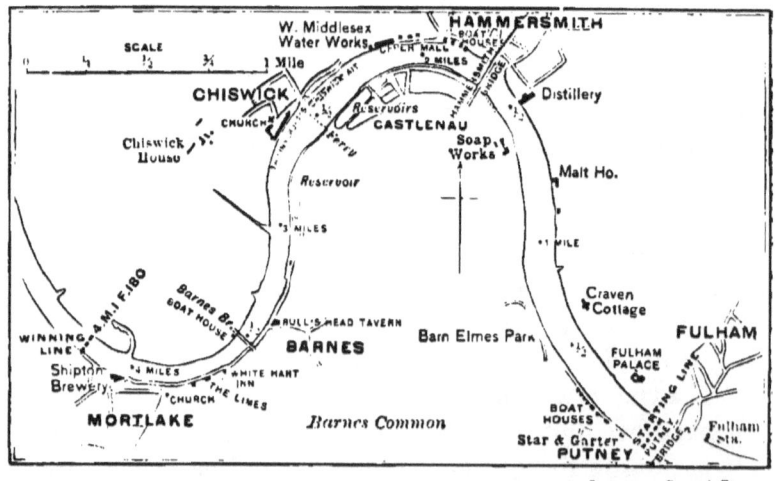

COURSE OF OXFORD-CAMBRIDGE ANNUAL RACE FROM PUTNEY TO MORTLAKE
Putney to Hammersmith, 1 mile, 6 furlongs. Putney to Chiswick, 2 miles, 4 furlongs. Putney to Barnes, 3 miles, 6 furlongs. Putney to Mortlake, 4 miles, 2 furlongs.

Only three boats are allowed on the English Thames between Putney and Mortlake during the inter-university race — the steam-launch of the umpire, which carries no one but the referee, or umpire, as he is called over there, and timers; the umpire's boat, so-called, which corresponds to our judges' boat, and carries the coaches and a limited number of old 'varsity oars, and the press boat. There is no possibility of a deviation from this arrangement, as in addition to the thorough patrolling of the river by the Thames Conservancy police, it is effectually blocked below Putney Bridge by a line of scows stretched from bank to bank, leaving one narrow and well-guarded entrance.

There are many ways of seeing the race, however, though none that gives the constant view afforded by our observation-train. The railway runs cars on to Barnes Bridge, which crosses the Thames at the $3\frac{1}{2}$-mile point of the course; Hammersmith Bridge is at the $1\frac{3}{4}$-mile, and is probably the best vantage-ground, as it gives a good view for the first two miles; and from Putney Bridge the crews can be seen at the start and followed to Hammersmith. Besides these the roofs of all the taverns and business buildings along the course are covered with seats, which are sold at a reasonable figure, and command an excellent view of the race. The immense concourse of people that turn out to witness this contest must be seen to be appreciated. I had the good-fortune to have an invitation for the umpire's boat, which follows directly astern of the referee's launch, and, consequently, a fine opportunity of seeing the race; but looking back on it now I scarcely know which attracted me more — the struggle of the sixteen oarsmen in front of me, or the thousands of spectators that literally blackened the banks, house-tops, and bridges, through which we steamed for four miles and a quarter.

OXFORD-CAMBRIDGE EIGHT-OARED RACES.

Year.	Date.	Winner.	Course.	Time.	Won by.
1829	June 10...	Oxford......	Henley...............	14 m. 30 s.	easily.
1836	June 17,..	Cambridge..	Westminster to Putney..	36 0	1 m.
1839	April 3....	Cambridge..	Westminster to Putney..	31 0	1 m. 45 s.
1840	April 15...	Cambridge..	Westminster to Putney..	29 30	¾ length.
1841	April 14...	Cambridge..	Westminster to Putney..	32 30	1 m. 4 s.
1842	June 11...	Oxford......	Westminster to Putney..	30 45	13 s.
1845	March 15..	Cambridge..	Putney to Mortlake.....	23 30	30 s.
1846	April 3....	Cambridge..	Mortlake to Putney.....	21 5*	2 lengths.
1849	March 29..	Cambridge..	Putney to Mortlake.....	22 0	easily.
1849	Dec. 15...	Oxford......	Putney to Mortlake.....	— —	foul.
1852	April 3....	Oxford......	Putney to Mortlake.....	21 36	27 s.
1854	April 8....	Oxford......	Putney to Mortlake.....	25 29	11 strokes.
1856	March 15..	Cambridge..	Mortlake to Putney.....	25 50	½ length.
1857	April 4....	Oxford......	Putney to Mortlake.....	22 35†	35 s.
1858	March 27..	Cambridge..	Putney to Mortlake.....	21 23	22 s.
1859	April 15...	Oxford......	Putney to Mortlake.....	24 40	Camb. sank.
1860	March 31..	Cambridge..	Putney to Mortlake.....	26 5	1 length.
1861	March 23..	Oxford......	Putney to Mortlake.....	23 30	48 s.
1862	April 12...	Oxford......	Putney to Mortlake.....	24 41	30 s.
1863	March 28..	Oxford......	Mortlake to Putney.....	23 6‡	43 s.
1864	March 19..	Oxford......	Putney to Mortlake.....	21 40	26 s.
1865	April 8....	Oxford......	Putney to Mortlake.....	21 24	4 lengths.
1866	March 24..	Oxford......	Putney to Mortlake.....	25 35	15 s.
1867	April 13...	Oxford......	Putney to Mortlake.....	22 40	½ length.
1868	April 4....	Oxford......	Putney to Mortlake.....	20 56	6 lengths.
1869	March 17..	Oxford......	Putney to Mortlake.....	20 5	3 lengths.
1870	April 6....	Cambridge..	Putney to Mortlake.....	22 4	1½ length.
1871	April 1....	Cambridge..	Putney to Mortlake.....	23 5	1 length.
1872	March 23..	Cambridge..	Putney to Mortlake.....	21 15	2 lengths.
1873	March 29..	Cambridge..	Putney to Mortlake.....	19 35§	3¼ lengths.
1874	March 28..	Cambridge..	Putney to Mortlake.....	22 35	3 lengths.
1875	March 20..	Oxford......	Putney to Mortlake.....	22 2	10 lengths.
1876	April 8....	Cambridge..	Putney to Mortlake.....	20 20	easily.
1877	March 24	Oxford...... Cambridge	Putney to Mortlake.....	24 8ǁ	dead heat.
1878	April 13...	Oxford......	Putney to Mortlake.....	22 13	10 lengths.
1879	April 5....	Cambridge..	Putney to Mortlake.....	21 18	3½ lengths.
1880	March 22..	Oxford......	Putney to Mortlake.....	21 23	3¼ lengths.
1881	April 8....	Oxford......	Putney to Mortlake.....	21 51	3 lengths.
1882	April 1....	Oxford......	Putney to Mortlake.....	20 12	7 lengths.
1883	March 15..	Oxford......	Putney to Mortlake.....	21 18	3½ lengths.
1884	April 7....	Cambridge..	Putney to Mortlake.....	21 39	2½ lengths.
1885	March 28..	Oxford......	Putney to Mortlake.....	21 36	2½ lengths.
1886	April 3 ...	Cambridge..	Putney to Mortlake.....	22 29	⅔ length.
1887	March 26..	Cambridge..	Putney to Mortlake.....	20 52¶	2½ lengths.
1888	March 24..	Cambridge..	Putney to Mortlake.....	20 48	7 lengths.
1889	March 30..	Cambridge..	Putney to Mortlake.....	20 14	2¾ lengths.
1890	March 26..	Oxford......	Putney to Mortlake.....	22 3	bare length.
1891	March 21..	Oxford......	Putney to Mortlake.....	21 48	½ length.
1892	April 9....	Oxford......	Putney to Mortlake.....	19 21	2¼ lengths.
1893	March 22..	Oxford......	Putney to Mortlake.....	18 47	1 length, 4 ft.
1894	March 17..	Oxford......	Putney to Mortlake.....	21 39	3½ lengths.

* The first University race rowed in outriggers.
† Used keelless boats for the first time.   ‡ From the High Bridge to Putney Pier.
§ Both crews used sliding seats for the first time.
ǁ The Oxford bowman damaged his oar.   ¶ No. 7 in the Oxford boat broke his oar.

Fifty-one matches have been rowed—Oxford winning 28, Cambridge 22; one dead heat.
  There is a tradition on the other side that the winning crew, once it has the race in hand, shall not extend itself—hence the distance separating the two on the finish line is of small value as indicating the actual superiority of the winner over the loser.

VI

ROWING

ON THE THAMES

No sport in England is cleaner than boating, and none older, for it rivals the age, I dare say, of the very Thames, whose troubled, muddy bosom is the scene of so much of its activity. Having in the preceding chapter gone into the antiquity of rowing, and, after considerable rummaging among dust-laden tomes of boating-lore emerged with about as much knowledge as when I entered upon the research—to wit, that the first date of boating at the public schools and universities has not been authentically determined, and that one knows only that before history took up the subject, boating was—I shall curb my ambition for further delving. We do know, however, a little more about the early days of rowing on the Thames, or rather non-collegiate boating, since it is a matter of record that the first race instituted on that course was founded by Mr. Doggett, a famous comedian, who, in 1715, offered the trophy for watermen, which, known as the Doggett Coat and Badge, has been raced for annually up to this day, authentic records existing since 1791. The Thames waterman, by-the-way, is quite an interesting worthy, and forms a rather picturesque background to boating history, for in the early university rowing days, as we have seen, he always sat in the cockswain's seat, and frequently pulled an oar in the college boats. He is a professional, but an honest one, and, as one of a class, commands the respect of all British oarsmen. It is safe to say that if interest was keen enough to provide a prize for watermen, the general rowing spirit at the beginning of the eighteenth century must have been spreading satisfactorily, a conclusion rather corroborated by the first Thames regatta, held in 1775, which shows that there was a great deal of previous rowing to have suggested it. Further evidence of its popularity may also be had in the histories that tell of the very considerable stir in boating circles along in the beginning of the present century, and especially of Westminster and Eton public-school crews that attracted quite the greatest attention of the then rowing season.

The first river clubs to have left any record are the Star and Arrow, which were in existence even so early as the last of the eighteenth century, and flourished at the beginning of the nineteenth, disappearing somewhere along 1820.

From one or the other or both of these the Leander Club, founded in 1825 or thereabouts, is said to have arisen. Within a few years after its organization it attained the distinction of being considered not only the first amateur boating club in Great Britain in point of birth, but in influence as well, and grew to be a sort of consolidating power, absorbing the best oarsmen of the numerous little clubs that sprang up along the river. As rapidly, however, as one lot of clubs dissolved, only to materialize again under Leander colors, another, nothing daunted, floated their insignia to the Thames breeze, and while in no case did they develop beyond a more or less indifferent life, yet it all went to prove the boating spirit not wanting, and that the rivalry was becoming keen even at so early a day.

The most important appearance of the Leander Club

TRAINING QUARTERS OF THE OXFORD CREW AT PUTNEY

during its infancy was in '31, when they rowed and defeated Oxford with watermen steering. The fact that it was a match race for £200 is evidence that the amateur definition of to-day did not then obtain. Nor was it necessary, for the sport had not yet attracted the elements that are more susceptible to pounds, shillings, and pence than to the laurel wreath. It was shortly after this race, however, that the question of trophies was raised and money prizes abolished as being too tempting to the "mug hunter."

This was the liveliest of the early periods of boating, and for a few years the interest continued to spread and the sport to thrive, the Leander, and the small clubs that were popping into life and dropping out again, furnishing the centre of a growing class of oarsmen. Naturally, with this continual increase in number of participants, and the ensuing matches, a common meeting, where all might enter and settle disputes on individual prowess, was to be expected as a certain sequence. Thus it came about that, in 1839, the Henley Regatta, starting with but one prize, the Grand Challenge Cup, which up to the present day is considered the most desirable trophy for an eight-oar crew to win, was called into existence. It was a successful and popular institution, as the speedy offering of other trophies argues, for the same year the Town Challenge Cup was added to the list; two years later the Stewards' Cup; in '44, the Diamond Sculls; in '45, the Ladies' Challenge Cup for eights; in '47, the Visitors' Challenge Cup; in '56, the Wyfold Challenge Cup, both for fours; followed by the Thames Challenge Cup for eights in '68, and the Public Schools' Challenge Cup for fours in '79.

Notwithstanding the auspicious beginning of the regatta, however, and a generous prize list, the unforeseen influence of an expanding trade filled the Thames with steamboats, and from about 1840 so lessened the popularity of rowing that in the early fifties even a scratch eight was rarely seen on the river. In those days suburban railway facilities had not reached the present standard, and clubs at Putney as they are to-day were not then a possibility. The increased river traffic and the churning steamboats made training almost impossible, so that really the only bit of good water any of the crews got was at the Henley Regatta itself. Even Leander during this period cut no figure in the aquatic world, appearing only once or twice at Henley, and absenting itself thereafter, and it was not until along towards '56 that there were signs of a reviviscence.

The revival of rowing on the Thames may be dated from the birth of the London Rowing Club (1856), which, on its first appearance at Henley, in '57, not only won the Grand Challenge Cup, but sent a thrill of new life throughout amateur boating that gave it such an impetus as has carried it up to its present popular pitch.

No institution in Great Britain, indeed, may be said to have done so much for English rowing as this London club. Besides being a powerful factor in competitions, and invariably turning out excellent crews, it had the good sportsmanship to encourage others, and by its generous aid and example several clubs sprang into life shortly afterwards, the most important of them being the Thames, which exists to-day as one of the three great rowing clubs on the river. With the coming of the Thames Club, a new rival appeared to spur on the eights of Leander and London, all striving for the honor of giving the Oxford and Cambridge 'varsities the best practice spins when they came to Putney for their final work. It was all clean, honest rivalry, and has remained so.

In the meantime the boating spirit grew apace.

Such a show of boating life on the Thames was certain to bring a response from the country, and although making haste slowly at first, it was not long before provincial oarsmanship began to be heard from, and the movement set in that has in the last twenty years placed it at its present excellent standard. Clubs were formed wherever there was a suitable course, regattas held, and keenest rivalry existed between the towns of the same and different counties.

Along the Thames clubs have not multiplied largely since the revival of river boating the latter part of the fifties, but the number of oarsmen, with the public schools and the universities as constant feeders, has greatly increased, and there has been no drag in interest. Each year has seen the Henley Regatta grow more and more important, until it is now regarded as unquestionably the most prominent amateur rowing event in the world.

With a boating spirit spreading to the farthermost corners of the kingdom, there came a time, along in the seventies, when it was apparent that the amateur definition stood in much need of clarification. Previous to the Henley Regatta of '71 an occasion for legislation had never arisen, but the qualification as "gentlemen amateurs" of one of the crews entered that year for the Town Cup being questioned, without specific charges, the necessity of deciding just what should constitute an amateur oarsman became apparent.

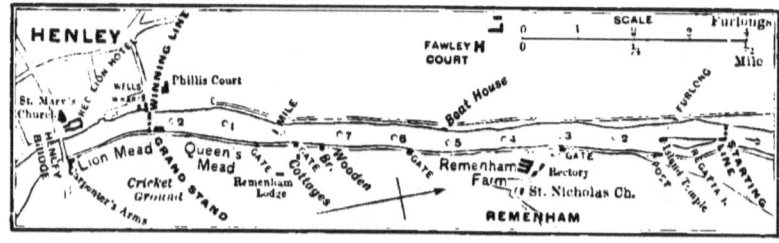

THE HENLEY COURSE—SCENE OF HENLEY REGATTA
1 mile, 550 yards

Refusing an entry was a radical departure at the time of which I am writing, and led to much general discussion among oarsmen, although it was not until '78 that a representative meeting eventually went into session, and a committee composed of the leading members of the clubs and universities determined upon this definition:

"An amateur oarsman or sculler may be an officer of her Majesty's army or navy, or civil service, a member of the liberal professions, or of the universities or public schools, or of any established boat or rowing club not containing mechanics or professionals; and must not have competed in any competition for either a stake or money or entrance fee, or with or against a professional for any prize; nor ever taught, pursued, or assisted in the pursuit of athletic exercises of any kind as a means of livelihood, nor have ever been employed in or about boats, or in manual labor; nor be a mechanic, artisan, or laborer."

The next year the executive committee of the Henley Regatta drew up a set of rules of their own, which, worded differently, were practically the same; and these have been changed slightly, until the following, that obtain to-day, are the result:

"1. No person shall be considered an amateur oarsman, sculler, or cockswain—

"A. Who has ever taken part in any open competition for a stake, money, or entrance fee.

"B. Who has ever knowingly competed with or against a professional for any prize.

"C. Who has ever taught, pursued, or assisted in the practice of athletic exercises of any kind for profit.

"D. Who has ever been employed in or about boats, or in manual labor for money or wages.

"E. Who is or has been by trade or employment for wages a mechanic, artisan, or laborer, or engaged in any menial duty."

These rules have created much criticism now and again, both in England and in the United States, but, despite some inconsistencies in application as to different trades, they have beyond question proved the salvation of honest amateur boating and the means of keeping it the cleanest of English sports. I have studied this subject very carefully on both sides of the water, and not only am I of the opinion that English amateur rowing would not occupy the high plane it does to-day were it not for this definition, but, strange as it may sound to our American ideas of democracy, I believe we must adopt some very similar ruling if we ever hope to attain a correspondingly high standard. There is no reason why we should not have a Henley in America; but we cannot under present rulings.

Why there should be such constant strife to bring together in sport the two divergent elements of society that never by any chance meet elsewhere on even terms is quite incomprehensible, and it is altogether the sole cause of all our athletic woe. Unlike the quality of mercy, which blesses him that gives and him that receives, this athletic philanthropy embarrasses both. We form associations, and rush into them, *nolens volens*, all manner of clubs, composed of men of all conditions, expecting these, whose education has not been such as to lead to an appreciation, or even an understanding, of the true amateur definition, to at once fall into the lines we have laid down, and forsake traditions and habits of a lifetime—nay, of several generations of lifetimes.

It sounds quite as senseless and impracticable as the theory of that other Utopian philanthropist who fondly expects the negro, lifted suddenly out of generations of bondage, to fraternize and favorably compare with the race whose individuals have always been the refined and cultured members of the civilized world.

Just so impossible is it for the amateur athletic organizations of Great Britain and America to bring together two elements in sport that do not harmonize in any other walk of life.

Even in England there has been in recent years an attempt by university men, whose sincerity cannot be doubted, even though their wisdom be questioned, to mix oil and water by the formation of the National (so called) Amateur Rowing Association, which should admit all men who pretended to row for sport, be their station in life what it may. But, sad to relate, their Christian efforts have been illy rewarded; for on several occasions these reclaimed amateurs are said to have sold challenge cups to which they had no title, and the annual regatta has dwindled to an affair of small importance and less respectability.

If this were not lesson enough for those who seem to believe that athletics, like love (according to popular report), levels all ranks, the present condition of track and field athletics and of football in England, in all of which their pet doctrine has been exploited, ought to be convincing proof of the utter impossibility of keeping amateur sport clean and throwing it open to the laboring (so called) classes; for we are all laborers on this earth—

TRAINING QUARTERS OF THE CAMBRIDGE CREW AT PUTNEY

laborers in our chosen professions or trades, laborers of different degrees of culture, according to the quality of refinement into which we are born or subsequently acquire.

We of America have only in the last five years begun to see this side of sport. We saw the introduction of the low element damn boxing; we know that the defunct Manhattan Athletic Club and its hireling athletes professionalized athletics; we see every day to what state bicycling has come; rowing is not what it should be; and we are grateful that football has not yet become so popular as to jeopardize its present health and respectability. But the day is coming when we shall have such an element to contend against just as certainly as it came in England, and we must profit by the mistakes of the sportsmen of the Old World.

No one rejoices more than I at evidences of the lower classes turning their attention to sport. It is a magnificent spectacle, of incalculable value to national manhood, and would it applied to the whole world. None is more democratic than I. I am more than willing to help my laboring brother of lesser refinement; to do all I can for him in his worthy efforts to attain a sound mind and healthful body; give him advice, time, aid, and to encourage in every possible manner his endeavors to make more of a man of himself. But I do not care to dine or play football with him.

We each of us have our own ways of doing, our own ideas of the fitness of things, and of the qualifications of an amateur. Let us therefore abide in them, neither trespassing on the prerogatives of the other. There is no reason why, because I prefer to use a fork, and my laboring friend is predisposed to the knife, that we should attempt to force our preferences one upon the other.

This is a free country, and life is too short to waste

W. H. Grove

LEANDER ROWING CLUB BOAT-HOUSE AT PUTNEY—USED BY CAMBRIDGE

time in fruitless endeavors. The laboring class are all right in their way; let them go their way in peace, and have their athletics in whatsoever manner best suits their inclinations. There is no reason on earth why they should play under our rules, or why we should open our rules to admit of their more liberal understandings of an amateur.

Let us have our own sport among the more refined elements, and allow no discordant spirits to enter into it. Let our best clubs hold meetings open to invitation entries only, and our college men after graduation keep up their rowing, as they do in England, and give us a few more crews like that the New York Athletic Club had two years ago, and of the kind Detroit has always turned out. Let us have a definition somewhat akin to the English Amateur Rowing Association, and, likely as not, in a few years it may be possible for us to hold such a regatta as they have at Henley, but not until then.

So thoroughly impressed has the better English athletic public become with the hopelessness of otherwise relieving the present condition that I expect to see in the next few years the few amateur clubs of Great Britain adopt a definition similar to that which obtains in rowing. It is sure to come, for to-day the better element, once it has left the universities, shuns competition, driven out by the lower.

Every boating-man in the universe knows the Henley Regatta, instituted in 1839, as not only the largest in the world, but the only one at which all the entries are *bona fide* amateurs beyond question. It more nearly approaches —indeed, it would probably be more correct to say that it surpasses—the scenes of our boat-race week at New London, wherein the Oxford-Cambridge event in March is lacking. Henley is a three days' festival of the gayest description in the first week of July; the river-banks are lined with college barges hired for the occasion, and brought down from Oxford and all lavishly decorated; the Thames swarms with small boats, which crowd to the banks to clear the course when a race is called, and the enthusiasm—for Englishmen—is considerable. It should be borne in mind that the much-criticised "gentlemen amateur" definition governs all the racing of this regatta, and it is the cleanliness of the sport that this rule assures and the character of the contestants that makes Henley so thoroughly enjoyable and sport-giving, and its cups represent the championships of two hemispheres. The programme includes: The Grand Challenge Cup for eights, open to any amateur crew in the world; the Stewards' Challenge Cup for fours, open to the world; the Ladies' Challenge Plate, open only to English university, college, and public-school eights; the Visitors' Challenge Cup for fours, open only to college and school crews; the Thames Challenge Cup for eights, open to the world—

"but no member of the winning crew, cockswain excepted, of the Grand Challenge or Stewards' cups may row, nor can the same man enter for this race and for others in the same year";

the Wyfold Challenge Cup for fours, open to the world under the same conditions as the Stewards' Cup; the Silver Goblets for pair oars, open to the world; the Diamond Challenge Sculls for singles, open to the world.

The entries at this regatta are from the colleges of both Oxford and Cambridge, the public schools, and the clubs,

LONDON ROWING CLUB BOAT-HOUSE AT PUTNEY—USED BY OXFORD

the three great clubs — Leander, London, and Thames — being the most important competitors, and the college-trained oarsman invariably shows to better advantage than the graduate of the river school.

Although there is no definite restriction to that effect, the Leander Rowing Club is to a great extent membered by university men, and consequently their crews are composed pretty much of past or present 'varsity and college oars. The London Club is not so exclusive, but its crew likewise is made up largely of similar material. The Thames Club does not confine its membership to college men, though all its oarsmen are desirable, and the amateur standard is maintained. There have been occasions when the club made a slight deviation, but, as a usual thing, it lives up to the lines pretty closely.

Following Henley, in about the middle of July, comes the race for the Wingfield Sculls, open only to "gentlemen scullers of the United Kingdom of Great Britain and Ireland." The trophies are silver sculls, presented in 1830 by Henry C. Wingfield to the "best amateur sculler of the Thames." Originally the course was from Westminster to Putney Bridge; then in 1849 it was changed to be rowed annually, August 10th, from Putney to Kew, a distance of 6 miles; but in '61 it was altered to the present course, 4¼ miles, from Putney Aqueduct to the Ship (Tavern) at Mortlake. The winning of this trophy carries with it the amateur championship of Great Britain, and the best oarsmen of the mother country are always to be found among the entries. Since '61 a badge has been given to the successful oarsmen, while the box in which the trophy itself is contained is literally covered with silver plates containing the names of its annual winners.

Directly after Henley, too, comes the Metropolitan Regatta, founded in '66, at which four cups are given — one

THE LONDON, LEANDER, AND THAMES ROWING CLUBS—LOOKING UP THE THAMES

W. H. Grove

each for Junior and Senior eights, one for fours, and one for scullers; Thames National Regatta for watermen—champion fours, pair oars, sculls, apprentice sculls, and the famous Doggett Coat and Badge race.

The waterman, to prove the place he occupies in the esteem of British oarsmen, is favored by several closely following regattas, and in August come the Windsor and Eton regattas, which furnish excellent sport, and the Amateur Punting Championships, where the most skilful pole-work in the world may be seen and enjoyed, for these punt races, as may be judged by the form of the craft, which is flat-bottomed, without stem, keel, or stern-post, the width at each end being at least one-half of the width at the widest part, are no end of fun as well as sport.

Besides all this boating on the Thames, there are innumerable regattas given by different cities—Chester, Bedford, Derry, Reading, Molesey, Ipswich, Mersey, Worcester, Leicester, York, Nottingham, Kingston-on-Thames, etc., to no end. It may be judged, therefore, from this list of regattas, which does not pretend to be complete, that the boating spirit in England is intense, and its influence felt throughout the kingdom.

In Ireland and Scotland there are a number of clubs which hold annual regattas, but rarely send a crew to Henley. Dublin University sometimes is represented, but is about the only one that has ever put in an appearance. There are clubs and rowing at Belfast, Dublin, Cork, Limerick, and Londonderry in Ireland, and at Edinburgh, Glasgow, Greenock, and Aberdeen in Scotland.

Although pretending to have no jurisdiction outside of England, I believe, nevertheless, the Amateur Rowing Association is looked upon as, and unquestionably is, the ruling spirit of the British Kingdom. It is to rowing, in fact, what the Marylebone Club is to cricket and Hurlingham is to polo, and this for the very evident and good reason that its guidance remains in the hands of gentlemen.

The executive committee has amongst its members the president of the Oxford and of the Cambridge boat clubs, the captains of the London, Leander, and Thames rowing clubs, and the Honorable Secretary of the association.

Its roster of membership numbers 36 affiliated clubs; besides, there are in great Britain 60 Metropolitan clubs, 30 of which are also members of the National Amateur Rowing Association, and the West End Amateur Rowing Association, 92 provincial clubs, 24 tradesmen's clubs, and 21 seacoast clubs.

It may be judged, therefore, that this great boating spirit, upon which I have commented so exhaustively, is not confined to Oxford and Cambridge.

HENLEY-ON-THAMES ROYAL REGATTA WINNERS

GRAND CHALLENGE CUP, for Eight Oars.—Established 1839.

Year	Winner	Time m. s.	Year	Winner	Time m. s.
1839	First Trinity, Cambridge	8 30	1867	Etonian Club, Oxford	7 54
1840	Leander Club	9 15	1868	London Rowing Club	7 23
1841	Cambridge Subs. rooms*	— —	1869	Etonian Club, Oxford	7 28
1842	Cambridge Subs. rooms	8 30	1870	Etonian Club, Oxford	7 18
1843	Oxford U. B. C. (7 oars)	9 0	1871	Etonian Club, Oxford	8 5
1844	Etonian C., Oxford	8 25	1872	London Rowing Club	8 37
1845	Cambridge U. B. C.	8 30	1873	London Rowing Club	7 58
1846	Thames Club, London	8 15	1874	London Rowing Club	7 43
1847	Oxford U. B. C.	8 0	1875	Leander Club	7 22
1848	Oxford U. B. C.	9 11	1876	Thames Rowing Club	7 27
1849	Wadham College, Oxford†	— —	1877	London Rowing Club	8 16
1850	Oxford U. B. C.	— —	1878	Thames Rowing Club	7 42
1851	Oxford U. B. C.	7 45	1879	Jesus College, Cambridge	8 39
1852	Oxford U. B. C.	— —	1880	Leander Club	7 3
1853	Oxford U. B. C.	8 23	1881	London Rowing Club	7 24
1854	First Trinity, Cambridge	8 15	1882	Exeter College, Oxford	8 11
1855	Cambridge U. B. C.	8 32	1883	London Rowing Club	7 51
1856	Royal Chester R. C.	— —	1884	London Rowing Club	7 27
1857	London Rowing Club	7 50	1885	Jesus College, Cambridge	7 22
1858	Cambridge U. B. C.	7 26	1886	Trinity Hall, Cambridge	6 53
1859	London Rowing Club	7 45	1887	Trinity Hall, Cambridge	6 56
1860	First Trinity, Cambridge	8 55	1888	Thames Rowing Club	7 1
1861	First Trinity, Cambridge	8 15	1889	Thames Rowing Club	7 4
1862	London Rowing Club	8 2	1890	London Rowing Club	7 4¼
1863	University College, Oxford	7 45	1891	Leander Club	6 51
1864	Kingston Rowing Club	7 40	1892	Leander Club	7 48¼
1865	Kingston Rowing Club	7 26	1893	Leander Club	7 45
1866	Etonian Club, Oxford	8 29	1894	Leander Club	7 22

* A foul claimed and allowed against the Leander Club.
† A foul claimed and allowed against Second Trinity, Cambridge.

LADIES' CHALLENGE PLATE, for Eight Oars.—Established 1845.

Year	Club	Time m. s.	Year	Club	Time m. s.
1845	St. George's Club, London	8 25	1870	Eton College Boat Club	7 47
1846	First Trinity, Cambridge	— —	1871	Pembroke College, Oxford	7 56
1847	Brasenose, Oxford	9 0	1872	Jesus College, Cambridge	8 39
1848	Christ Church, Oxford	— —	1873	Jesus College, Cambridge	7 54
1849	Wadham College, Oxford	— —	1874	First Trinity, Cambridge	8 9
1850	Lincoln College, Oxford, r o	— —	1875	Trinity College, Dublin	7 28
1851	Brasenose, Oxford	8 10	1876	Jesus College, Cambridge	7 31
1852	Pembroke College, Oxford	— —	1877	Jesus College, Cambridge	8 22
1853	First Trinity, Cambridge	8 15	1878	Jesus College, Cambridge	8 52
1854	First Trinity, Cambridge	7 55	1879	Lady Margaret, Cambridge	8 53
1855	Balliol College, Oxford	7 58	1880	Trinity Hall, Cambridge	7 26
1856	Royal Chester R. C.	— —	1881	First Trinity, Cambridge	7 51
1857	Exeter College, Oxford	7 57	1882	Eton College Boat Club	8 37
1858	Balliol College, Oxford	7 51	1883	Christ Church, Oxford	7 50
1859	First Trinity, Cambridge	7 55	1884	Eton College Boat Club	7 37
1860	First Trinity, Cambridge, r o	— —	1885	Eton College Boat Club	7 21
1861	First Trinity, Cambridge, r o	8 17	1886	Pembroke College, Cambridge	7 17
1862	University College, Oxford	8 17	1887	Trinity Hall, Cambridge	7 10
1863	University College, Oxford	7 23	1888	Lady Margaret B. C., Cambridge	7 18
1864	Eton College Boat Club	7 56	1889	Christ Church, Oxford	7 22
1865	Third Trinity, Cambridge	7 38	1890	Balliol College B. C., Oxford	7 16
1866	Eton College Boat Club	8 16	1891	Balliol College B. C., Oxford	7 20
1867	Eton College Boat Club	7 56	1892	First Trinity B. C., Cambridge	7 43½
1868	Eton College Boat Club	7 25	1893	Eton College Boat Club	7 32
1869	Eton College Boat Club	7 56	1894	Eton College Boat Club	7 36

THAMES CHALLENGE CUP, for Eight Oars.—Established 1868.

Year	Club	Time m. s.	Year	Club	Time m. s.
1868	Pembroke College, Oxford	7 46	1882	Royal Chester Rowing Club	— —
1869	Oscillators B. C., Surbiton	— —	1883	London Rowing Club	8 5
1870	Oscillators B. C., Surbiton	— —	1884	Twickenham Rowing Club	7 48
1871	Ino Rowing Club, London	8 3	1885	London Rowing Club	7 36
1872	Thames Rowing Club	8 42	1886	London Rowing Club	7 54
1873	Thames Rowing Club	8 2	1887	Trinity Hall B. C., Cambridge	7 20
1874	Thames Rowing Club	8 19	1888	Lady Margaret College, Cam.	7 19
1875	London Rowing Club	7 33	1889	Christ Church, Oxford	7 16
1876	West London Rowing Club	7 37	1890	Thames Rowing Club	7 21½
1877	London Rowing Club	8 29	1891	Molesey Boat Club	7 18
1878	London Rowing Club	7 55	1892	Jesus College B. C., Cambridge	8 10
1879	Twickenham Rowing Club	8 55	1893	Thames Rowing Club	7 49
1880	London Rowing Club	7 43	1894	Trinity College B. C., Oxford	7 53
1881	Twickenham Rowing Club	7 50			

VISITORS' CHALLENGE CUP, for Four Oars.—Established 1847.

Year	Club	Time m. s.	Year	Club	Time m. s.
1847	Christ Church, Oxford	9 0	1871	First Trinity, Cambridge	9 8
1848	Christ Church, Oxford	— —	1872	Pembroke College, Oxford	9 28
1849	Christ Church, Oxford	— —	1873	Trinity College, Dublin	— —
1850	Christ Church, Oxford	— —	1874	Trinity College, Dublin	8 50
1851	Christ Church, Oxford	9 0	1875	University College, Oxford	8 20
1852	Argonauts Club, London	— —	1876	University College, Oxford	8 5
1853	Argonauts Club, London	— —	1877	Jesus College, Cambridge	9 7
1854	St. John's, Cambridge	8 48	1878	Columbia College, U. S. A	8 42
1855	St. John's, Cambridge	— —	1879	Lady Margaret, Cambridge	9 21
1856	St. John's, Cambridge	— —	1880	Third Trinity, Cambridge	8 16
1857	Pembroke College, Oxford	8 40	1881	First Trinity, Cambridge	8 22
1858	First Trinity, Cambridge	— —	1882	Brasenose College, Oxford	9 23
1859	Third Trinity, Cambridge	— —	1883	Christ Church, Oxford	— —
1860	First Trinity, Cambridge	— —	1884	Third Trinity, Cambridge	8 39
1861	First Trinity, Cambridge	8 5	1885	Trinity Hall, Cambridge	7 41
1862	Brasenose College, Oxford	9 40	1886	First Trinity B. C., Cambridge	8 20½
1863	Brasenose College, Oxford	— —	1887	Trinity Hall B. C., Cambridge	8 8
1864	University College, Oxford	— —	1888	Brasenose College, Oxford	7 59
1865	Third Trinity, Cambridge	— —	1889	Third Trinity B. C., Cambridge	8 6
1866	University College, Oxford	8 49	1890	Brasenose College, Oxford	7 42
1867	University College, Oxford, r o	— —	1891	Trinity Hall B. C., Cambridge	7 45
1868	University College, Oxford	8 15	1892	Third Trinity B. C., Cambridge	8 23
1869	University College, Oxford	9 7	1893	Third Trinity B. C., Cambridge	8 21
1870	Trinity College, Dublin	8 37	1894	New College	walk over

DIAMOND CHALLENGE SCULLS—Established 1844.

		Time. m. s.			Time. m. s.
1844	T. B. Bumpsted, Scullers' Club, London	10 32	1871	W. Fawcus, Tynemouth R. C.	10 9
1845	S. Wallace, Leander	11 30	1872	C. C. Knollys, Magdalen College, Oxford	10 48
1846	E. G. Moon, Magdalen College, Oxford	— —	1873	A. C. Dicker, St. John's College, Cambridge	9 45
1847	W. Maule, First Trinity, Cam.	10 45	1874	A. C. Dicker, St. John's College, Cambridge	10 50
1848	W. L. G. Bagshawe, Third Trinity, Cambridge	— —	1875	A. C. Dicker, St. John's College, Cambridge	9 15
1849	T. R. Bone, London	— —	1876	F. L. Playford, L. R. C.	9 28
1850	T. R. Bone, Meteor Club, London	— —	1877	T. C. Edwards-Moss, Brasenose College, Oxford	10 20
1851	E. G. Peacock, Thames Club, London	— —	1878	T. C. Edwards-Moss, Brasenose College, Oxford	9 37
1852	E. Macnaghten, First Trinity, Cambridge	— —	1879	J. Lowndes, Hertford College, Oxford	12 33
1853	S. Ripplngall, Peterhouse, Cam.	10 2	1880	J. Lowndes, Derby	9 10
1854	H. H. Playford, Wandle Club, London	— —	1881	J. Lowndes, Derby	9 28
1855	A. A. Casamajor, Argonauts Club, London	9 27	1882	J. Lowndes, Derby	11 43
1856	A. A. Casamajor, Argonauts Club, London	— —	1883	J. Lowndes, T. R. C.	10 2
1857	A. A. Casamajor, L. R. C.	— —	1884	W. S. Unwin, Magdalen College, Oxford	9 44
1858	A. A. Casamajor, L. R. C.	— —	1885	W. S. Unwin, Magdalen College, Oxford	9 22
1859	E. D. Brickwood, Richmond	10 8			
1860	H. H. Playford, L. R. C.	12 4	1886	F. I. Pitman, Third Trinity B. C., Cambridge	9 5
1861	A. A. Casamajor, L. R. C.	10 0			
1862	E. D. Brickwood, L. R. C.*	10 40	1887	J. C. Gardner, Emmanuel College, Cambridge	8 51
1863	C. B. Lawes, Third Trinity, Cambridge	9 43	1888	Guy Nickalls, Magdalen College, Oxford	8 36
1864	W. B. Woodgate, Brasenose College, Oxford	10 3	1889	Guy Nickalls, Magdalen College, Oxford	8 56
1865	E. B Michell, Magdalen College, Oxford	9 11	1890	Guy Nickalls, Magdalen College, Oxford	9 57¼
1866	E. B. Michell, Magdalen College, Oxford	9 55	1891	V. Nickalls, Magdalen College, Oxford	— —
1867	W. C. Crofts, Brasenose College, Oxford	10 2	1892	J. J. K. Ooms, Neptunus R. C., Amsterdam	19 9½
1868	W. Stout. L. R. C.	9 6			
1869	W. C. Crofts, Brasenose College, Oxford	9 56	1893	Guy Nickalls, Magdalen College, Oxford	9 12
1870	John B. Close, First Trinity, Cambridge	9 43	1894	Guy Nickalls, Magdalen College, Oxford	9 32

* After a dead heat with W. B. Woodgate, Brasenose College, Oxford, 10m. 22s.

WYFOLD CHALLENGE CUP, FOR FOUR OARS.—Established 1855.*

1855	Royal Chester Rowing Club	— —	1875	Thames Rowing Club	8 10
1856	Argonauts Club, London	— —	1876	West London Rowing Club	8 26
1857	Pembroke College, Oxford	8 30	1877	Kingston Rowing Club	— —
1858	First Trinity, Cambridge	— —	1878	Kingston Rowing Club	8 44
1859	First Trinity, Cambridge	8 21	1879	London Rowing Club	9 56
1860	London Rowing Club	10 8	1880	London Rowing Club	8 4
1861	Brasenose College, Oxford	— —	1881	Dublin University Rowing Club	8 8
1862	London Rowing Club	9 20	1882	Jesus College, Cambridge	8 58
1863	Kingston Rowing Club	8 50	1883	Kingston Rowing Club	8 51
1864	Kingston Rowing Club	— —	1884	Thames Rowing Club	8 58
1865	Kingston Rowing Club	8 23	1885	Kingston Rowing Club	— —
1866	Kingston Rowing Club	— —	1886	Thames Rowing Club	8 4
1867	Kingston Rowing Club	— —	1887	Pemb. Coll. B. C., Cambridge	7 50
1868	Kingston Rowing Club	8 32	1888	Thames Rowing Club	7 59
1869	Oscillators B. C., Surbiton	8 58	1889	London Rowing Club	7 58
1870	Thames Rowing Club	8 34	1890	Kingston Rowing Club	7 46
1871	Thames Rowing Club	— —	1891	Royal Chester Rowing Club	7 50
1872	Thames Rowing Club	10 8	1892	Molesey Boat Club	8 42
1873	Kingstown Harbor Boat Club	8 37	1893	Molesey Boat Club	8 28
1874	Newcastle A. R. C.†	8 58	1894	Thames Rowing Club	8 16

* In 1847, and for some years following, the Wyfold Cup was given to the best crew among the challengers for the Grand Challenge Cup.

† Rowed without a cockswain.

SILVER GOBLETS, for Pair-Oars.—Established 1845.

Year	Crew	Time m. s.
1845	F. M. Arnold and G. Mann, Caius, Cambridge	— —
1846	W. H. Milman and M. Haggard, Christ Church, Oxford	— —
1847	Falls and Coulthard, St. George's, London	— —
1848	W. H. Milman and M. Haggard, Christ Church, Oxford	— —
1849	Peacock and F. Playford, London	— —
1850	Chitty and Hornby, Bal. and B. N. C., Oxford	— —
1851	Chitty and Aitken, Bal. and Exeter, Oxford	— —
1852	Barker and Nind, Christ Church, Oxford	— —
1853	Barlee and Gordon, Christ's, Cambridge	10 0
1854	Cadogan and Short, Christ Ch. and New, Oxford	9 5
1855	Nottidge and Casamajor, London	— —
1856	Nottidge and Casamajor, London	— —
1857	Warre and Lonsdale, Balliol, Oxford	9 22
1858	H. Playford and Casamajor, L. R. C.	— —
1859	Warre and Arkell, Balliol and Pembroke, Oxford	9 0
1860	Casamajor and Woodbridge, L. R. C.	11 5
1861	Woodgate and Champneys, B. N. C., Oxford	— —
1862	Woodgate and Champneys, B. N. C., Oxford	9 45
1863	Woodgate and Shepherd, B. N. C., Oxford	— —
1864	Selwyn and Kinglake, Third Trinity, Cambridge	9 27
1865	May and Fenner, L. R. C.	9 7
1866	Corrie and Woodgate, K. R. C.	9 30
1867	Corrie and Brown, K. R. C.	9 49
1868	Crofts and Woodgate, B. N. C.	— —
1869	Long and Stout, L. R. C.	9 20
1870	Corrie and Hall, K. R. C.	— —
1871	Long and Gulston, L. R. C.	10 17
1872	Long and Gulston, L. R. C.	— —
1873	C. C. Knollys and A. Trower, K. R. C.	9 22
1874	Long and Gulston, L. R. C.	10 3
1875	Chillingworth and Herbert	9 3
1876	S. Le B. Smith and F. S. Gulston, L. R. C.	8 55
1877	W. H. Eyre and J. Hastie, T.R.C.	— —
1878	W. A. Ellison and T. C. Edwards-Moss, Oxford	9 14
1879	R. H. Labat and F. S. Gulston, L. R. C.	11 16
1880	W. H. Eyre and J. Hastie, T.R.C.	8 45
1881	W. H. Eyre and J. Hastie, T.R.C.	9 4
1882	D. E. Brown and J. Lowndes, Hertford, Oxford	— —
1883	G. Q. Roberts and D. E. Brown, Twickenham Rowing Club	9 22
1884	J. Lowndes and D. E. Brown, Twickenham Rowing Club	9 1
1885	H. McLean and D. H. McLean, Oxford Etonians	— —
1886	F. E. Churchill and S. D. Muttlebury, Third Trinity, Cam	8 40
1887	C. T. Barclay and S. D. Muttlebury, Third Trinity, Cam	8 15
1888	N. P. Symonds and E. Buck, Cambridge and Oxford U.B.C.	— —
1889	J. C. Gardner and S. D. Muttlebury, Cambridge U. B. C.	8 25
1890	Lord Ampthill and Guy Nickalls, O. U. B. C.	8 38
1891	Lord Ampthill and Guy Nickalls, Leander Club	8 36
1892	V. Nickalls and W. A. L. Fletcher, O. U. B. C.	9 7
1893	V. Nickalls and W. A. L. Fletcher, O. U. B. C.	8 44
1894	G. and V. Nickalls	9 35

STEWARDS' CHALLENGE CUP, for Four Oars.—Established 1842.

Year	Crew	Time
1842	Oxford Club, London	9 16
1843	St. George's Club, London	10 15
1844	Oxford U. B. C.	9 16
1845	Oxford U. B. C.	— —
1846	Oxford U. B. C.	— —
1847	Christ Church, Oxford	— —
1848	Christ Church, Oxford	— —
1849	Leander Club	— —
1850	Oxford U. B. C.	— —
1851	Cambridge U. B. C.	8 54
1852	Oxford U. B. C.	— —
1853	Oxford U. B. C.	8 57
1854	Pembroke College, Oxford	9 38
1855	Royal Chester Rowing Club	— —
1856	Argonaut Club, London	— —
1857	London Rowing Club	8 25
1858	London Rowing Club	— —
1859	Third Trinity, Cambridge	8 25
1860	First Trinity, Cambridge	9 26
1861	First Trinity, Cambridge	9 35
1862	Brasenose College, Oxford	9 40
1863	University College, Oxford	8 24
1864	London Rowing Club	8 45
1865	Third Trinity, Cambridge	8 13
1866	University College, Oxford	9 28
1867	University College, Oxford	8 45
1868	London Rowing Club	8 22
1869	London Rowing Club	8 34
1870	Etonian Club, Oxford	8 5
1871	London Rowing Club	9 2
1872	London Rowing Club	9 21
1873	London Rowing Club*	8 25
1874	London Rowing Club	9 0
1875	London Rowing Club	7 56
1876	London Rowing Club	8 32
1877	London Rowing Club	9 7
1878	London Rowing Club	8 37
1879	Jesus College, Cambridge	9 37
1880	Thames Rowing Club	7 58
1881	Hertford College, Oxford	8 15
1882	Hertford College, Oxford	— —
1883	Thames Rowing Club	— —
1884	Kingston Rowing Club	— —
1885	Trinity Hall, Cambridge	7 53
1886	Thames Rowing Club	7 39
1887	Trinity Hall, Cambridge	7 53
1888	Trinity Hall, Cambridge	8 25
1889	Thames Rowing Club	7 53
1890	Brasenose College B. C., Oxford	7 37
1891	Thames Rowing Club	7 45
1892	Royal Chester Rowing Club	8 38
1893	Magdalen College B. C., Oxford	7 45
1894	Thames Rowing Club	8 20

* Rowed without a cockswain

WINGFIELD SCULLS—Established 1830

Year	Winner	Time m. s.	Year	Winner	Time m. s.
1830	J. H. Bayford	— —	1863	J. E. Parker	25 0
1831	C. Lewis	— —	1864	W. B. Woodgate	25 35
1832	A. A. Julius	— —	1865	C. B. Lawes	27 4
1833	C. Lewis	— —	1866	E. B. Michell	27 26
1834	A. A. Julius	— —	1867	W. B. Woodgate	— —
1835	A. A. Julius	— —	1868	W. Stout	26 52
1836	H. Wood	— —	1869	A. de L. Long	— —
1837	P. Colquhoun	— —	1870	A. de L. Long	— —
1838	H. Wood	— —	1871	W. Fawcus	26 13
1839	H. Chapman	— —	1872	C. C. Knollys	28 30
1840	T. L. Jenkins	— —	1873	A. C. Dicker	24 40
1841	T. L. Jenkins	— —	1874	A. C. Dicker	25 45
1842	H. Chapman	— —	1875	F. L. Playford	27 8
1843	H. Chapman	— —	1876	F. L. Playford	24 46
1844	T. B. Bumpsted	— —	1877	F. L. Playford	24 41
1845	H. Chapman	— —	1878	F. L. Playford	25 14
1846	C. Russell	— —	1879	F. L. Playford	24 50
1847	J. R. L. Walmisley	— —	1880	A. Payne	24 2
1848	J. R. L. Walmisley	— —	1881	J. Lowndes	25 13
1849	F. Playford	— —	1882	A. Payne	27 40
1850	T. R. Bone	— —	1883	J. Lowndes	— —
1851	T. R. Bone	— —	1884	W. S. Unwin	24 12
1852	E. G. Peacock	— —	1885	W. S. Unwin	25 2
1853	J. Paine	— —	1886	F. I. Pitman	24 12
1854	H. H. Playford	— —	1887	Guy Nickalls	25 23
1855	A. A. Casamajor	— —	1888	Guy Nickalls	23 36
1856	A. A. Casamajor	— —	1889	Guy Nickalls	— —
1857	A. A. Casamajor	— —	1890	J. C. Gardner	26 20
1858	A. A. Casamajor	— —	1891	Guy Nickalls	— —
1859	A. A. Casamajor	— —	1892	Vivian Nickalls	23 40
1860	A. A. Casamajor	— —	1893	G. E. B. Kennedy	24 56
1861	E. D. Brickwood	29 0	1894	Vivian Nickalls	23 30
1862	W. B. Woodgate	27 0			

VII

UNIVERSITY FOOTBALL

ALTHOUGH football is the oldest of all organized English out-door sport, its introduction into the universities is of comparatively recent date. Comparatively, when we consider that rowing goes quite back to the very beginning of the present century, and that football in England was flourishing most actively as early as 1300. It does appear curious, at first thought, that the game should have thrived so wondrously among the people, and yet be ignored by Oxford and Cambridge; but the explanation is found in the very fact of its being the people's game, and it seems never to have arisen to the social distinction accorded it in America. It was not in those first days by any means fashionable, and while, since being added to the list of university sports, it has, of course, attained a much higher plane in that respect, and is, to a certain extent, one of "society's" outing fixtures, yet it has never quite become the vogue as in America, or as cricket in England. You will not see the same large percentage of cultured spectators at the Oxford-Cambridge football contests as at Springfield and in New York attentively following the struggles of the Harvard-Yale-Princeton elevens. Certainly you will see graduates and undergraduates at the English university matches, but not in such numbers as in America when our great universities meet on the gridiron field.

Somehow football in England has never lost the original stamp that made it the property of the populace. Contemporary with its modern popularity, there sprang up such noisome scandal from deeply-rooted professionalism that the better element, which in America lends the game distinctive and distinguished coloring, in England is scarcely large enough to give a lighter shading to the sombre effects of the mass.

Just a few words now of the early days of football in England, that we may reach its introduction in the universities. The first we hear of the game is about 1300, when from all accounts it must have been very popular, since it flourished, despite no end of vigorous opposition, up to the seventeenth century, growing meanwhile quite as phenomenally as we in America have seen it expand during the last few years, and absorbing even more of the people's attention. It was a crude game, with, I dare say, still cruder rules, and, from all historians tell us, must have been a more or less lustily sustained contest between different towns or counties, in which the inhabitants of each engaged with all the ardor of rival sections. The side having the ball (usually an inflated bladder) endeavored to carry it into the town of their opponents and to touch some door or house or tree previously agreed upon as goal. Oftentimes the field of play might be several miles in length or breadth, and, indeed, these early contests may be likened to the advance of an army, with its skirmishers thrown out along the lines, and its closed bodies of fighting-men struggling to reach the coveted goal in the enemy's territory. The use of both hands and feet was permitted, and tackling must have been one of the most important features.

It is easy to understand why this hurlyburly game did not find favor with the fashion—especially the dilettante fashion of the fifteenth and sixteenth centuries—and why it led so tempestuous a life, frowned on by the nobility, and discouraged and even forbidden by the ruling sovereigns. Bitterly opposed by the government, king after king on ascending the throne issued proclamations against football, while the merchants in the cities appealed to the local authorities against the play of the very boys in the streets. Probably no other game ever struggled through and prospered under such bitter opposition.

There is no opposition to the game in England to-day, but in America we have had some experience in that line the last two years, and know what silly objections timorous and bigoted people may put forth in their ignorance, and how strenuously they can urge them.

To these, more particularly to those whose unsound exploitations found harbor in the winter of '93-'94 with one or two American editors equally prejudiced, I commend a gem I discovered in an old English history of the game, which, among other reasons given for a belief in the ending of the world in 1583, was that "football playing and other devilishe pastimes" were occupying too much of the people's attention. And I think it eminently fitting to record here also, as one of the curiosities left by the

RUGBY UNION SCRIMMAGE

futile but bigoted wave that swept over us last winter, the unsuccessful effort of the Cambridge Member of the Massachusetts State Legislature to introduce, in February, 1894, a bill providing for the punishment of one "who takes part in a game of football when such a game is played in the presence of persons who have paid an admission fee to witness the same, or who promotes the playing of a game of football when money is charged for admission to the same, or who offers or sells a ticket of admission to a game, or who, while a student in an institution of learning, and while engaged in a game of football, beats, strikes, or intentionally wounds or bruises another person engaged in playing such game."

However, despite the opposition and all the threats of imprisonment, football thrived in its early days in England just as it has with us, notwithstanding the clamoring of people who neither can nor would if they could understand the benefits derived by young men from so hardy a game.

Until the beginning of the seventeenth century football flourished healthfully, but with the political ascendency of the Puritans a rigid veto was put upon the sport; all Sunday playing was stopped entirely, and week-day matches so thoroughly discountenanced that popular interest waned with great rapidity. The people were discouraged, and, so long as the Puritans remained the dominant power, sport of all kinds entered upon a period of stagnation, out of which some never fully came; it took over two hundred years to revivify football.

At the beginning of the present century practically all play had ceased—the game was almost a reminiscence of the past; and, indeed, if discussed at all, spoken of as a relic of an ancient pastime.

It was not to be supposed, however, that a sport which

had fought so valiantly for recognition, and one of such sterling quality, would long remain a mere memory, and it is no surprise, therefore, to find it beginning to show signs of life again along about 1820. Between the thirties and forties, without actually attaining popularity, the game continued to work its way in favor, until the fifties and sixties, when England's great public schools took it up, and the second wave of football interest was set in motion, not again to be checked.

Each school adapted play in accordance with the capacity of its own ground, and as one ground differed from the others in dimensions and surroundings, it came to pass that Rugby, Eton, Harrow, Winchester, Westminster, and Charterhouse each developed a distinctive game of football, some of them rather curious, and all retained to this day. Because of this there are no inter-school matches.

Eton has two, the wall and the field game. The first is altogether too complicated to explain in the few lines that I am going to give. Suffice it to say that the field is 120 yards long by 6 wide, with a wall about 10 feet high running its entire length on one side, and along which most of the play is made. A door 4 feet wide by 5 feet high at one end, and a large elm-tree at the other, constitute the goals. The game is unquestionably a development of what we as boys in the long ago used to know as "passage" football, played stealthily about the dormitories at an hour when we were supposed to be sleeping the sleep of good and tired youngsters.

The Eton field game is chiefly a kicking one, the ground being from 100 to 120 yards long, 80 to 100 yards wide, and the goals 12 feet wide by 6 feet high, and placed, as they are with us, at the base-lines.

The Harrow game permits of catching and free kicking; but, although they have much more room than at Eton, there is no running with the ball and no tackling.

At the Charterhouse and Westminster schools the early boys were restricted to the cloisters for play-ground, and theirs was the original dribbling game.

Rugby was the only school that seems to have had abundant space, and therefore the only one that originally played the game where tackling and running with the ball were recognized features.

The Winchester game, again, is different from all the others. The field is about 80 yards long by 25 yards wide—a shape that appears to have been likewise the result of necessity, since, cricket being the more favored sport, the football men were consigned to the edges of the playing-field, while the centre was reserved for the other. This originated an extraordinary sort of play, in a field surrounded by a net. The game is really a prolonged scrimmage (called a "hot"), and there is no dribbling whatever.

Naturally, with each public school developing a distinctive game and graduating its own players, to sow the seeds of so many different styles of play at the universities, it was a matter of several years before the introduction of a common game. So, while the public-school boys had football in plenty between the fifties and sixties, it was not until well on in the sixties that the game began to be played at Oxford and Cambridge to any great extent. Cambridge appears to have had football earlier than Oxford, as there are records of a dribbling game having existed in 1855, and an old Etonian, cousin of E. T. Gurdon, who was up at Trinity 1849-52, says they used to play at that time a sort of compromise between the Rugby and Eton game, more exercise than science. No attempt at an organization of players was made at this time, however, and such life as the sport had so early was probably of a desultory character.

Along in the seventies there had sprung up quite a football spirit in the public schools and in the universities, and some outside clubs had even begun to organize teams. In 1863 Cambridge men, who were playing a dribbling or what afterwards became the Association game, organized, though, together with Westminster and Charterhouse, they had no off-side play until 1867, when the rule was

A WINCHESTER "HOT"

passed as it now stands. The teams playing Rugby football were not associated, but had an off-side rule that was enforced at Eton and Harrow, and with especial severity at Winchester.

In 1871 the popularity of football was increasing tremendously; all the public schools had teams playing one style or the other of the game, the Rugby Union Association was organized, and immediately instituted an international championship series with Scotland, which, together with the Ireland series (formed later), has ever since been the most interesting feature of the Rugby season. In 1872 the Association followed in the same lines, but at the first Rugby developed a greater number of players and increased more rapidly in popularity.

In 1873 Oxford and Cambridge played their first match, and from '75 to '76 one may say the game dates the beginning of its present popularity, which, increasing year by year, has reached the farthermost corners of the kingdom.

Let us have a glance over the periods of our own game. We have seen that the earliest football of the English universities was in 1849, at Cambridge, and that they did not take up the game to any very great extent until well on in the seventies, although playing somewhat during the sixties; that Oxford and Cambridge had their first match in 1873. Turning to our own universities, we know there was football at Yale in 1840, that the undergraduates played until 1858, when, the city authorities refusing the use of the town green, the sport was discontinued, and we know that during all this time the game was not unknown at Harvard.

In 1871 football was revived at New Haven, and in 1872 the Yale Football Association was organized, and a game played and won by their university team against Columbia.

In 1874 the Intercollegiate Football Association was organized by Yale, Princeton, Columbia, and Rutgers; and Yale won the first championship. From that year American university football dates, if not its birth, at least its first attempt at independent life. How vigorous the youngster proved is a familiar story; its creeping days were short, and it ran long before it was booked to

"DRIBBLING" IN THE ASSOCIATION GAME

walk. Thus we find that although the English universities had been rowing many years before us, in football we stand on a much more equal basis.

As may be supposed, football is one of the most favored of English university games. It may be said, I think, to occupy the second place in popularity, though I am aware in making such assertion that cricket is so strong a rival, and the two stand so very near together in interest, that a choice is difficult. Particularly do I know that cricket men—indeed, all Englishmen—are exceedingly solicitous that their game, which has been called the national one, should continue to be so ranked, and I doubt if the average Britisher will agree with me in placing rowing first and football second at Oxford and Cambridge; however, it impressed me that the summing up of the case depends entirely on the Englishman's predilections; I know I had some difficulty in arriving at an unbiassed decision after estimates gathered from many sources.

Every college at Oxford and Cambridge maintains an

Association and a Rugby Union team, and some support even a second.

Of their system of training little remains to be said that I have not already covered. There is very much less preparation for contests than that made by boating men, nor do they receive the consideration bestowed upon the members of college eights. No pretence is ever made of going into rigid training, and only in the last week or ten days before the match do the men go into training at all; still it must be remembered that these men are always more or less in condition. Those who go in for sport at Oxford and Cambridge are, as a rule, of natural athletic inclination, and if they are not playing football they are playing cricket, or they are rowing, or they are actively interested in one or another of the many seasonable sports; as this goes on the year round, it stands to reason that the physical condition of the average English undergraduate is rather high — probably higher than would be found in an American college. Football men are as often as not cricketers, and sometimes even members of the track athletic teams; this year, for instance, C. B. Fry, of Wadham College, Oxford, was the captain of the University Association Football team, president of the University Athletic Club, competitor in the hundred yards, a fast man over the hurdles, holder of the English University running-broad-jump record, and a member of his 'varsity cricket eleven.

All English university football men, however, are not Frys.

The management of the teams I touched upon in the first chapter of the university series, which is, briefly, that in most of the colleges the athletic interests are amalgamated in one common treasury, from which all money is drawn for the support of teams.

The costumes of English football men are quite dissimilar to ours, as the illustration will show. They wear breeches like our track athletes, a sleeved shirt, and heavy stockings that reach up to but do not cover the knee, and it stirs an American college man apprehensively when for the first time he sees a team come on to the field with bared knees. The head-gear of the forwards looked more natural, for I observed ear-protectors were both known and appreciated.

It is true that our padded football trousers are not a necessity in their less vigorous game, but it seemed to me the Englishmen could do something for themselves by adopting our canvas jackets, as with their loose jersey shirts a clean tackle is not now an 'absolute essential.

Before I go on to talk of their form I must tell how curiously the indifferent reception given by the spectators to the Oxford and Cambridge university football teams, at their annual Association match at Queen's, impressed me. I am sure no situation in which I found myself on the entire trip seemed so strange as standing in that crowd of university men, all apparently keen on the match, and yet never a one of them raising his voice in a cheer when the elevens came on to the field. As a matter of fact, the university players received no more greeting than do our scrub elevens when they come out to make practice for the 'varsity. I noticed this same lack of enthusiasm throughout all English university athletics. On no occasion did I hear a cheer given except at the boat-race when each crew pulled away from its landing-stage for the staked boats at the starting-point. Even down at Oxford and Cambridge, on the banks of the river, during their college races, one never hears a cheer. There are guttural murmurs of approbation given by the crowd of college men that run along the banks with the boats;

murmurs that rise and fall like the vocal demonstrations of the conventional dramatic stage mob, but they rarely reach the point of utterance, or when they do are confined to repeated cries of "Well rowed!" At the football match of which I am speaking you would hear "Well played, Oxford!" or "Well played, Cambridge!" but that was the limit of encouragement. At the athletic sports, "Well run!" or "Well jumped!" was the vogue, in addition to the more prevalent and general method of approval by hand-clapping. Throughout English university athletics concerted cheering, as we know it, is absolutely unheard, and, indeed, unknown.

Now as to the football play. Candidly, I must confess I was disappointed; probably I expected too much, or, what is more likely, perhaps my standards were too high. Our own American university game is so superior in point of scientific preparation and skilful play that I felt exactly as though, for instance, I had gone to see the Princeton 'varsity team, and, instead, the scrub eleven had been brought out for my entertainment. I could not help the feeling, as I stood on the side lines, that I was a spectator of an undeveloped game — that there were so many ignored opportunities. One who knows American football must, on first seeing a Rugby Union match, feel he is watching an elementary game. You recognize instantly whence came our advanced quarter-back play and the formation of our forwards with the centre rusher in full possession of the ball. You appreciate at once how this sort of touch-and-go, haphazard game was the beginning of our scientifically developed play of to-day. After seeing a great deal of Rugby Union football in England, I cannot instance a single feature of it that approaches our own game, and I saw it played by the universities and by some of the best outside teams. No matter how well drilled the men are, you feel they are losing sight of some of the most interesting possibilities of the play, and you can hardly restrain yourself from coaching them, then and there. To begin with, it is a slower game; the forwards in their scrimmage seem to get wedged in so compactly that when the ball comes out it takes them an appreciable instant of time to break up and get into the play. In fact, they do not get into the play, as we understand it. I have seen a forward occasionally get

"PASSING"

out to the side and be up with the ball, but it is somewhat of a rare sight, except when a team has such exceptional players as were the two Gurdons of Cambridge a few years ago. It is usually the case that the ball is out and in play before the forwards have got going at all.

The *modus operandi* of a scrimmage, or scrummage, as they call it, will be interesting to Americans. The forwards form practically a circle with their heads down, their arms not exactly interlocked, but the upper arm in position to hold the upper arm of the *vis-à-vis* and aid in pushing him; the ball is thrown in by the half-back of the side in possession of it (the side which kicks out of touch loses the ball); once thrown in, the forwards on one side endeavor to shove their opponents down the field, or, I believe, the skilful way is to screw them around, thus seeking an opportunity to get the ball out at the most advantageous point. In the meantime the half-backs are watching for the ball to come out of the scrimmage, and the three three-quarter-backs are just a little behind the halves and lined out towards the side of the field on which the play is likely to go. Instantly the ball comes out the three-quarter-backs get in motion, and the half-back passes it to the three-quarter nearest him, who, if in danger of being tackled, passes it to the other three-quarter, and this one in turn passes it to the third—the idea in passing from one to the other being to get well out to the side and around the forwards and the backs of the opponents, and thus nearer their goal. If a back is hard pushed, and has not a chance to pass the ball, he punts it out of touch, and it is then brought in by the other side, and the scrimmage begins again. With three three-quarter-backs the half-back ought, when the ball comes out of the "scrum," to get past his opposing half-back, draw an opposing three-quarter on to him, and then pass to his own three-quarter, whom he has by this time got well into his stride. With four three-quarter-backs he has seldom time or room to do this.

The skill of this game is supposed to rest largely in clever passing. I had expected a great deal from it, having been led to understand that it was too clever for any tackling, but I am disposed to disagree with English football men over their faith in this style of game. The passing is clever—of that there is no doubt; and it is equally certain that it is too clever for the kind of tackling they do in England; but I am quite sure that their passing would not be very effective against our tackling. Its effectiveness seems to me to be largely due to the slowness of the men in getting into the play. It is well enough to be able to pass the ball from one three-quarter-back to the other if only there is one opponent who has been fast enough to closely follow it, but I need not tell American university men that such a condition could not exist with our football players in the game, for with their rapidity of getting into a play every one of those three-quarter-backs would certainly have down on him one determined tackler, who would not be likely to give the back a chance to pass the ball. The slowness (as compared with our game), therefore, of the men getting into the play I consider to explain why the passing is so successful in the Rugby Union game. And apropos of slowness, in a match I saw between the Oxford university eleven and a strong club team, one of the Oxford

PUTTING THE BALL IN PLAY FROM SIDE LINES IN RUGBY UNION
The line-up in Association is practically the same

backs sat on the side lines for several minutes mending a shoelace while the play went on! There was no calling of time.

Of their getting down the field under kicks, I can only say it is excessively slow. Certainly their off-side rule makes the play slower than with us, for a man may not go ahead of the ball, and is not allowed to get within five yards of the opposing half-back on his catch, but, even so, they waste many an opportunity of gaining ground by going to the other extreme.

Their tackling does not compare with ours. In the first place, it is high. Occasionally you will see a man down his opponent at the knees, but usually he gets him about the upper part of his body, and quite frequently around his neck. Nor do they bring their man down when they tackle him. One player riding another's back in an unskilful effort to bring him to earth was rather a frequent sight on my pilgrimage. They appear to know nothing whatever of the science of tackling, as we have perfected it.

Perhaps what impressed me most in the Oxford and Cambridge fifteens was the, to my mind, lack of what we consider 'varsity form. There was a great deal of fumbling, and I could easily have picked out three or four men that I should not have cared to have on a second team. Then, again, the men do not "go into" the play just as our men do. You see many a yard gained that could have been stopped by a determined tackle. They do not seem to have the resolution of our football men, and the gaining of a few yards appears not to be of so much moment, which of course is explained somewhat by the difference of our games, for the Rugby Union field is not marked up in five-yard lines like ours (it has only a line at twenty-five yards from each goal-line, and one

PUTTING THE BALL IN PLAY—RUGBY
Edward Airy

in the centre), and they are not obliged to gain five yards or lose possession of the ball. There is no rule laid down as to how many yards they should gain. They keep the ball as long as they can, whether they gain or lose, but it changes hands quite frequently, for, as I have said, when a man is about to be tackled, and does not see a good opportunity of passing, he kicks into touch.

The English and the American Rugby games are radically different, insomuch as in the former all plays are more or less haphazard, whereas in the latter they are the result of previous study—the ball is put in play by a system of signals, and every man has a clearly defined duty to perform in carrying it to a successful issue. To be sure, in the English game there is a certain definite idea of the best means to the desired end, and a general scheme of the manner to attain it. The half-back knows when he gets the ball out of the "scrum" that he is to pass it to the three-quarter, and the three-quarter understands that he is to run with it until he is likely to be stopped, and then pass it to another three-quarter, and if fortune favors them they hope to get down to the enemy's goal, and, failing in that, to punt the ball into touch; but that, so far as I could make out, is the beginning and end of the system. When the play starts off it comes very near being a case of "every man for himself, and the devil take the hindmost."

The full-back has rather a dull time of it, for he does not play up as our full-back does, and this year there has been some attempt, though it has not been received with universal favor, to put him even more out of touch with the general play by increasing the number of three-quarter-backs to four.

It is not exactly my mission to criticise, since whatever developments they make can never affect our play one way or the other; but, as my impressions are from an American point of view, so my criticisms must likewise be considered. It appeared to me that the Englishmen have not done so much with their game as they might; and it seems, too, that they are making a great mistake in laying such stress on passing. In watching their play, I noticed this feature absorbed all the attention of the players, and that every other was really of secondary consideration.

It is obviously true that, as all efforts are concentrated on passing, players attach less importance to tackling, practice it less, and the average of the tackling skill becomes proportionately lowered. I say frankly that I was exceedingly astonished at the poor quality of tackling, and, in my opinion, the great predominance of passing is directly responsible for it. The average English football player is firmly convinced that his passing game is too clever for any tackling game, though I endeavored to explain to some of them that it would not live a natural life against the sharp tackling of the American player, and I dare say nothing short of practical demonstration will shake his faith in it. I am quite sure an American university football eleven, with a single season's practice, would work disaster with a Rugby Union team devoted to passing.

And still another of what seem to me to be evils of the prevalence of passing is the likelihood of its making a very inferior sort of game on a wet day; for in order to pass successfully and cleverly men must keep their feet, and if it happen to be a muddy, slippery field, the standard of play is so materially lowered as to bring a team from first-class to mediocre.

Earlier in this chapter I said there was no single feature of the Rugby Union game worthy of recommendation in America, but as I write it comes to me that there is no "slogging," and their play is particularly free of "roughing." In all the games I witnessed in not one did I see the slightest attempt at anything savoring of slogging. Indeed, I am told the written and unwritten law on the subject is extremely severe, and that the transgressor would not only be ruled off the field for that game, but stand a good chance of being ruled off for the season. Of course I am alluding now to the universities; of the general play outside the universities it is another matter, although Rugby Union is much freer of unnecessary roughness than our game as it is oftentimes played.

Of Association football there is little to say that would interest an American, for as university men we ceased playing it many years ago; but I noticed there has been very little improvement in the play since I captained my prep.-school eleven away back in 1874 and '75. Of course dribbling has been carried to a more scientific point, which is merely the perfection of longer practice, but beyond the use of the head, which has become so much a feature that skill in this direction cuts quite a figure in the player's general qualifications, I could not discover any innovations of especial skill. The head is used as they use their feet—to receive the ball on a kick and butt it in the desired direction—and might, indeed, aptly be called the third leg.

The costumes of the men are the same as in Rugby, with the exception that they wear no head-gear, for of course there is no tackling, the use of the shoulder only being permitted, and no scrimmage.

Although not so popular in the universities as Rugby Union, yet to me it was more interesting, for the dribbling of the ball down the field requires a great deal of skill, and gives an opportunity for very clever work. Probably its greater interest for me is explained by the fact that, as I watched Rugby Union (always making mental comparisons with our own), I never could shake off the feeling of looking on a game that had been neglected from infancy.

It is not my province here to go into the English football rules and give an exhaustive explanation of the games. I am touching only such points as are considered interesting to American players. It is only necessary to say for the understanding of Americans that in Association the hands are not used at all, and there is no running with the ball. It is a game consisting exclusively of dribbling, and the ball may be handled (except by the goal-keeper) only when it has been kicked into touch; then the sides line up, and it is thrown in by a player on the "opposite side of that which kicked it out, who, facing the field of play, shall throw the ball over his head in any direction." There is a pretence, of course, in throwing a ball from the side lines, to place it advantageously for your own team, but the opposing side is more often than not just as apt to get hold of it. In Rugby the ball may also be thrown in from the side lines instead of being put in play by a scrimmage, and when this method is chosen the players line up about the same as in Association, but the ball must be thrown in "so as to alight at right angles to the touch line."

Match play is governed by a referee, whose duties are similar to those of ours, and by two umpires—one for each side—who carry flags, with which they signal when and where the ball goes into touch, and who are touch-line judges only.

As may be supposed, in games where the element of chance cuts so large a figure, and where plays are not the result of previous planning, coaching amounts to a minimum. In Rugby Union it is expended chiefly on the three-quarter-backs, whose passing to be most successful should be the result of team-work. In Association coaching is largely devoted to the forwards, where, in dribbling, team-work is also necessary, and I should say this game required more team-work and more coaching than the Rugby Union, but neither one of them receives a great deal of it.

They do not approach that systematic coaching and drilling given our teams; in fact, their style of play does not require it. Some 'varsity player who happens to be in residence at the time takes them in hand, but more often it devolves upon the captain, and the general preparation of English university football men consists largely of what practice play they have on their own fields against outside teams.

"HEADING"

This is, in fact, the best practice work they get, for with the many teams in England it must be understood that the average of general play is pretty high.

Association university elevens are not so good as some of the club teams, and never up to the standard of the professionals. The university Rugby Union fifteen is usually the strongest in England, with the possible exception of Yorkshire, though it is not uncommon for Oxford or Cambridge to be scored against, and it is quite usual for them to continue playing outside teams some time after they have decided the inter-university match, which differs materially from our system, and seems not so good, since it makes a series of anticlimaxes where there is nothing to gain and everything to lose.

There is not the same chance of bruising a man in Rugby Union as there is in our game, but there is infinitely more danger in the Association, where, when players meet on a ball and attempt to kick it in different directions, broken legs may result, besides the further danger, entirely unknown to our game, of kicking a man in the head or body.

Altogether, after a careful study of English football, I am more devoted than ever to the American game, more firmly convinced of its exceptionally good qualities, its skill, its ruggedness, and its demand on brain and brawn.

VIII

CLUB FOOTBALL

WHEN I say that Oxfordshire, with a population of about 186,000, supports upwards of one hundred teams, some idea may be gained of the popularity of football in England—a popularity so wide-spread, in fact, as to be the most obstinate thorn in the flesh of the two governing bodies, or, rather, in that of one of them — Rugby — since the Association seems long ago to have given up the fight for purity and decency in the sport it is alleged to direct. So rapid and so far-reaching has been the popularization of the game in the last decade, that it has ceased to be mere recreation, and become, instead, a commercial speculation, particularly in the more flourishing Association centres, where regular limited-liability companies live and prosper, with football as their sole *raison d'être*. These companies own grounds, maintain teams, arrange matches, pocket the gate receipts, pay the players, and altogether are organized for business on a business basis, to make trading in football-players as profitable as they would have it in cattle or groceries.

And yet this Association, which proclaims itself amateur, countenances it all. Fancy! And it is this class of football-players that is now loudly knocking for admittance on the door of the Rugby Union, and to whom many thoughtless people are urging the Union to open, and follow the example of the Association in legalizing what it cannot exterminate. These unthinking ones put forth the weak argument that Rugby is losing prestige because of its persistent refusal to let down the bars to professionalism; that in declining to permit payment of players it is narrowing its recruiting-field by turning all that lower element which breeds this class over to the Association.

That Association football has outpaced Rugby of late years in popularity among the masses is perfectly true, but who that has made a careful study of the situation will declare the growth healthful or the Association to be envied? From the very day the Association, yielding unwisely to a pressure it had not the courage and good sense to withstand, opened its ranks to professionalism, it has been declining in tone and in healthful, vigorous growth. As rapidly as the game has spread among the masses, so rapidly has it been dropped by amateurs, until to-day there is probably not a single amateur club playing the Association game in the north of England or the Midlands, while, with rare exceptions, it is in disrepute everywhere.

And what has the professional done for Association football in return for being taken into the fold? He has given it great popularity among his kind, a popularity which, like a flash in the pan, will die away as quickly as it flamed, once deprived of artificial kindling; he has killed the game so far as amateurs are concerned, and infested it instead with a depravity as deep-rooted as it is far-reaching; he has, in fine, vitiated the football atmosphere of the British Kingdom. One may well ask, Has the game been worth the candle?

How he came to gain admittance reads curiously enough. It was claimed for football, just as it is being claimed now for rowing by some who, strangely, indeed, seem unable to profit by experience, that in the matter of

BLACKHEATH FOOTBALL GROUNDS AND CLUB-HOUSE

sport it was not democratic to draw distinctions between the lower and higher elements of society; that admitting the lower to the games of the higher meant popularization, and that it would be only fair, and not harmful, to permit adequate compensation for those players who could not afford to give the time to sport.

Ah me! what a headlong scamper after the shadow! Is it not wondrous that, with generations of experience to be had for the reading, such illusive argument could—yes, can, to this very day—make converts? Is it conceit or ignorance that impels us to experiment where there are no new lessons to learn, if we would but profit by the experience of others? Are not, indeed, conceit and ignorance synonymous?—but I am straying from the subject, and if I may be pardoned for this bit of mind *vs.* matter, I'll turn from psychological digression to practical argument.

It is absolutely true that, wherever or whenever an element enters sport for profit, corruption is certain to follow. Will any one tell me of one game which professionals have dominated that has not, starting out with a boom, ended in final decay, after a life of corruption and scandal? How runs the history of professional foot-racing, boating, and pugilism? How that of our so-called national game of baseball, which came so near collapse through the intrusion of greed and corruption, and the popularity of which has never since reached the point it once enjoyed before our faith in its integrity had been shaken? Why is it that even horse-racing, with its government partly in the hands of gentlemen, has degenerated to a mere gambling-machine, while Association football in England has gone the same way, and racing bicycling, in both England and America, is fast reaching a similar condition, if it is not that money, and not sport, has been the moving spirit in every instance?

And so long and so sure as grass grows and water runs, just so long and so sure will the result be identical.

Must we, then, give over all our sport outside of the schools and universities to professionals to run its scandalous course until overtaken by collapse and disgrace? Is the worship of the almighty dollar to obtain in recreation as it does in trade? Shall the man who plays football, or runs, or rides a bicycle for money have preference in our support over the one who plays for the love of it?

No sophistry can be more harmful than that which suggests, as a means of developing sport, the encouragement of the professional to the detriment of the amateur. What is more absurd than the argument, advanced for the benefit of the lower element, that the man who cannot afford the time to play should be compensated for such loss? Why should any man be paid for the time he loses from his business? Why should such a one play at all? There are plenty just as good that have the time. And why, if compensation is in order, should only the lower element be considered? There are hundreds of young men graduated every year from our universities who, if they were cads enough to permit of being "approached" by athletic "managers," would perform quite as well, and certainly be a more acceptable lot to spectators. But, thank Heaven, the college man, as a class, remains an amateur and a gentleman!

And what drivelling talk is all this that prates of ignoring the poor "laborer"—as if we were not all laborers in this work-a-day world—and wants to drag him into our sport, putting him under restrictions with which he has no sympathy, and paying him for the time he may lose from his trade! What sporting "Coxeyism" is this that has neither rhyme nor reason to warrant its serious consideration by intelligent mankind!

The only wholesome way to develop sport is to encourage amateurs, not by bands of travelling star performers, but by local stimulus; and the only basis upon which sport will ever remain firm and healthful is that of honesty, and sport for sport's sake only.

Those who call me a crank on the subject I ask to watch the career of racing bicycling in America the coming two years, meanwhile thinking of what was prophesied for athletics a few years ago by the same crank.

The Rugby Union deserves the greatest credit for withstanding the influences brought to bear towards its rec-

A BRADFORD CLUB FOOTBALL CROWD
Edward Airey

ognition of professionalism. It has suffered somewhat maybe in the popular eye, but it has continued to prosper, and, more than all, it has retained the respect and admiration of all English sportsmen. However, despite its good intentions and its discountenancing of all attempts to pay players, a certain professional taint has crept in among the lower classes that play the game in some sections of England. Where the football spirit is keen, men who could ill afford several months of idleness in their trade unless compensated are found playing on club teams and remaining in training throughout the season, and the obvious conclusion is that such are practically supported by the large clubs, of which there are a number, organized for business pure and simple. It looks as though the Union would eventually be obliged to give up attempting to reclaim the great unwashed, and leave them to go their way, while it went back to the definition that has kept rowing (next to cricket) the cleanest sport in England.

There are such an infinite number of football clubs in Great Britain that it would take quite a volume to chronicle them all; but, as in athletics, a few only own grounds, and fewer yet have club-houses. Those that have fields are of the limited-liability class, which throw open their gates to football, cricket, athletics, or whatever attracts gate money enough to make the venture profitable, but only rarely have these companies maintained a team of their own. The largest is the Huddersfield Cricket, Football, and Athletic Club, which has three enclosed fields, and pays dividends to its members; and next in importance is, probably, the Bradford Club, which has a cricket and football field, and is one of the few with a club-house. Blackheath, the oldest Rugby club in England, rents grounds, and has provision for cricket and lawn-tennis as well; the London-Scottish, also Rugby, rents its grounds, as do also the largest clubs in Liverpool, Manchester, Salford (all Rugby), and Birmingham (Association). The London Athletic Club has no team; it had a Rugby fifteen, but gave it up several years ago. In Association, clubs of all sorts and kinds are constantly springing into existence, each a breeding-den of strife, and every one trying, by bribery and by every other foul means, to outdo the other. In order to check this migration of players from one club to another, the Association has been obliged to inaugurate a system like the one which obtains in our professional baseball leagues. Each club puts a price on every one of its men, according to his value, and no one of them may be transferred to another club without its paying to that player's club the sum set against his name. Thus, for instance, John Brown is valued at £100, and the club that wants to enlist his services must first pay that amount to the organization to which he belongs.

Association clubs play one against the other for the county championships, the successful ones deciding the supremacy in a further series of cup ties; and from the winning teams in these ultimate results the International elevens are chosen, on which are frequently university men, though they are becoming fewer every year. Rugby Union, generally speaking, is not predisposed to cup ties, experience having shown that they did not work to the most healthful encouragement of the game; but they remain in vogue in Yorkshire and in the Midlands, and unfortunately in some other counties too. There is, therefore, no actual championship trophy or round in Rugby Union as in Association, and the international matches with Ireland, Scotland, and Wales are the great features of its season. Many counties that formerly played Rugby have gone over to professionalism and the Association.

The club match is really the life of Rugby, and, outside Oxford and Cambridge, the most interesting games of the year are between the Richmond, Blackheath, and London-Scottish clubs, all of which play the universities; while in the north the Bradford and Manchester clubs are considered to furnish the best sport. In the south the Oxford-Cambridge-London match usually determines the best team, while in the north Yorkshire is the accepted power.

Yorkshire, indeed, where they do have cup ties and a championship, which, however, some of the best clubs do not enter, is generally acknowledged to turn out the strongest team next to Oxford and Cambridge. Besides being the biggest county in England, it is the great Rugby centre, and the people are so very keen that its gates are the largest of all amateur teams.

Although professionalism has practically killed the amateur in Association football, the desire for a purer condition is shown by the recent organization of a distinctive amateur body. The taint, however, seems to cling to it, for when in England I heard of one club that had offered to "scratch" for a consideration (surely a curious suggestion for an amateur club); while in a game under the new Association's auspices the referee was so roughly handled after a decision that his clothes were literally torn off him, and a half-back who went to his defence was knocked senseless by a rap on the head with a stick. Notwithstanding this poor beginning, there is considerable agitation in England over the desirability of a body that will maintain strictly amateur Association football, and a determination that there shall be a reform from present methods, and a union of amateur clubs that will provide sport somewhat on university lines.

Despite the gates at the matches of the professional teams, which run from $6000 to $12,000, with entrance fees at sixpence to one shilling *per capita*, the clubs are nearly all in debt, because of the large salaries paid players, and it looks to me very much as if professional football in Great Britain were rapidly going the way that professional baseball went with us a few years ago, as a result of artificial propagation, extravagant salaries, and general depravity. Their games are very rough, and not infrequently break up in a general mêlée; a match I attended,

YORK *VS.* ENGLAND
Edward Airey

between a club and Army Association team, ended in a free fight, the soldier spectators using their belts so effectively as to necessitate a call for doctors and police.

Such scenes are not witnessed in Rugby, where the ruling on rough play is severe, and the referee respected. A player may be warned or ordered off the field for a first offence, but for a second, in addition to being ruled off, he is reported to the Union.

The Midlands and Lancashire are the centres of Association football, but within the Association again is a league comprised of fourteen of the best professional clubs in the north, which play home-and-home games, and legislatively and every other way is quite as powerful as the alleged governing body.

Scotland has been until very recently the recruiting-ground for the English professional teams, but the Scottish Association not long ago legalized professionalism, and thereby not only insured the strength of their future teams, but narrowed the English field of supply.

In the foregoing chapter I have shown that, after the first general wave of football had spent its force, the public schools of England taught the game, and old schoolboys and university men created clubs.

Before the Union came into being the Blackheath Club, formed in 1857, and the Richmond Club, organized in the early sixties, occupied the attention of enthusiasts, and their matches were the most keenly followed of the day.

But there was in fact very little of Rugby so early as the sixties, not more than a score of clubs about London all told, and hardly any in the provinces, except Lancashire and Yorkshire, which furnished some of the players in the first international match with Scotland in 1871. That there is nothing new in the world seems to be verified even by sporting research, for I found that, well back in the sixties, the old Blackheath Club had played a primitive interference game, which we have developed with such consummate skill, their forwards charging down the field in defence of the half-back running behind them with the ball: it was a winning play too, and gave many a victory before it was finally disallowed.

The Rugby Union was organized in the early part of 1871, with E. C. Holmes, captain of the Richmond team, in the chair, whose club, together with the Blackheath and the Civil Service clubs, was the most important of the original members, though Scotland should not be forgotten as having furnished three of the first thirty-three clubs.

For some years previous to this there had been attempts to codify the rules, but the existence of so many different styles of play made compilation a matter of time and patience.

Previous to such defining, the Rugby and Association games were more or less analogous, but with the organization of the latter in '63, followed by the former in '71, the two began to drift apart until they reached the entirely dissimilar conditions of play that exist to-day. At first the Union had jurisdiction over the entire British

Kingdom, but as the football interest developed it was found the one body did not answer, and in '73, '75, and '80 Scotland, Ireland, and Wales formed unions of their own. At this time twenty were a team, and contests consisted chiefly of compact scrimmages and wearisome shoving matches. This number of players continued until '77, when, at the instance of Scotland, it was officially decreased to fifteen (though Oxford had begun playing fifteen in '74 and in '75, with Cambridge agreed to that number for their inter-'varsity matches), leading instantly to a more open style of play. This, together with increasing the number of three-quarter-backs to their present number of three, followed by the inauguration of the system of passing that is so great a feature of the game to-day, constitutes two of the very few improvements that have been made in Rugby Union football. Passing was first brought into prominence by the Blackheath Club, though it was not until '82 that the Oxford team developed the long-passing now prevalent.

During the shoving age, hacking, tripping, and scragging, the last being a very effective if not pleasing method of making the opponent cry "down" by twisting his neck, were prominent and important features, though abolished with the limit at fifteen players and the beginning of looser play; but the penalty of a free kick for off-side play was not adopted until '88.

Although the forwards were having a pretty hard time of it during this shoving period, the half-backs enjoyed opportunities for brilliant play they have never since had, for about all the "gallery" work fell upon them before the rise into prominence of the three-quarter-back. The halves stood farther back of the scrimmage than they do now, and did practically all the running with the ball, as may be understood by the fact that even when they were playing twenty a side only one three-quarter-back was used.

The introduction of the loose game is claimed by several clubs. The Scotch believe they were the first to play it; by some, Blackheath is given the honor; others maintain that Richmond was the first; and still others, with very good reason, are of the opinion that the change came from Oxford. However that may be, as the system of tight scrimmages gave way to loose play, the brilliancy of the half-back dimmed, and he found he was fulfilling his mission if he succeeded in snapping up the ball and getting it to the single three-quarter, who, as the forwards became more skilful in breaking up, required a companion in order to advance it with any degree of certainty.

Thus it came about that the number of three-quarter-backs was gradually increased until, even in the last year, some of the teams have taken back another forward. While the four three-quarter-back system has not yet become universal, the development of the play has brought the three-quarter into the greatest prominence, and it is he nowadays who is given the opportunities, and not the half, who rarely runs with the ball, and serves in about the same position as our quarter.

The Rugby Union is governed by a committee composed equally of southern and northern members, who choose their representative teams. The selection of international teams is made by a subcommittee of six— three representing northern England, three southern— while international contests generally are governed by a board of twelve, on which England has six, Scotland two, Ireland two, and Wales two members each.

The international fifteens of Scotland, Ireland, and Wales are chosen by their respective governing unions, and on practically the same basis.

They have always played good football in the home of Bobby Burns, the Rugby game having flourished there certainly since the formation of the Union, and was popular even long before that body was dreamed of. Scotland seems, in fact, to have always been predisposed to football, and her sons have played it enthusiastically as boys and men time out of mind.

Ireland, though not having made such progress as Scotland, has, nevertheless, a history dating well back, and of much interest. They have, indeed, three kinds of football—Rugby, Association, and Gaelic—the relative conditions and amateur status of which may be judged when, as it is said, that in Rugby they kick the ball; in Association they kick the man if they cannot kick the ball; and in Gaelic they kick the ball if they cannot kick the man. Ireland played its first international match with England in '74, though not until '82 did they begin to send out the strong teams that now rank with the best.

Wales is the youngest but most energetic Rugby centre of the four. They played England for the first time in '80, and not until the last year or so have they succeeded in putting out a strong team. But to-day nowhere is the game played with greater energy.

At the time of the organization of the Association in 1863 the

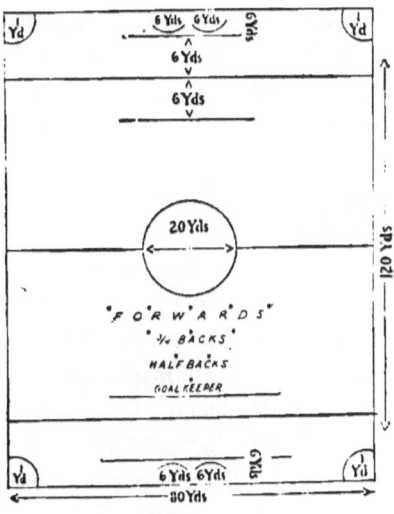

ASSOCIATION FOOTBALL FIELD.

Rugby off-side rule was in force, but this was changed in '67 to the present ruling, and from that date both passing and dribbling have been features of the game. Since then there has been no particular development other than the perfection of skill in dribbling, and the introduction of heading the ball, which has become a most clever and important feature. In the very first years there was some experimenting with different plays, but the game had settled down about '75, and has remained practically the same ever since. Of late years, to facilitate the umpire's work, a net has been spread back of the goal, from post to post and beneath the cross bar (under which the ball must go to count), since which disputes over goals have ceased.

The earliest years of the Association game were amateur, and the Wanderers' Club was famous for the very clever team it turned out, and with which it won several years in succession. It was in 1872 that cup ties were established, which started the popular wave that had spread in '75 to the provincial districts, and in a year or so later had taken full possession of the country, and bade farewell to all hopes of the amateur. There was only one club playing Association football in Birmingham in '74, but two years later the number had increased to nearly half a hundred, and this was only the beginning of the interest that has extended throughout the kingdom. So many provincial clubs sprang up that the system of cup ties had to be changed in '79, the clubs being divided into districts for the preliminary rounds. In '83 a provincial club won the championship, and from that year the successful team has always come from those sections.

With the increase of provincial clubs and the absorption of football by the lower elements, teams became more and more professional, until finally offences were so flagrant that the Association in its weakness openly recognized what it could not stamp out. That day sounded the knell of the amateur in Association football. He endeavored for a while to stem the current, but it was too strong for him, and, realizing he must either get out or be carried along in the polluted sea, he left the field to the professional, who has held undisputed sway ever since.

Whether this decadence in amateur football may ever be repaired is a serious question, but I incline to the opinion that the present extravagant professional furor will run its course, and the amateur live once again in all his pristine purity.

IX

UNIVERSITY ATHLETICS

ATHLETICS have been one of the characteristics of town and country life in England as far back as anything that has ever been written on the subject carries us, and to comment, therefore, on present-day university athletics without touching a bit on the earlier history would be to put forth an incomplete story. Besides which, Oxford and Cambridge fathered the Amateur Athletic Association of Great Britain, and university history in its turn becomes really that of (comparatively) modern English athletics.

Of the very earliest English athletics it is only pertinent to say here that there appears to have been no period when they did not thrive, even, though somewhat less vigorously, during the political ascendency of the Puritans. Their determined warfare waged against football lost much of its bitterness when directed upon athletics, and opposition was chiefly confined to Sunday playing. Unlike football, too, athletics received much consideration at the royal court, and were not only looked upon with favor, but became a not-inconsiderable feature of its out-of-town entertainment. Royalty itself, both by precept and example, encouraged the people in running and jumping, wrestling, and games with the weights. Some pretty tall stories, that go to prove the lonely fisherman not to have been, indeed, the first of Ananias's many descendants, are handed down to us of the prowess of these early athletes, among others that Henry V. was so swift and tireless a runner that it was quite common amusement for him, aided by two of his lords, to run down and capture a deer in the royal park! It is not unlikely the said king's quarry was the prototype of the present queen's half-tamed stags, which, after having their antlers sawed off, are carted to the meet, and turned out to be chased by hounds (that are on terms of perfect familiarity with them), and followed by a large field of mounted men and women, who fancy they are having great sport. Still another story is of a man who ran twenty miles in less than one and a half hours, which puts Mr. W. H. Morton's (amateur) world-beating performance of 1 h. 52 m. 51½ sec. (March 22, 1890) rather in the shade.

However impossible these yarns may be, the fact is that athletics were very popular during the fifteenth and sixteenth centuries, waned a bit under "Puritan England" the first half of the seventeenth, but, during the latter part of the seventeenth, after the Restoration, entered upon a regular nineteenth-century boom. An athletic wave set in that spread throughout the kingdom, and each holiday was made an excuse for fairs, at which sports of every known description were held. Some of these games were more curious than sporting, as, for instance, I find the programmes included such extraordinary novelties as "girls running for smocks, old women drinking hot tea for snuff, grinning through horse-collars, jumping in sacks for a cheese, hunting a pig with a soaped tail, whistling and spinning matches," besides foot-racing at various distances –a programme that, while more startlingly unique, is not so sporting as the following list of events for an all-round competition that was given along in the fifties of the present century: "A mile run, walking backwards a mile, rolling a coach-wheel a mile, leaping over fifty 3 ft. 6 in. hurdles, stone-picking, and weight-putting."

With all the great activity in sport, and the innumerable opportunities afforded athletes of this time, it is passing strange that there were no distinctive amateur meetings. It is true that these fair games had, of course, a certain percentage of contestants who entered for sport rather than for personal aggrandizement, yet no distinguishing line had been drawn, and amateurs neither held recognized meetings nor were systematically organized. In the latter half of the eighteenth century they made a movement towards uniting, but little came of it, and that little had almost entirely disappeared by 1825. It was not until between the forties and fifties that amateurs began earnestly to bestir themselves, and even then their first appearance in games was under assumed names, curiously enough, too, since the never-withdrawn patronage of royalty, which had unbounded faith in leaping and running as the best physical training for the nation's soldiers, would seem to have placed rather an honorable mark upon such recreation.

The sport of "the people," however, which by this time had developed a wide-spread professional element, went on uninterruptedly, though the growth of a class that sought it as a means of livelihood raised a standard of skill that lessened popular participation, and gradually decreased the number of fairs until they disappeared entirely.

The first professional athlete was evolved from the running footman of the gentry. It was quite the thing, at the time of which I am writing, for country gentlemen to match their foot-grooms at short distances, and thus they developed from being carriers of messages into carriers of their employers' wagers, and into trained athletes

OXFORD ATHLETIC FIELD AND CLUB-HOUSE

H. W. Taunt & Co.

hired and kept because of their qualifications as sprinters rather than as serving-men. A speedy foot-groom became as necessary an acquisition to every gentleman's establishment as his hunter, and, although probably not costing so much, was regarded with equal solicitude. It was an easy transition into professionalism for those running grooms, who would naturally after a time turn their skill to their own account instead of to their masters', from whom they received only a good servant's berth in return for their athletic prowess.

Although undoubtedly there had been English school games at which running was an important feature, and we do know for a certainty that the Rugby "crick run" was begun as early as 1837, while personal diaries tell of 100-yard hurdle-races at Eton the same year, yet the first organized amateur athletic meeting was not held until 1840, and is accredited to the Royal Military Academy, Woolwich, which, however, abandoned the event four years later.

Exeter College, at Oxford, has the most authentic record and the clearest title to the honor of being the first (in 1850) to inaugurate annual athletic meetings, a direct result, as detailed in the chapter on rowing, of steeple-chasing among members of the same college. Among the colleges, Lincoln (Oxford) was next, followed by St. John's and Emmanuel at Cambridge; while at Oxford, Balliol, Wadham, Pembroke, and Worcester gave games in '56, Oriel in '57, Merton in '58, Christ Church in '59, and two years later all the colleges were holding separate meetings.

Of the schools, Rugby was of course first to give attention to athletics by the "crick run" in '37, but it is not credited with regular athletic meetings until '56, whereas Eton, in addition to its claims to hurdle-races in '37, began its athletic meetings with steeple-chase, sprint, and hurdle-races in '45, while Kensington Grammar-school was on the field in '52; and Harrow, although some years behind its great rival, was at work in '53, and thus among the athletic pioneers. Of the others, Winchester began in '57, and Westminster and Charterhouse both in '61. Previous to these regular meetings nearly all the schools had hare-and-hound chases, which were, I have no doubt, in various forms, the very beginning of all organized sport among boys.

Of the more skill-requiring games, the hurdle seems to have been the earliest at all the first college athletic sports, since, as already stated, Eton had introduced it in '37, while C. N. Jackson, the athletic mentor of Oxford, so early as '65 made a 16-second record for 120 yards that has not yet been excelled and only once equalled in England.

Cambridge as a university turned its attention to athletics in '57, three years before Oxford, but the latter from the very first made it an annual event, whereas Cambridge did not do so until '63. The first Oxford-Cambridge meeting was held in '64 at Oxford, on the Christ Church cricket-grounds, the programme consisting of eight events, of which each won four; but in '67 they went to London, where, on the Queen's Club grounds, the contests have since been annually decided. Trinity College, Dublin University, had athletic games in '57, but the first meeting of Edinburgh University is not recorded.

Once the universities and public schools had taken to athletics, its adoption by the young men of the country generally followed as a natural sequence. So it happened that, after having lain dormant for many years— for by this time all the great activity and fairs of the earlier period had become mere memories of the past— there came once again a boom, as track athletics renewed its youth. It was rather more of a babyhood at first, and

toddled along uncertainly for several years; but the need of just such exercise was felt in the land, and, with the additional impetus given by the annual contribution from the universities, strength and surety replaced feebleness and uncertainty. Yet the meetings were few and far between for some time, and the amateur remained uncared for; he competed under his own name or a fictitious one for money or trophies, and against whomsoever he pleased. The Honorable Artillery Company held a meeting in '58 that made a worthy effort to give him his rightful standing, but little came of it, and really the first games for amateurs only were given in '62 by an enterprising promoter of professional handicaps. The meeting was very successful, and, as a result, the following year gave birth to the Mincing Lane Athletic Club, which held games in '64, and for a couple of years enjoyed the distinction of being the only athletic club in Great Britain that made any pretence of fostering amateurs.

It was not to be supposed that a club formed through the commercial zeal of a man associated with professional running would satisfy the awakening amateur spirit, and in '66 a number of university men organized the Amateur Athletic Club for the purpose of supplying the want of an established field, upon which their contests could be decided without rubbing elbows with professionals. They gave the first amateur championship of England that same year, and in 1868 opened the famous Lillie Bridge grounds, which forthwith became the amateur headquarters of Great Britain.

The Amateur Athletic Club did much for the good of sport, and stood alone as the champion of the amateur (outside Oxford and Cambridge and the public schools), and without an athletic rival until the London Athletic Club sprang into existence a year or so later. For a time the L. A. C. held its meetings on the grounds of the A. A. C. at Lillie Bridge, and the two worked harmoniously in the good cause. But the London Club, with its more active members and more vigorous constitution, soon made it evident that the older club was losing position, and in '76 there came a rupture between the two, which led to the London Athletic Club securing its present ground at Stamford Bridge. Although fast reaching a moribund condition, the A. A. C. was not inclined to surrender its prestige without a struggle; therefore, that year two championships were held, and a division of interests created which ended finally in the collapse of the weaker A. A. C.

Added to this conflict was a growing feeling among non-university athletes that the date of the championships should be changed from the spring to summer, on the ground that the Oxford and Cambridge men, by reason of having their own athletic sports in February and March, had a considerable advantage in the championships over the club athletes, who were not able to get "fit" so early in the year. All of which led to a very unsatisfactory condition of affairs generally, until a conference between the older heads of the universities and the more prominent club officials resulted, in 1880, in the formation of the present Amateur Athletic Association of Great Britain, and the selection of summer for the English championships.

From the day of the organization of the A. A. A., university and non-university athletes have been drifting further and further apart, until to-day the meetings of the London Athletic Club are about the only outside ones in which Oxford and Cambridge entries are made. Oxford and Cambridge have no distinct ruling body of their own, such as our Intercollegiate Athletic Association, and hold their meetings under the auspices of the Amateur Athletic Association. The chief reason for this state of affairs is found in the unwholesome condition of English athletics, which, since the popular wave set in, have been absorbed by the lower elements of society, and tainted from one end of the kingdom to the other by disguised (the worst sort of) professionalism.

Comparisons being always in order between our English cousins and ourselves, perhaps it will be interesting, before going into the systems that obtain at Oxford and Cambridge, to glance over our own university athletic history.

Event	Oxford-Cambridge, 1864 Performance	American Inter-collegiate, 1876 Performance
100 yards	10 1-2 sec.	10 3-4 sec.
440 "	56 "	56 "
880 "		2 min. 16 1-2 "
Mile walk		8 " 7 "
Mile run	4 min. 59 "	4 " 58 1-2 "
120-yard hurdle	17 3-4 "	18 1-2 "
Running high jump	5 ft. 5 in.	5 ft. 4 in.
Broad jump	18 ft.	8 " 3 1-2 "
16-lb. shot		30 " 11 1-2 "

American inter-university athletics were given their first impetus through the sportsmanship of James Gordon Bennett, who in 1873 offered a $500 cup for a 2-mile race, to be run in July, after the inter-university boat-races, which were then rowed at Saratoga, and followed it up the next year by one cup each for a 100-yard run, 3-mile run, 120-yard hurdle-race, 1-mile run, and 7-mile walk. Yale held a meeting under the auspices of the "Navy Base and Foot Ball Clubs" in the autumns of '73 and '74, at which there were a hurdle-race, running high jump, standing broad jump, 100-yard dash, half-mile run, mile walk, hop, step, and jump, throwing baseball, and wrestling. Harvard in '74 held its first athletic meeting, at which the 100 yards was run on a grass course, and won in 13 seconds, and where August Belmont aroused great interest by the spike shoes he wore in one of the sprints, and George Walton Green shocked the natives by walking with bare legs and in the short running-breeches that are the conventional dress of to-day. Yale in '75 formed an athletic association, and held a meeting in the autumn, at which the 16-pound shot was won at 32:5; 100 yards in 10¾; mile walk, 8:13; high jump, 5:3; half-mile run, 2:10; 3-mile run, 19:27; 120-yard hurdle, 19¼; 440 yards, 57; mile run, 5:20; throwing baseball, 327 feet.

While the discussion of the formation of an intercollegiate athletic association was rife in '75, a meeting was held at Saratoga, at which the 100 yards was won in 10¾ seconds, the mile in 4:44½, the quarter in 55¼, and the half-mile in 2:06¾. It should be remembered that this was on a horse track, and also that the timing in those days was not nearly so accurate as it is to-day.

OXFORD-CAMBRIDGE ATHLETIC MEETING, MARCH, 1894

Event	Performance	Winner	University
100 yards	10 3-5 sec.	Jordan	Oxford
440 "	50 4-5 "	"	"
Mile run	4 m. 19 4-5 "	Lutyens	Cambridge
3-mile "	15 " 7 "	Horan	"
120-yard hurdle	16 3-5 "	Oakley	Oxford
Broad jump	22 ft. 4 in.	Fry	"
High "	5 " 10 1-4 "	Swanwick	"
16-lb. hammer	101 " 4 1-2 "	Robertson	"
16-lb. shot	37 " 6 "	Rivers	"

Hammer thrown from 30-foot circle; shot put from 10 foot square.

AMERICAN INTER-COLLEGIATE ATHLETIC MEETING, MAY, 1894

Event	Performance	Winner	College
100 yards	10 sec.	Ramsdell	Pennsylvania
220 "	22 "	"	"
440 "	50 2-5 "	Merrill	Harvard
880 "	1 m. 59 1-5 "	Kilpatrick	Union
Mile run	4 " 26 4-5 "	Jarvis	Wesleyan
Mile walk	7 " 14 3-5 "	Houghton	Amherst
120 yd. hurdles	16 "	Cady	Yale
220-yd. "	25 1-5 "	Bremer	Harvard
2-mile bicycle	5 " 18 1-5 "	Goodman	City of New York
Running high jump	5 ft. 10 1-2 in.	Paine	Harvard
" broad "	22 " 1 "	Ramsdell	Pennsylvania
Pole vault	10 " 9 "	Kershaw	Yale
16-lb. hammer	123 " 9 "	Hickok	"
16-lb. shot	42 "	"	"

Hammer thrown first time with 7-foot run; shot put from 7-foot circle.

QUEEN'S CLUB, LONDON—FOOTBALL AND ATHLETIC FIELD

W. H. Grove

At the Oxford-Cambridge 1864 meeting there was a 200-yard hurdle-race and 2-mile steeple-chase, won in 26¾ seconds and 10:34 respectively. The following year the 2-mile run, putting the 16-pound shot, and throwing the cricket-ball were added, the last being replaced, however, at the third meeting, by the 16-pound hammer, and thus the list stands to-day. The half-mile run, mile walk, two-mile bicycle-race, 220-yard dash, and pole vault are not included in the Oxford-Cambridge sports, and only occasionally in any of the college games, though there is no lack of ability in the half-mile. With us the '76 meeting (the birth-year of the Intercollegiate Association) was the first of the shot, and the following year saw the first of the pole vault and hammer, with records of 7 ft. 4 in. and 75 ft. 10 in. One of the ludicrous sights of this meeting was a young man clad in green silk tights liberally spangled with gold fringe, who heroically whipped his legs throughout the walk, undoubtedly in emulation of Weston the pedestrian, at that time in the public eye.

COMPARATIVE TABLE ENGLISH AND AMERICAN UNIVERSITY RECORDS

Event.	English.				American.			
	Record.	Name.	Year.	University.	Record.	Name.	Year.	University.
100 yards	10	Wharton	1886	Darlington	10	{ Sherill / Wendell / Cary }	1880 / 1881 / 1889	Yale. / Harvard. / Princeton.
440 "	49 4-5	Moneypenny	1882	Cambridge	47 3-4	Baker	1886	Harvard.
880 "	1:54 2-5	Cross	1888	Oxford	1:54 1-2	Dohm	1890	Princeton
Mile run	4:19 4-5	Lutyens	1884	Cambridge	4:26 4-5	Jarvis	1894	Wesleyan.
3-mile "	14:44 2-5	Horan	1892	"	15:41 4-5	Lane	1888	Yale.
120-yd. hurdle	16	{ Joyce / Bulger }	1884 / 1892	Dublin / Cambridge	15 4-5	Williams	1891	"
2-mile bicycle	5:36 2-5				5: 7 2-5	Elliott	1894	Harvard.
High jump	6 ft. 2 1-2 in.	Brooks	1876	Oxford	6 ft. 4 in	Page	1887	Penn.
Broad "	23 " 6 1-2 "	* Fry	1893	"	23 " 6 1-2 in.	Reber	1891	Wash'n.
16-lb. hammer	136 ft. 6 in	† Hales	1876	Cambridge	123 ft. 9 in. 7-ft. run.	Hickok	1894	Yale.
16-lb. shot	39 ft. 1 in. 10-ft. run.	Ware	1886	Oxford	42 ft. 7-ft. run.	"	1894	"

* See comment on English measuring.   † Unlimited run.

While it has been only in the last half-dozen years that our records have approached the English, yet since 1889 they have been raised steadily at almost every meeting, until they stand now at the very top in a majority of the events, as a glance at the tables makes patent. The greatest meeting our universities ever had was that of '91, when records were made in ten out of fourteen events on the programme, two of them being world's records.

With so large a variety of athletic interests at the English universities it is surprising how many men become candidates for the track athletic teams of the different colleges. Every college at Oxford and Cambridge has its athletic team, and holds sports open only to its own undergraduates. As I have already intimated, there is very little preparation, as we understand it, among the track athletes for their university contests, and there is less to be seen at these purely college meetings, which show more of a good sportsmanlike feeling than of excellent form.

The general athletic schedule of the universities is arranged for the year by the "Blues" committee, which includes a blue in every branch of sport, and they decide on dates for rowing, cricket, football, and athletic contests.

The athletic year begins with the Freshmen's sports in November, after which candidates for college teams are chosen, and the slight training that they do is begun. Active work is in order shortly after Christmas, and college meetings are continued throughout January and February. By the last of February the colleges have pretty nearly all held their meetings, and interest then centres in the make-up of the 'varsity athletic team, the candidates for which are chosen at the university sports, held usually about the first week in March for that purpose. The first and second men are chosen, two only in each event—except in one and three mile events, in which there are three—being sent up to London for the Oxford-

Cambridge contest, decided annually at Queen's on or about the day of the boat-race. The winners are called the first string, and receive a full " blue "; the second men form the second string, and receive a half " blue " — the difference being that the first may wear the blue cap and jacket, whereas the halves have only the blue trimming on their shirt and running breeches. This team is generally selected about three weeks before their contest, and, once chosen, settle down to more serious training, usually going to the sea for the final ten days of preparation.

I have told of the manner of meeting the expenses of athletic teams, but I think I have neglected to say that

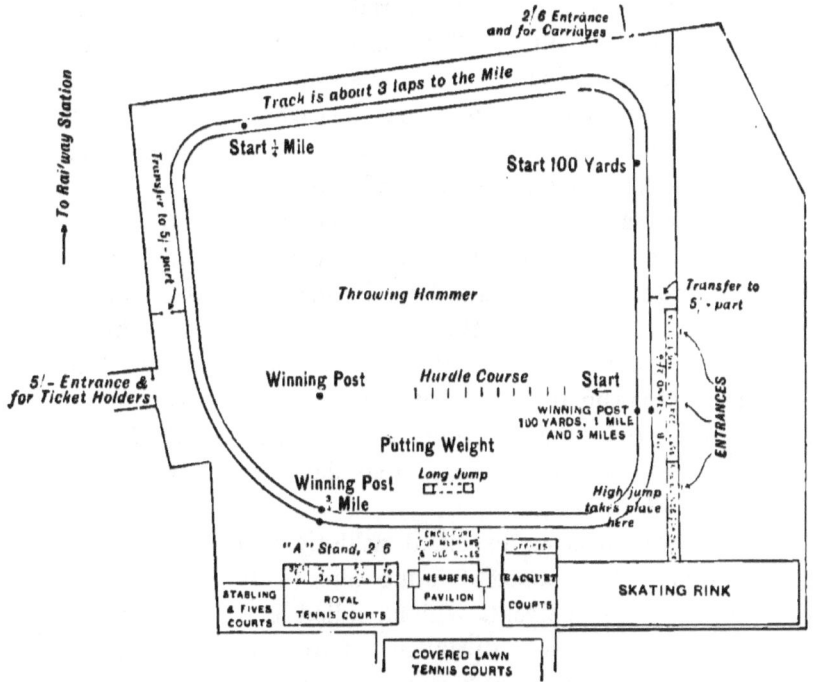

DIAGRAM OF QUEEN'S CLUB GROUNDS
Site of the Oxford-Cambridge football and athletic contests

the university athletic ground at both Oxford and Cambridge is open for training purposes to those only who have joined the U. A. C. and paid their fee. The colleges are permitted to hold their games on the 'varsity grounds, and on that day only may athletes not members of the U. A. C. use the track. As a result, a large proportion of the athletes do become members of the University Club.

The sportsmanlike spirit is very much in evidence at these meetings. The afternoon is generally given the coloring of a social gathering, and made the more pleasurable by an excellent band of music — an idea that might well be adopted by our universities, which do not have music even at the intercollegiate championships. The prizes are simplicity itself, being silver medals of precisely the same value for the first and second men—a plan long ago inaugurated, and one that has worked most advantageously in fostering the excellent feeling which greets you at every turn at Oxford and Cambridge.

I have said that there is no trainer at the English universities; but Oxford until lately had the advantage of retaining in residence, as a don of Hertford College, one of its most famous old athletes — C. N. Jackson — who, as Honorable Treasurer of the Association and general adviser, gave the athletics of his *alma mater* a great deal of personal and valuable attention ; and the Rev. E. H. Morgan, of Jesus College, bears a similar relationship to athletics at Cambridge.

Oxford owns an excellent athletic field, with a fully equipped club-house, dressing and reading rooms, etc., while Cambridge rents a field, called Fenner's, from the cricket club, with the privilege of its club-house. There is a movement now making at Cambridge to raise money for the purchase of grounds. The tracks, cinders on clay

OXFORD RACQUET AND FIVES COURTS

at both, are about one-third of a mile, measured 12 inches (instead of 18, as with us) from the inner side of the path, and kept in very excellent condition by their groundsmen. Their curves are rather easy, though not raised for cycling, and there is a good 100-yard stretch, though Oxford has not a 220-yard straightaway, and, in fact, neither requires one, since that distance is not used for flat or hurdle-racing.

The hurdling—and the hurdles (single ones) 3 ft. 6 in., are rather more primitive than ours, and driven into the ground—is done on the very best of English turf, which is the finest imaginable, and must be seen and walked on to be appreciated. The costumes of the athletes are worthy of our emulation, the shirts being invariably quarter-sleeved, which is a decided improvement on the rowing shirts seen at our college meetings. The American Intercollegiate Association should pass a law compelling athletes to wear shirts with sleeves, if not quarter, at least covering the armpit; it would make no difference whatever in the freedom of motion, and certainly be infinitely more decent. The Yale team that made the recent athletic invasion of England were requested by Oxford to wear shirts with quarter-sleeves.

The form of English university athletes, with the exception of distance running, does not average so good as ours. Of course there are individuals who approach our best, but where they have one such, we have dozens. In the sprints, which are run in lanes, the men are much less steady on the mark, due, I think, largely to the starting, which is by no means so careful or so skilful as that to which we are accustomed in America. I was amused by the pistol of the Oxford starter, which is a muzzle-loading affair, rivalling the college buildings in antiquity, and when exploded sounded like a huge cannon fire-cracker. The men as a rule adopt the standing start. I think I observed only one who started from his hands and knees, and he did not get the advantage (steadiness) that is supposed to belong to that style of getting off the mark. I have come to the conclusion that the time of year at which their games are held has much to do with the sprinting records. The atmosphere was emphatically chilly at all the sports I attended, as it is invariably in February and March, and it must have a certain influence on the performances of the athletes.

The hurdling form is rather poorer. A few negotiate the sticks in excellent style, but the average top them very awkwardly, many taking their jumps straight on without regard apparently to their stride. The same criticism applies to the average high-jumping form, the measuring of which, but particularly of the broad jump, I consider faulty. Along the landing-bed sides of the broad jump are permanently fixed measuring-boards marked in feet and inches. The take-off is a piece of joist sunk flush with the earth, as with us; but instead of measuring, as do we, from the scratch-line (outer edge of joist) with a steel tape to the first break in the ground made by the jumper's last heel, they measure with a linen tape (I saw none of steel at either Oxford or Cambridge) to the *final* impression of the last heel, where a pole placed across the measuring-boards on the sides indicates the distance jumped. This method of measuring is neither accurate nor even fair to the contestants, as the nature of the earth in the landing-bed makes a difference of several inches in a performance, and the groundsman's spade in turning up and loosening the soil largely influences results; thus one man may have more favoring conditions than another in the same competition. Nor are my deductions speculative, since I found just such dissimilar conditions existing at the Oxford and at the Cambridge college and university sports. Moreover, I carefully noted on the afternoon of the Oxford University meeting the performance of Mr. Fry, whose jumps in three trials, as announced, varied from three to five inches greater than they would have been had the tape been stretched to the first break made by the last heel, and not to where it sank into the loose earth of the landing-bed. Given a yielding landing-bed, a rainy day, a strong sprinter without too much rise to his jump, and this measuring system, and there is no record beyond the limit of the Englishmen. Mr. Fry is credited on the English and American record tables as dividing the world's running broad-jump record of 23 ft. 6½ in. with the American, Mr. C. S. Reber; and while the Oxford man is an exceptionally good all-round athlete, and a jumper for whom the world's record is a possibility, yet I certainly do not regard his alleged record as entitled to consideration, nor any other long-jump-

TYPE OF ENGLISH HURDLE

ing performances of the Englishmen, until they have cast aside their present manner of measuring, and adopted the fair one in vogue in the United States.

My comment on this broad-jump measuring, printed first in HARPER's WEEKLY, created so much discussion on both sides of the Atlantic that I publish herewith what Mr. W. B. Curtis, editor of the *Spirit of the Times*, and the highest authority on athletic legislation and records in the United States, had to say on the subject:

BROAD JUMPING IN ENGLAND
From *The Spirit of the Times*, August 4, 1894.

DURING the past three months there has been much newspaper discussion concerning the methods of measuring the running broad jump as practised in England and America. In the conduct of this argument English athletes and English editors have shown more temper than wisdom in dealing with a subject whose proper adjudication depends on fact rather than argument, and cannot be furthered by ill-natured protest against statements made in good faith by American newspapers. With the purpose of eliminating from this discussion all extraneous rubbish, and bringing the interested parties face to face on a platform of common-sense, we give below a brief history of the contention.

Early this spring the proprietors of HARPER's WEEKLY sent their athletic editor, Mr. Caspar W. Whitney, to England, with instructions to study English amateur sport. Mr. Whitney incorporated his impressions in a series of articles published after his return. His contribution of May 19th treated of athletic sport at the English universities, and included the following sentences—

(Then follows the paragraph containing my broad-jump criticism.—C. W. W.)

The Spirit of the Times of May 26th reprinted those portions of Mr. Whitney's article quoted above, and commented as follows:

"The measurement rule of the Amateur Athletic Union is as follows: 'When jumped on earth, a joist five inches wide shall be sunk flush with it. The outer edge of this joist shall be called the scratch-line, and the measurement of all jumps shall be made from it at right angles to the nearest break in the ground made by any part of the person of the competitor.'

"The alighting ground for the running broad jump is dug up to the depth of a foot, so as to furnish a soft place for the descending jumper, and after each jump an attendant rakes the earth over until it is smooth and without mark. At the time a jumper alights his motion is diagonally forward and downward, and after he first touches the top of the soft earth he goes on forward as well as downward several inches before his feet come to a full stop.

"The extent of this forward and downward motion would vary with the softness of the ground and the different angles at which different jumpers end their flight. But the 'heel mark' named by the English rule will always be several inches below and in front of the 'nearest break in the ground' given in the American rule. The difference would certainly average three inches and probably four inches or more.

"It would appear from these facts that all American records at running broad jump are really of several inches more value than English records of the same announced length, and that Reber's 23 feet 6½ inches, and Goff's 23 feet 6 inches, are actually several inches better than Fry's 23 feet 6½ inches.

"Or the difference might be stated in another way. The English record, 23 feet 6½ inches, if measured by American rules, would have been about 23 feet 1 inch or 23 feet 2 inches; while the American record, 23 feet 6½ inches, if measured by English rules, would be 23 feet 11 inches or 24 feet.

"We shall await with interest English comment on these statements."

The first English athletic authority to answer was London *Pastime*, whose edition of June 7th published the following:

"There is no record to which so much international rivalry attaches as that for the long jump, the best-known performance in which is 23 feet 6½ inches, by both C. B. Fry at Oxford, and C. S. Reber in the United States. The conditions for such contests in America are slightly different from those in this country, but it has not been suggested until recently that a performance in one country is, through the method of measurement, of less value than that in another. But an American visitor to the Inter-University meeting of March last, and also to the sports of both universities and certain college meetings, viz., Mr. Caspar W. Whitney, the athletic editor of HARPER'S WEEKLY, has recently published some remarks on the management of our competitions. In the first place he draws attention to the using of a linen tape instead of a steel tape. But his more serious contention is that the measurements from the scratch-line are taken, not to the first disturbance in the soil, but to the 'final impression of the last heel.' Such a notion as this is quite incompatible with A. A. A. laws. Mr. Whitney's argument is as follows:"

(Here followed the pertinent portions of Mr. Whitney's article, as reprinted above.)

"However true the last remark may be, there is no question that all good judges in long-jump performances are well aware that the measurement should be made to the nearest disturbance made in the earth by the foot, and the words 'the nearest heel-mark' are surely thus understood."

The next English answer came from the well-known journalist who writes over the signature of "Vanderdecken." Concerning the statements made by him and by *Pastime*, *The Spirit* of July 7th commented as follows:

"And now we have been favored with advance proofs of an article written by 'Vanderdecken,' one of England's most intelligent and impartial editors. It is as follows:

"'When the Yale athletes arrive in England, it will be well if the Oxford athletic authorities, with the experienced Mr. C. N. Jackson at their head, discuss a matter which has recently received prominent attention in United States prints. A Mr. Whitney has been publishing in HARPER'S WEEKLY the results of some investigations made by him in England in the spring. He has discovered that the English method of measuring long jumps is open to the serious objection of always favoring the jumper, his allegation being that we do not measure to the first break, but to the spot where the athlete's heel "sank in the loose earth of the landing-bed." The conclusion arrived at by Mr. Whitney and by *The Spirit of the Times* is that all English records are necessarily some inches behind American ones—a somewhat sweeping assertion to make on the strength of observations made at Oxford and Cambridge. *The Spirit of the Times* asks: "What answer will Englishmen make to this?" Speaking for myself, the result of my inquiries is simply that Mr. Whitney is a bad observer. Neither in the case of C. B. Fry (whose claims to a record are ridiculed) nor any one else is the final heel-mark taken, but the spot where the rearmost heel first cuts the earth. This is not necessarily the spot where the first falling away of the earth is observed, and what the judges have to do is to decide where the first contact of the last heel with the earth has taken place. I have it from one of the judges who measured Fry's record jump of 23 feet 6¼ inches, that the first mark made by the heel was one of the most clearly defined he had ever seen, and that the three judges were unanimous in assigning the position of the first break.'

"'Vanderdecken' does not 'speak by the card' when he states that Mr. Whitney and *The Spirit of the Times* have concluded, etc. If he will read our article (reprinted above) he will note that our conclusion was specifically predicated on the correctness of the facts stated by Mr. Whitney. If these be in error our conclusions have no standing.

"Nor is he wholly ingenuous in stating that 'the conclusion arrived at by Mr. Whitney and by *The Spirit of the Times* is that all English records are necessarily some inches behind American ones—a somewhat sweeping assertion to make on the strength of observations made at Oxford and Cambridge.' In making this criticism 'Vanderdecken' has overlooked the fact that the best English amateur records at running broad jump have been held continuously for more than twenty years by members of Cambridge or Oxford universities, and that each of the several successive records thus held has been made at university games. Therefore the methods of measurement in vogue at Oxford and Cambridge have controlled all of England's best amateur broad-jump records for more than twenty years, and the conclusions of Mr. Whitney and of *The Spirit of the Times* were fully justified by the facts.

"We regret that neither *Pastime* nor 'Vanderdecken' has been able to make a more satisfactory and explicit denial of the statements made by Mr. Whitney.

"*Pastime* admits that the English rule is unsatisfactory, but claims that all good judges understand it correctly and apply it properly. This would seem to leave the correctness of measurement entirely at the mercy of the judges, and suggests that all English records at broad jumping should carry a foot-note specifying whether the judges were good or bad.

"'Vanderdecken' practically admits all that Mr. Whitney claimed. He says 'the spot where the rearmost heel cuts the earth is not necessarily the spot where the first falling away of the earth is observed.' This frank admission deserves a little explanation. In the running broad jump, as contested at reputable athletic meetings in England and America, the jumpers run along a smooth, hard approach, take-off from a board sunk flush with the surface of the ground, and alight in a plot of earth freshly spaded up so as to be loose and soft. Before each jump this plot is raked until its surface is smooth, level, and without any marks save those of the rake. After the athlete jumps and walks away there will be found in this soft plot an irregular hole or break in the soft dirt, caused by the jumper alighting in it. In America the jump would be measured from the board at which the jumper started to that part of the hole or break in the ground nearest to the starting-board, no matter whether that nearest part of the hole was made by the jumper's heel or his leg or his body or his arm or his hands or his elbows or his back or by the shock consequent on his alighting. This hole was not there before he jumped, and must have been caused by his jump, directly or indirectly, and the measurement is made to the nearest part of that hole, no matter what made it, or where the jumper's rearmost heel first cut the earth. 'Vanderdecken' admits that in England the measurement would be made to the point where the judges thought the jumper's rearmost heel first cut the earth, and that this point would sometimes be different from and farther away from the starting-board than the first falling away of the earth, which is the point to which measurement would be made in America.

"As this is exactly what Mr. Whitney claimed, there seems to be nothing on which to base further discussion."

That Mr. Whitney's original article clearly represented his convictions is proven by the following note, published in *The Spirit* of July 14th:

"FRANKLIN SQUARE, NEW YORK, July 6th.

"I have read the comments of the English journalists in this week's *Spirit of the Times* with interest. I note that 'Vanderdecken' says that measurement in a broad jump is made from 'where the rearmost heel first cuts the earth.'

"I am afraid that 'Vanderdecken' was not using his eyes very carefully at whatever broad-jumping contests he may have been a witness. What I told you about the measurement of the broad jump, and that which I wrote in HARPER'S WEEKLY, were my observations on the field of contest at both the Oxford and the Cambridge sports. The measurement is not taken to where the rearmost heel first cuts the earth, but to the firm imprint in the ground of the rearmost heel.

"Very truly yours, CASPAR W. WHITNEY."

The London *Sportsman* of July 14th published an interview with Mr. Charles H. Sherrill, of the Yale Graduate Advisory Committee, who accompanied the team to England. One paragraph of this article is as follows:

"'I see that your journals are trying to misrepresent our athletic methods,' I observed. 'Yes,' rejoined Mr. Sherrill, 'and nothing could be more inaccurate or in worse taste. Of the fairness of your starting, judging, and measurement I cannot speak too highly In our country a man is penalized and disqualified for the slightest thing. In the broad jumping, too, our method is far too strict. That is why I think Sheldon will have quite an appreciable look in, for his distance is according to American measurement, not English, and he will perhaps do his 23 feet when he tries.'"

It is not impertinent to remark that nine-tenths of all the published articles of which Mr. Sherrill now says "nothing could be more inaccurate or in worse taste" consisted solely of statements made by Mr. Sherrill to various American reporters during the three weeks next preceding his departure for England. It is also worthy of note that Mr. Sherrill's only stated reason for preferring the English method of measuring the running broad jump is that it would make Mr. Sheldon's performances longer than by the American method

And, finally, the London *Sporting Life* of July 16th says:

"On Saturday afternoon Mr. C L. Lockton and Mr. C. Herbert examined the jumping-bed, and expressed perfect satisfaction with the ideas of Messrs. C. N. Jackson and C. B. Fry, and their mode of measurement. They clearly stated, notwithstanding American papers to the contrary, that the English method is perfectly fair; that is to say, measurement to the place where the hindermost heel cuts the soil, not to the farthest point of the drivage of the heel. English judges take no account of the break back of the soil behind, but simply the cut of the hindmost heel, thus giving the actual distance fairly covered."

In commenting on the documents printed above, we wish, first of all, to express our complete confidence in the honesty and accuracy of Mr. Whitney's statements He is an intelligent gentleman, of liberal education, and has no personal interest in or prejudice for or against either English or American athletic customs. He occupies an honorable and responsible position on the editorial staff of one of America's most reliable and respectable journals. At the suggestion of his employers he visited England to study and report upon English amateur athletic sport. The series of articles published after his return were uniformly courteous and notably laudatory of almost everything he saw or heard in England; so much so, in fact, that many readers, who did not know Mr. Whitney personally, supposed that the articles were written by an Englishman. His statements concerning the measurement of the running broad jump were not censorious or written in carping mood, but merely rehearsed in temperate language what he had seen during his sojourn in England. We are firmly convinced that his statements on this point are absolutely and wholly correct; that at the various Oxford and Cambridge sports, and at the annual inter-university meeting, he saw the several broad jumps measured to the final resting-place of the rearmost heel, thus making each jump several inches longer than if properly measured.

It is also true that the best English amateur records at running broad jump have been held continuously for more than twenty years by members of Cambridge or Oxford universities, and that each of the several successive records thus held has been made at university games. Remembering these facts, we are fully convinced that each of these successive record-holders received credit for several inches more than was fairly his due, because measurement was made to the final imprint of the heel instead of the first break of the ground. The present English amateur record, 23 feet 6¼ inches, was made by C. B. Fry, of Wadham College, Oxford University, at the games of Trinity College, Oxford University, March 4, 1893, and we firmly believe that this jump was measured to the final imprint of his rearmost heel, and that, if measured under American rules, it would not have been more than 23 feet 1 inch or 23 feet 2 inches. We are satisfied that this unfair system of measurement has been for years and is still in use at the English universities, and that all published performances made in their games need correction by deducting from 4 inches to 7 inches, which would be the distance gained by the erroneous measurement.

The Athletic Rules of the English Amateur Athletic Association are most curiously divided. Rules 1 to 24, inclusive, are called "Laws for Athletic Meetings and Competitions," and all amateur clubs must obey and enforce these 24 laws. Then Rules 25 to 37, inclusive, are labelled "Recommendations," and clubs can obey them or not, as they choose. This point is plainly set forth in an article entitled "The Conditions of the Contest," published in the London (Eng.) *Sportsman* of July 14th, and also in the London *Sporting Life* of July 16th. One paragraph of this article is as follows:

"With reference to the Oxford and Cambridge regulations, it has been repeatedly stated by some critics in London that the Oxford and Cambridge athletes every year in the conduct of their sports violate two or three of the laws of the Amateur Athletic Association. It may be as well to correct this mistake once for all. Such a mistake obviously arises from the said critics confusing the laws and the regulations of the A. A. A. Oxford and Cambridge, like all other amateur clubs in England, cannot and dare not break any of the essential laws formulated by the A. A. A. The regulations of the Amateur Athletic Association are quite another thing, being merely recommendations with respect to the most desirable rules of racing. Any body of amateurs is therefore at liberty to adopt these recommendations or to follow any rules of racing which they themselves may prefer."

It will be seen from the above that the Constitution, Rules, and Laws of the A. A. A., corresponding to the Constitution, By-laws, and half of the General Rules and Athletic Rules of the Amateur Athletic Union of America, are binding on all English athletic organizations; but that the recommendations of the A A. A., corresponding to the other half of the General Rules and Athletic Rules of the Amateur Athletic Union, carry no mandatory power, and every English athletic club is at liberty to adopt or reject any or all of them.

The English universities not only can but do discard some of the athletic recommendations of the A. A. A., and substitute rules of home manufacture. They put the shot from a ten-foot square instead of the seven-foot square prescribed by the recommendations of the A. A. A., and throw the hammer from a thirty-foot circle instead of the nine-foot circle specified in the A. A. A. recommendations. They also measure the running broad jump in a style which violates the established custom, if not the letter of the Laws of the A. A. A. Oxford and Cambridge have a right to go still further and to adopt such other unique rules as they wish. They have a right to measure their cinder-paths 12 feet instead of 12 inches from the curb, and on tracks thus measured to run miles in 4 m. 12 s., beating all amateur or professional records of the world. They have a right to cut the hurdles down a foot, and then run hurdle races in 15 s. In fact, they have an undisputed right to ignore the athletic recommendation of the A. A. A. and manage their games as they please.

And any other English athletic club or sports committee has the same right.

This is certainly a curious condition of affairs, and until reformation is effected no performance reported at any English athletic meeting deserves credence until it is known under what rules it was made, and how it was timed or measured.

Having thus announced our full confidence in the statements made by Mr. Whitney, it is now proper to state that we also believe in the honesty and accuracy of "Vanderdecken" and the athletic editors of *Pastime*, *Sportsman*, and *Sporting Life*. We believe that English university officials at English university sports measure the running broad jump as described by Mr. Whitney; but we also believe that many English judges, serving at other English athletic meetings, measure to what they believe to be the point where the rearmost heel first cuts the earth. This imaginary or rather indeterminable point would be somewhere between the point of measurement used at the English universities and that adopted in America—probably a little nearer the latter than the former.

Omitting for the present any consideration of Mr. Whitney's recital, and confining ourselves exclusively to the published statements of "Vanderdecken," *Pastime*, *Sportsman*, and *Sporting Life*, it is not hard to discover some points which are admitted by both sides.

First, there is a difference in the rules governing the measurement of the running broad jump, as laid down by the Amateur Athletic Union of America and the Amateur Athletic Association of England.

Secondly, when the alighting place is turf or hard ground the measurement would be the same by either rule.

Thirdly, in all well-managed athletic meetings, either in England or America, it is the custom to spade up the alighting ground for the running broad jump like a garden bed and rake its surface smooth between each jump, thus giving to the contestants a spot so soft that they can extend themselves fully without fear of injury. When a competitor takes a trial and walks away there will be found in this soft earth an irregular hole, varying in size and shape according to how much of the jumper's person came in contact with the ground. Under American rules the measurement would be made from the scratch-line to that point of the perimeter of this hole which was nearest to the scratch-line. Under the English methods measurement would be made to some point farther from the scratch-line than the point used in the American measurement, thus making the jump measure more than under American rules. The exact point to which this English measurement is made has been variously described by different English athletic authorities. *Pastime* claims that it is to "the nearest disturbance made in the earth by the foot." "Vanderdecken" describes it as "the spot where the rearmost heel first cuts the earth, which is not necessarily the spot where the first falling away of the earth is observed." And, finally, London *Sportsman* and *Sporting Life* agree that it is "to the place where the hindmost heel cuts the soil. English judges take no account of the break back of the soil behind, but simply the cut of the hindmost heel."

Fourthly, these English authorities differ slightly in detail, but all admit that the English method of measurement makes each jump longer than it would measure under American rules.

Fifthly, owing to this difference in measurement, English and American records do not stand on a level footing, and cannot be compared without explanation. It is evident that C. B. Fry, of Oxford, does not share with C. S. Reber, of St. Louis, the honor of the world's best record, for it is admitted by all interested parties that Reber's jump would have measured more than Fry's if measured by English methods. E. W. Goff's record, only half an inch behind Reber's, would also, if measured by English methods, be longer than Fry's.

These five propositions are proven by the above-quoted statements of four English athletic authorities—"Vanderdecken," *Pastime, Sportsman,* and *Sporting Life*—and those English athletes and editors who have been snarling at such American newspapers as had ventured to speak the truth on this subject would do well to change front and quarrel with their own neighbors and friends, who admit all the essential points ever claimed by an American newspaper.

The English rule seems to be somewhat inexplicit, and its provisions have been variously interpreted by different officials. Note "Vanderdecken's" language:

".. And what the judges have to do is to decide where the first contact of the last heel with the earth has taken place. I have it from one of the judges who measured Fry's record jump of 23 feet 6½ inches, that the first mark made by the heel was one of the most clearly defined he had ever seen, and that the three judges were unanimous in assigning the position of the first break."

If these words mean anything, they mean that the judges frequently have difficulty in establishing the proper point of measurement, and that when the three judges agree, the circumstance is so unusual as to be noteworthy.

If English officials sometimes differ as to the practical application of their own law, it is not strange that American athletes should be unable to understand the method of making a correct measurement under the English rule. There is one point about this measurement which is especially mysterious to Americans, and we appeal to our English friends for enlightenment.

The recondite point is as follows: After the jumper has made his effort and withdrawn from the alighting ground, there remains in the soft earth an irregular hole caused by the jumper alighting. The heels of the jumper strike the surface of the dirt and then plough forward and downward until they come to a full stop, the distance thus travelled, both forward and downward, varying with the softness and dryness of the earth and the depth to which it is loosened. If the jumper does not fall down after the jump, and steps squarely out of the soft earth, the final resting-place of his heels can be plainly seen at the bottom of the hole caused by his jump. Under American rules the jump would be measured from the scratch-line to that part of the hole nearest to the scratch-line, and as the scratch-line and the hole are in plain sight, intelligent and honest judges cannot disagree as to the point of measurement. The Englishmen measure, not to the nearest part of the hole, but to the point where the judges think the jumper's rearmost heel first struck the dirt. They claim that the soft earth usually breaks back and tumbles in behind this point of first impact, and that the correct distance cleared by the jumper is found by measuring, not to the edge of the hole, but to the point where the rearmost heel of the jumper first touched the ground. Granting, for the sake of argument, that their contention is just, the practical question is to devise a method of exactly locating this true point of measurement. Mr. Sherrill states that Sheldon's winning jump, 23 feet 11 inches, at the Oxford-Yale sports, measured only 23 feet $9\frac{1}{2}$ inches by the American rules, and it is probable that the difference between the two styles of measurement would average about that distance. The inside of the hole made by the jumper slopes from its edge downward and inward to its bottom, and no part of its inner surface is as high as its edge. If the spot where the jumper's rearmost heel first touched the surface of the alighting ground is farther from the scratch-line than the nearest edge of the hole, which is claimed by the English judges, then that spot, which was necessarily level with the surface of the alighting ground, must be in mid-air, as the inner faces of the hole slope downward and inward from the edge. There can be no dirt nor anything but air at the spot where this first impact is claimed to have been made. If a spirit-level were laid across the hole, the desired spot would be on the under-side of that spirit-level, an inch or two over the inner sloping surface of the hole, level with the edges of the hole, and in mid-air, an inch or two away from the nearest dirt.

Now, the conundrum is, How do those English judges find, and measure to, this point in mid-air?

We shall send copies of this article to "Vanderdecken" and to the editors of *Pastime*, *Sportsman*, and *Sporting Life*, and trust that one or all of them will instruct us how to locate, and measure to, a point in mid-air whose distance and direction from any material substance except the atmosphere are matters of guesswork.

Meanwhile we venture to suggest to our English cousins that it seems quite possible to discuss this question without ill-nature or undue acerbity.

My criticism of the methods that obtain in the high jump touches the length of pegs, which project from the upright fully four inches. What so long a peg means, moreover, was instanced in the performance of Swanwick, the Oxford winner at the Oxford-Cambridge games, March 17, '94, at Queen's Club, who hit the bar so violently in one of his trials (and the last one, by-the-way) that it bounced into the air and fell down on the pegs quite at their end. Had they been the length of ours (three inches), the bar must have fallen to the ground, and Mr. Swanwick would not have been credited with 5 ft. 10¼ in., though he made a record of 5 ft. 11 in. last year. I noticed, too, that the bar sagged in the centre, which, however, seemed a matter of indifference to the measurers.

There is nothing in the rules of the Amateur Athletic Association of Great Britain to cover these points I have criticised: in fact, the A. A. A. rulings, although verbose, are quite loosely put together. Regarding the high jump, the length of pegs is ignored, and they might be a foot long for all the rules to the contrary: as to measuring the broad jump, it is set forth only that "all jumps shall be measured to the taking-off line from the edge to the heel-mark nearest that line, along a line perpendicular to that line"— certainly more redundant than lucid.

The average hammer-throwing and shot-putting form is not very good, though I was told this year's performances fell below the usual standard. The hammer weighs the same as ours, sixteen pounds, including the 3 ft. 6 in. handle, which differs from the ones we use in being stiff; the head, too, is not of similar shape, but oval, looking very much like an enlarged pecan-nut. Instead of the seven-foot circle we have, the English university athlete has a thirty-foot circle, and the performers start from the edge farthest from the scratch, and after getting into their swing usually make three progressive turns before reaching the scratch and letting go the hammer. The event was won this year by 101 ft. $4\frac{1}{2}$ in., though the best university record is 138 ft. 3 in., made in 1876, at which time there was no circle, measure being taken from the last footmark, and the handle was not limited in length. Outside the universities the hammer is thrown from a nine-foot circle.

The 16-pound shot is put from a ten-foot square, again an advantage over our seven-foot circle, and the seven-foot square that is customary at non-university games in Great Britain, and was won this year by a performance of 37 ft. 6 in., which is five inches behind the English university record.

The annual dual meeting of Oxford and Cambridge on the Queen's Club grounds is the greatest athletic event of England, and the one I had the pleasure of witnessing this year proved a record-breaker in the matter of attendance, I believe, as 12,000 spectators passed through the gates. It draws out a class of society equalled in quality at no other sporting event except the cricket match at Lords, and there are more top-hats to be seen, in proportion to the number of heads, than at any other one-afternoon gathering in Great Britain. The small number of officials on the field at this meeting appealed to me strongly as a most sensible departure from the score or more that obstruct the view of spectators at American meetings. There were only nine at Queen's, including but one timer, which is the rule; consequently they carried off the events promptly, and did not get in their own and everybody else's way. Another pleasing arrangement is the manner of announcing results. There is no announcer, but the winner's number and performance are put on two large blackboards, placed so as to be visible to all spectators, while his university color, over that of the second man's university, is floated from a flag-pole. Each event is scheduled on the programme for a certain hour, and is brought off on time, the clerk of the course being a groundsman with a large-sized bell, to the vigorous ringing of which the men respond promptly, or run the risk of losing their place.

With all our American progression there seem to be yet a few simple and effective customs in the mother-country we have not, up to date, improved upon.

The universities of Scotland just about absorb what little there is of athletics in that country, the wave that spread over England having spent its force at the Tweed. There are ample grounds in and about Edinburgh, most beautifully laid out and picturesquely situated; but notwithstanding the opportunities there are few athletic clubs of which one ever hears, although football clubs flourish abundantly, a statement that applies likewise to Glasgow and Aberdeen. The universities and schools of these cities hold their own games, but there are no joint meetings. The Scottish Association has labored to put more life into athletics among the better classes, but with little if any avail; the average Scotchman of the best sort usually fills a place in the work-a-day world he cannot neglect, and when he does take an outing he picks up a rifle or his beloved golf-club. There is some pretty fair polo in Scotland, likewise a little hunting, but not at the universities.

There is more activity in athletics in Ireland, Trinity College, Dublin, having fine grounds, and being undoubtedly the best-known college, athletically speaking, outside Oxford and Cambridge. Queen's Colleges at Cork and Belfast hold games also, but, even so, as in Scotland, there are no inter-university meetings, and a representative is rarely seen away from home. There are a number of Irish clubs which do not attract the best element, and without the dual university meetings, as in England, athletics in Scotland and Ireland maintain but an indifferent existence.

And now that I have come to the last of this university series, I wish to dwell for a few lines on the influence athletics have had upon the English undergraduate in lessening dissipation and raising the average of scholarship, a side of this great question of sport in our universities at home and abroad that to me, at least, seems the most important.

I found athletics in the English as in American universities to have worked appreciably in raising the general tone of the colleges, singly and collectively, in giving a more wholesome aptitude for study, in strengthening the *morale* of the student body, and in better fitting men for not only their work at the university, but for the serious business of life when they had gone out into the world. Old graduates of both Oxford and Cambridge who have kept in touch with the *alma mater* assured me my investigations did not belie the facts, and that there is tangible evidence at every hand to prove the inestimable value of judicious participation in sport.

It is true, however, I did not find the results in the

English universities so marked nor so general throughout the undergraduates as in the American institutions, and for two very good reasons: In the first place, it is an undoubted fact, as I have already written, that the average Englishman is naturally more athletically inclined than the average American, and that the former, being no stranger to athletic influences, would, therefore, be less susceptible to its workings, and the results not so noticeable as in the case of the latter; secondly, a class of men is to be found at Oxford and Cambridge that goes there merely for the experience of university life, and with no preconceived idea of subsequently using its lessons in any profession or business. These men may or may not remain throughout the course for a degree, and the system extant at both universities permits the existence of such a class. There is no examination on matriculation at Cambridge except a college one, which is not universal. The ordinary pass man has "Little Go," "General," and "Special" to pass at the end of his first, second, and third years respectively. The honor man has "Little Go," and then his Tripos at the end of his time, and college examination at the end of each May term. At Oxford there is an examination on matriculation, and an intermediate university examination both for honors and a pass degree. At Cambridge there is no intermediate examination for honor men, and at both there are annual college examinations, but they are not followed up so strictly as in our universities.

Unless he goes in for honors, the Oxford or Cambridge undergraduate may arrange to have a rather easy time of it throughout his course, whereas the American university man must attend recitations to keep up his standing and pass an examination every term of his course, or be dropped. I must conclude, after looking the field over carefully, that the American university man will average higher in scholarship than the Englishman.

The average man, or, it may be said, practically every man who goes to an American university, has a definite purpose of utilizing the education acquired there in whatever business or profession he may have chosen for his life's work; and the average American does choose a life's work, even if he is blessed with an ample fortune.

In England nearly every man of gentle birth one meets seems to have at least a competency from some source; and as one can live as well over there on two thousand dollars a year as on six over here, one finds an astonishingly large class of young men of moderate incomes and large prospects, with ample leisure to spend the one and await the other. To these the importance of study and its influence on their subsequent life decreases in proportion as prospects increase, and an education becomes a matter of culture, and not necessarily a matter of usefulness in their after-career. As a considerable percentage of this class is always to be found in residence at Oxford and Cambridge, it follows that the university average is lowered to just that extent.

It may be a popular, but it is certainly a fallacious, American conception that those of noble birth receive especial distinction at the English public schools and the universities. Rank takes no precedent in either social or sporting life at Oxford, Cambridge, Eton, or Harrow; nor is a man put on the team or crew because his name happens to be prefaced with a "Lord" or a "Sir." He takes equal chances with the rest, and all that is expected of him, or any man, is to be a good "chap" and a gentleman; if he is not, all the blue blood in England won't float him into the clubs (there are no societies, as with us), or into the rooms of those who are good chaps when they are "sporting" their "oaks." Nor is the man with nothing to commend him but his athletic prowess made the lion he is at some of our universities. If he is a boor, all the athletic ability in Christendom will not prove an open sesame for him.

Before I put down my pen I must bring to the surface a fact that gave me considerable pleasure in the discovery.

It is rather a unique departure for England to show us the enlightened path, and yet, thanks to the joint promulgation of our Secretaries of War and Navy against football between West Point and Annapolis, the Old World is just at present holding the torch aloft for the New.

The honorable Secretaries, whose opinions on sport would lead to the conclusion that their personal experience had stopped short at croquet and mumble-the-peg, have proclaimed against inter-academy contests, despite the report of the West Point Commandant that football has proved a stimulant to discipline, by bringing about a kindlier feeling between the officers and cadets, and that its dangers are no greater than the prescribed horseback riding, and that athletics have been beneficial to scholarship and an aid to discipline.

The Royal Naval College at Greenwich, the Royal Military Academy at Woolwich, and the Royal Military College at Sandhurst, which correspond to the United States Naval Academy at Annapolis and the United States Military Academy at West Point, not only are encouraged by the government to foster athletics, but hold annual inter football, athletic, and cricket contests as well. They have never found that these sports interfered with the cadets' duties nor affected their discipline, but, on the contrary, military and naval men of Great Britain are openly the stanchest advocates of such athletic training.

THE WATER HAZARD ON THE RANELAGH GOLF LINKS

Apropos of which I quote the following from the *Saturday Review:*

MILITARY VALUE OF SPORT

The value of sport as a means of developing and training soldiers has always been recognized in all armies, and, as regards officers, at any rate, has been well appreciated by us. A distinguished cavalry officer stated in public a few years ago that, in his opinion, no man was fit to hold a commission who did not ride fairly well to hounds. The immortal Jorrocks, too, was not slow to appreciate the relation between war and its image, with only 25 per cent. of its danger. In India we encourage our men to go out into the country on shooting expeditions, and a few enthusiasts at home have even allowed the "woollies" an occasional sight of the hounds. The Great Duke kept a pack in the Peninsula, and a race meeting has not seldom formed the closing act of many of our little wars. But it has been left to our friends the Russians to definitely organize sporting expeditions on a large scale, with a view to giving realistic instruction to their rank and file. Hunting fosters nerve and manly qualities. It cannot fail to improve horsemanship; but it makes a man far more than a mere rider. It teaches him to husband and save his horse's energies, study his idiosyncrasies, and, above all, perhaps, bring home to him the need of thoughtful stable management and careful fitting of saddles and bridles. A man who hunts grows accustomed to finding his way about in a strange country; he acquires an eye for ground, and becomes resourceful in danger or difficulties. Thus it affords, perhaps, the best training-ground a mounted man can have.

But victories are won mainly by infantry, and nowadays especially, when formations are loose, a foot-soldier must have a head on his shoulders. It was stalking deer and antelope that made the Boers the dangerous foes we found them, and the man who has been brought up as a gamekeeper is the most valuable prize of the recruiting sergeant. The Germans, for this reason, have called their smartest regiments "Jägers," and the French "Chasseurs" illustrate, too, the appreciation which the same class meet with, and have ever met with, on the other side of the Rhine. Our riflemen are distinguished by no such characteristic title, but are clothed in the traditional green affected by the natives of the woods. However, "Jägers" and "Chasseurs" can no more all be sportsmen than kilted men in our service can all claim a birthplace north of the Tweed, and the name is but a survival of the olden time.

In France and Germany game-preserves and tillage have destroyed any chance there might ever have been of allowing the natural instincts of men a free outlet. But in Russia there is more scope, and the chance a sparsely populated country offers has not been thrown away. Hunts have of late years been set on foot in the neighborhood of military stations in which whole battalions occasionally have taken part. The quarry has usually been a bear marked down by the villagers in an adjoining forest, and the excitement of pursuing an animal with a reputation in popular imagination for ferocity forms a delightful break in the weary monotony of barrack life. So far, however, as we have gathered from some accounts of these expeditions, poor Bruin has but a small chance, indeed, and is simply surrounded by a howling crowd of excited men, who destroy him by sheer weight of numbers. Little of value in war or anywhere else can be derived from such performances; but all hunts are not of this character, and better management is displayed in many districts. The Russian military authorities are now, indeed, quite alive to the benefit that may be derived from encouraging a real love of sport, and definite rules and regulations have quite recently been drawn up with a view to making the most of the special opportunities many of their troops enjoy.

But, after all, only a small proportion of troops can taste such joys, and in most places there may be a good deal of hunting and very little game, while equipments, and what our Indian officers would term "bandobasts," have to be on a particularly modest scale. Indeed, in most parts of European Russia the "Jägers" have to be contented with but the image of their craft, and there is considerably more of instruction than amusement about their expeditions. Scouting and reconnaissance duties against an imaginary foe are hardly so exciting as stalking and tracking beasts of prey; but the man who is an adept at one will probably excel at the other, and the same qualities will be developed by practice at either. Marksmanship will of course be the first essential when either animals or men are the quarries, and target practice is, therefore, an obvious part of training. Judging distances, too, will be attended to, while a man's muscles may be usefully developed by gymnastics, fencing, running, and leaping.

THE OXFORD-YALE TRACK ATHLETIC MEETING,

July 16, 1894

Although the result of the Oxford-Yale athletic meeting was not unexpected, the contest furnished much food for thought and some surprises that had been entirely unlooked for. If there is any one branch of track athletics more than another in which we have flattered ourselves on being invulnerable, it certainly was sprinting, where our notable quickness in getting off the mark would count for much. Yet Sanford and Pond (Yale), with records of 10¼, were third and fourth in the 100 yards, to Fry and Jordan (Oxford) in 10⅖ sec., and only Fry had ever bettered that time previously. Again in the hurdles, Cady (Yale), with a 16-second record on cinders, was run down and off his stride, so that he went to pieces and fell at the last hurdle, in 16⅔ on turf by Oakley (Oxford), whose best previous performance had been 16¾. There is no doubt that the turf was heavy, but not so much so as to keep the Oxford man from going the distance in his top form. In the quarter-mile dash, the best race by all odds of the day, Sanford (Yale), with a 50⅔-sec. record, was beaten out after a gallant struggle in 51 sec. by Jordan (Oxford), whose record is the same as Sanford's. In the half-mile, Woodhull (Yale), record 1:59¼, was defeated in 2 min. ⅔ sec. by Greenhow (Oxford), who had previously run a mile in 4 min. 24⅔ sec., and had no previously established record for the half.

In other words, in the very department of athletics in which we have always considered ourselves strongest we turned out to be weakest, and instead of excelling where speed and agility are essential, we lost every event but two where those attributes are requisite (one of which was a tie). Of nine men comprising the Yale team, two only, Hickok and Sheldon, saved it from an utter rout, and only four secured points.

Before going deeper into the subject let me hasten to say to those who might incorrectly interpret what is here written that there is no intention of either criticising the Yale athletes, or excusing their defeat; they trained conscientiously, made a hard struggle to win, and were fairly beaten. Unquestionably the strange surroundings handicapped them to a certain extent, but in no case may the result of the meeting be set down to "hard luck," since in the only event where such an element might be thought to have figured, *i.e.*, the hurdles, the Oxford man was a winner before Cady fell. In all contests where the teams are evenly matched, the home men invariably have whatever advantage familiar surroundings and climate are supposed to give, but these differences do not appear in this instance to have been sufficient to turn defeat into victory. Oxford won the day on its merits, and because every man turned up fit to stand the wear and tear and excitement of an important struggle, and did all that was expected of him.

In three events on the programme, the 100 and 880 yards and 120-yard hurdles, Yale did neither so well as had been expected, nor reached normal form; and I have plunged into all this detail to bring the case up to this point, and to ask our universities whether there is not a good, wholesome lesson to be learned from this Oxford-Yale meeting. Are we not training our college athletes too much? Have we not been carrying preparation too far in all branches of our college sport? I have already commented on the great difference that exists between English and American university athletes in this particular. I have shown, to come to the point under discussion, how little of it is done in track athletics, especially as compared with the superlatively trained American university men. And yet these Oxford sprinters, with poorer rec-

OXFORD YALE TRACK AND FIELD

Event.	Oxford.			Yale.		
	Firsts.	Seconds.	Winner.	Firsts.	Seconds.	Winner.
100-yard dash.........	1	1	{ C. B. Fry, } { G. Jordan. }			
440-yard run.........	1		G. Jordan.		1	G. F. Sanford.
880-yard run.........	1	1	{ W. H. Greenhow, } { F. W. Rathbone. }			
Mile run.............	1	1	{ W. G. Greenhow, } { G. M. Hildyard. }			
120-yard hurdle......	1	1	{ W. J. Oakley, } { T. S. Scott. }			
Running high jump..	1-2		E. D. Swanwick.	1-2	1	{ L. P. Sheldon, } { E. H. Cady. }
Running broad jump.		1	W. J. Oakley.	1		L. P. Sheldon.
16-lb. shot...........				1	1	{ W. O. Hickok, } { A. J. Brown. }
16-lb. hammer.......				1	1	{ W. O. Hickok, } { A. J. Brown. }
	5 1-2	5		3 1-2	4	

ords than the Yale athletes they met, were equal to beating them, and in one or two instances with something to spare.

The Oxford team averaged neither older nor heavier than Yale. To what, then, may be ascribed the reversal of Yale's form, say in the 100 and 880 yard events? I do not think the heavy track nor the strange surroundings explain it. I have always been convinced that we do too much "training," and these Oxford-Yale games strengthen my conviction. Boys are put through a gruelling that none but a seasoned athlete should be called upon to undergo. They are worked up to practically the last hour, and enter the race so "fine" that, when unusual circumstances arise, having no reserve fund, they go to pieces.

Unless one has stood on the mark in an exciting, important contest, he cannot appreciate what it means to be so fine that one's nerves are on the ragged edge, and likely to collapse at the first intimation of the unexpected. You need your nerves in a race, and you want them in good working condition, otherwise when you get on the mark your muscles seem suddenly to have lost their power and elasticity, and, unless you are an exceptional mor-

ATHLETIC MEETING, JULY 16, 1894.

Performance.	Performance at Oxford-Cambridge Games, March, '94.	Performance at Harvard-Yale Games, May, '94.	English University Record.	American University Record.
10 2-5 sec.	10 3-5 sec.	‡10 2-5 sec.	10 sec.	10 sec.
51 "	50 4-5 "	‡50 "	49 4-5 "	49 1-2 "
2 m. 4-5 "		1 m. 59 4-5 "	1 m. 54 2-5 "	1 m. 54 1-2 "
4 " 24 2-5 "	†4 m. 19 4-5 "	4 " 31 2-5 "	4 " 19 4-5 "	4 " 26 4-5 "
16 3-5 "	16 3-5 "	‡16 "	16 "	15 4-5 "
5 ft. 8 3-4 in.	5 ft. 10 1-4 in.	‡5 ft. 9 1-2 in.	6 ft. 2 1-2 in.	6 ft. 4 in.
22 " 11 "	22 " 4 "	21 " 9 1-2 "	*23 " 6 1-2 "	23 " 6 1-2 "
41 " 4 1-4 "	†37 " 6 "	40 " 1 1-2 "	{ 39 " 1 " }	{ 42 " }
(7-foot run.)	(10-foot run.)	(7-foot run.)	(10-foot run.)	(7-foot run.)
110 ft. 5 in.	101 ft. 4 1-2 in.	113 ft. 11 in.	{ 138 ft. 3 in. }	{ 123 ft. 9 in. }
(7-foot run.)	(30-foot run.)	(7-foot run.)	(unlimited run.)	(7-foot run.)

* English Measurement.   † Won by Cambridge.   ‡ Won by Harvard.

tal, you are rattled, and as a natural result fall far short of your form. I do not pretend to say these Yale men were under-trained or over-trained; they were unquestionably prepared on the approved American university system, and made as good a showing as any others would have done under the same conditions.

The performances of these men are a mere incident, though they furnish the first opportunity of testing our way with that of the Old World university methods, and I take it as a text for reiterating what I have preached at more or less length at different times on the questionable policy of giving our college athletes so much "training." It has always seemed to me a matter deserving much more serious consideration than has been given; and having been brought home by the Oxford-Yale meeting in the most practical of illustrations, may we not hope that it will receive the discussion it merits among American college authorities and alumni?

Nothing results from forced development; healthful growth may only be obtained by common-sense and natural methods. We make too much of a business of our sport. Let us invest it with a little more of the recreative feature. We will win just as many points, and give it more of a wholesome tendency. Entirely apart from an ethical point of view, we will place our teams afield much better fitted to win athletic honors for the *alma mater*. If any further illustration is needed to emphasize what I say on this subject of excessive training, let me recall the Yale-Princeton game which closed the football season of 1893. The Yale eleven had been prepared in the same old way of driving the men early and late, late and early, until about all the life and ginger had been worked out of them. Princeton, on the other hand, had taken a step in advance of all the colleges, and trained its team on a

G. JORDAN, University College
(100-yard and quarter-mile)

C. B. FRY, Wadham
(broad jump and 100-yard dash)

H. R. SYKES, Christ Church
quarter-miler

W. H. GREENHOW, Exeter
(half-mile and mile runs)

THE OXFORD TRACK ATHLETIC TEAM

G. M. HILDYARD, University College
(mile run)

W. J. OAKLEY, Christ Church
(hurdles)

E. D. SWANWICK, University College
(high jump)

C. B. ROBERTSON, New College
(hammer and shot)

WHICH MET AND DEFEATED YALE

more rational system, *i.e.*, of giving them hard, sharp work, but with intervals of lighter practice. As a result they faced Yale with quite as much endurance and muscles just as hard, but with a dash in their movements that made Yale seem loggy in comparison. Such a practical demonstration we have never had in rowing, simply because the Harvard and Yale eights are trained on the same system, and the perfection of the latter's crew-work and the perpetuation of a winning stroke have kept the blue too far in advance of the crimson on the water to permit of a test. Something of a comparison, however, may be drawn between Yale and Cornell, although they have not met in recent years. Cornell crews do nowhere near the amount of training of either Harvard or Yale, yet their four-mile rowing in the last two years against Pennsylvania shows they have both speed and endurance to such a degree that only an actual race could determine the faster. Again, the few Western college crews, although their form is crude, all evince endurance at a good rate of speed, and on a great deal less training than any of the Eastern university eights.

I have digressed a long way from the athletic meeting on the Queen's grounds July 16, '94, but if I have in the slightest degree brought home to our universities the folly and unwholesomeness of excessive training, I shall not begrudge the space.

The 100-yard dash, the first event of the Oxford-Yale meeting, was thought even by the Englishmen to be a sure first for Yale, but Fry upset all calculations by getting off the mark from a Sheffield start before Pond, who used the crouching position, and went away with such a burst of speed that he was never caught, finishing a yard ahead of his mate, Jordan. The hammer and shot were very easy wins for Hickok and Brown, who took first and second in each, completely outclassing the Oxford men.

Despite the fact of its being run on turf, the 120-yard hurdle was also considered a Yale event; but although Cady got away first, Oakley was too strong for him, and when he struck his pace, cut down the lead rapidly, having the race in hand when Cady fell at the last hurdle. The mile run had been conceded to Oxford, Greenhow's performance in the Oxford-Cambridge sports last March having stamped him a class above Morgan. Both Oxford men, Greenhow and Hildyard, led Yale from the start, Hildyard cutting out the pace for a third the distance, when Greenhow went to the front and won by over fifty yards, Morgan being third.

The quarter-mile was regarded an even thing, with the odds in favor of Oxford, and it turned out to be the best race of the day. Sanford made a game struggle, but Jordan was too strong for him on the finish, and won in the last twenty yards handily. The half-mile was a great surprise, Woodhull being thought a sure winner, but he seemed to go to pieces, and could get no better than third in slower time than he has shown this year. Probably the greatest surprise of the day, certainly for Oxford, was Fry's defeat in the broad jump by Sheldon; but the latter is one of those athletes, with his heart in the right

---

YALE ATHLETIC TEAM

Ernest Hyde Cady, '95 S. S. S., Hartford, Conn.
William Sayre Woodhull, '96 Acad., Orange, N. J.
Lewis Pendleton Sheldon, '96 Acad., Rutland, Vt.
Alexander Brown, Jr., '96 Acad., Philadelphia, Pa.
George Bates Hatch, '96 Acad., Cincinnati, O.
George Foster Sanford, Law School, Woodmont, Conn.
William Orville Hickok, '95 S. S. S., Harrisburg, Pa.
Ashley Pond, Jr., '96 S. S. S., Detroit, Mich.
Joseph Elias Morgan, '94 Acad., Essex, Conn.

CAPP   SANFORD   WORTHINGTON   SHELDON   HICKOK   FOSTER   ERDMAN   MORGAN   HYATT
hurdles   [?], quarter-mile   half mile   high jump, broad jump   hammer and shot   quarter-mile   hammer and shot   mile   half-mile

THE YALE TRACK ATHLETIC TEAM WHICH MET OXFORD

H. W. Laughn & Co.

place, who can always be depended on to do his best and a little more; he invariably rises to the occasion, and this time his work saved two events that on paper belonged to Oxford. His 22 ft. 11 in. jump was a fine performance, though it must be remembered this is English measurement, and even had it beaten it, could have had no bearing on the American inter-collegiate record, 22:11¼, held by Victor Mapes. Tying the high jump with Swanwick was equally notable, for the Oxford man had done 5:11, while Sheldon's best is an inch lower.

From beginning to end the games were conducted in a sportsmanlike manner, and the meeting has unquestionably brought English and American universities nearer together than they have ever been.

Now that we have finally brought off an international inter-university meeting, there seems to be no good reason why they should not be made an occasional feature. It will be wiser, however, and undoubtedly create a more wide-spread interest, to broaden the idea so as to include the full strength of Harvard and Yale against Oxford and Cambridge.

Whatever the future may provide, Americans are deeply grateful for the spirit that prompted Yale to send a team, and proud of the manly bearing of the individual athletes, who even in the hour of unexpected defeat bore themselves like sportsmen and Americans. The following summary, from London *Field*, gives detail of this first meeting between English and American university teams:

100 *Yards Race.*—C. B. Fry, Wadham, Oxford, 1; G. Jordan, University, Oxford, 2; G. F. Sanford, Woodford, Conn., 3; A. Pond, Detroit, Mich., 0. Fry had the station nearest the stand, which had been erected the whole length of the sprint track, and so was completely sheltered from the rather strong breeze blowing across the ground. It is open to question, however, whether even Sanford, who ran next the grass, was in the slightest degree prejudiced. The start was not a bad one, but Fry was much the quickest into his stride, and he ran so straight

and hard that at fifty yards he led by a yard. Sanford was at this stage of the race second, though his advantage over Jordan, who had made a rather slow start, was very slight. For some score yards it was a desperate race between Jordan and Sanford, but Fry continued to hold his place. However, with twenty yards to go, the Oxford president seemed to slacken. The contrary was the case with Jordan, who, finishing very resolutely, was beaten by a foot only; half a yard separated Jordan and Sanford. Time, 10 sec. The Yale men started with their hands touching the ground.

Throwing the Hammer.—W. O. Hickok, Harrisburg, Pa., 1; A. Brown, Philadelphia, Pa., 2; G. W. Robertson, New, Oxford, 0. After overstepping the limits of the circle three times, Hickok threw 110 ft. 5 in. Brown's first and fourth throws were 104 ft. each; his others 99 ft. 5 in. and 103 ft. 8½ in. Robertson's best throw was 101 ft. 10 in., his first; he also threw 100 ft. 7 in. The Americans threw from a 7-ft. circle, and used a hammer measuring 4 ft. Robertson used a 3 ft. 6 in. hammer, and threw from a 30-ft. circle.

Hurdle Race, 120 Yards, 10 flights.—W. J. Oakley, Christ Church, Oxford, 1; D. B. Hatch, Cincinnati, O., 2; T. G. Scott, Hertford, Oxford, 3; E. A. Cady, Hartford, Conn., fell. Both Americans adopted the "hand spring" or "all-fours" method of starting, and both were quicker in getting away than either of the Oxonians. Cady reached the first hurdle half a yard in front of the Dark Blues, and Hatch had an advantage of a foot. However, this was soon lessened, and at the seventh hurdle Oakley, Hatch, and Scott were as nearly as possible level, with Cady just leading. Approaching the next hurdle Oakley had almost overtaken Cady, and the excitement was growing, when the Connecticut man, failing to rise sufficiently at the eighth hurdle, came a cropper, the fall carrying him almost to the foot of the ninth obstacle. This settled matters, Oakley keeping his place, and finishing three-quarters of a yard in front of Hatch, who beat Scott by rather less than a foot. Time, 16⅗ sec.

One-Mile Race.—W. H. Greenhow, Exeter, Oxford, 1; J. E. Morgan, Essex, Conn., 2; G. M. Hildyard, University College, Oxford, 0. The last-named set the pace, followed by Morgan to the first corner, where Greenhow became second. Along the stretch on the eastern side of the ground Morgan drew up to Greenhow's shoulder, but at the finish of the first lap, ran in 1 min. 19 sec., Greenhow was next to Hildyard, and this was the order on to the main entrance, where Greenhow took command, and Hildyard, slowing down gradually, gave way to Morgan. At the close of the second lap (2 min. 51½ sec.) Greenhow was forty yards ahead of Morgan. Hildyard retired on reaching the pavilion in the last lap, and Greenhow went on increasing his lead of Morgan, until at the close it amounted to ninety yards. Time, 4 min. 24⅖ sec. The quarter-mile times were 56⅕ sec. (Hildyard), 2 min. 5⅕ sec. (Greenhow), and 3 min. 15 sec. (Greenhow). Morgan's time was 4 min. 41⅘ sec.

Long Jump.—L. P. Sheldon, Rutland, Vt., 1; W. J. Oakley, Christ Church, Oxford, 2; C. B. Fry, Wadham, Oxford, 3; D. B. Hatch, Cincinnati, O., 0. Sheldon's jumps were 22 ft. 1¼ in., 22 ft. 1¼ in., 21 ft. 6½ in., and 22 ft. 11 in.; Oakley's were 22 ft. ⅜ in., 22 ft., 21 ft. 6¼ in., and 22 ft. 1½ in. Fry cleared 22 ft. ⅜ in., and made two no jumps. Hatch went over the mark three times, and his only jump was not measured. Sheldon's jump was also measured according to the American method— *i. e.*, to the first break of the ground; it was found to be 22 ft. 9¼ in., which beats the previous Yale record by 3½ in.

Quarter-Mile Race.—G. Jordan, University, Oxford, 1; G. F. Sanford, Woodford, Conn., 2; A. Pond, Detroit, Mich., 3; H. R. Sykes, Christ Church, Oxford, 4. Sykes was the first to show in front, and for 150 yards was followed by Pond, with Sanford third. The last-named then went next to the leader, and half-way took up the running with Pond at his heels, and Jordan, very close up, third. Turning into the long straight by the club premises, Sanford had, so far as could be seen from the enclosure in front of the pavilion, a substantial lead, and the American's chance was not lessened by Jordan having to turn wide in his endeavor to go by Pond. This accomplished, Jordan set to work in most resolute fashion, and seventy yards from home he was running level with Sanford, whom he headed in the next few yards. The American struggled gamely, but without avail Inch by inch Jordan gained, and eventually he breasted the tape two yards from Sanford, who beat Pond by three yards. Time, 51 sec.

Putting the Weight (16 *lb.*).—W. O. Hickok, Harrisburg, Pa., 1; A. Brown, Philadelphia, Pa., 2; A. F. Maling, Exeter, Oxford, 3; D. H. Meggy, Christ Church, Oxford, 4. Hickok's puts were 41 ft. 7¼ in., 41 ft. 4¼ in., 41 ft. 2 in., and 40 ft. 10½ in.; Brown's best were 40 ft. 2 in. and 39 ft. 11½ in. Maling put 35 ft. 3½ in. and 33 ft. 7½ in. The Americans put from a 7-ft. circle and the Englishmen from a 10-ft. square.

High Jump.—L. P. Sheldon, Rutland, Vt., and E. D. Swanwick, University, Oxford, tied at 5 ft. 8¾ in., after a protracted competition. E. A. Cady, Hertford, Conn., cleared 5 ft. 7¾ in., and G. A. Gardiner, New, Oxford, 5 ft. 6¾ in.

Half-Mile Race.—W. H. Greenhow, Exeter, Oxford, 1; F. W. Rathbone, New, Oxford, 2; W. S. Woodhull, Orange, N. J., 3; J. E. Morgan, Essex, Conn., 0. The last-named, as in the mile, set the pace, and was followed by Woodhull for about a third of the distance, when places changed quickly, Woodhull going to the front, to be directly afterwards passed by Greenhow, Rathbone occupying third place just later. Along the stretch on the far side of the ground Rathbone drew on Woodhull, and the pair closed up with Greenhow as the home straight was reached, making matters very exciting. About seventy yards from home Woodhull got in front again, but the lead was scarcely gained ere it was lost, and as, when the American fell back, Rathbone came up, the cheers for Oxford were loud and long. There was a grand finish between the Oxonians, who were in the end separated by a few inches only; but Woodhull, having found pursuit hopeless, eased up slightly, and was four yards off when the worsted gave way before the pressure of Greenhow. Time, 2 min. ⅜ sec. The first quarter occupied 59 sec.

X

CLUB ATHLETICS

We have seen that modern organized athletics began with the Rugby School crick run in 1837, that the Royal Military Academy gave games in '49, followed by Exeter College at Oxford in '50, and that, after '55, the sport was taken up quite generally by the colleges one after the other at both universities. We know that Oxford and Cambridge held their first inter-university meeting in '64, and that the same year gave birth to the Amateur Athletic Club—England's first club devoted to amateurs.

We know that this club opened the Lillie Bridge grounds, which instantly became amateur headquarters, and remained so until the appearance of the London Athletic Club. This younger and more vigorous rival speedily outgrew the old order of things, and secured grounds of its own at Stamford Bridge, leaving the pioneer institution struggling for life until eventual collapse came to its relief. With the coming of this new athletic power, the sport entered upon a veritable heyday of prosperity that in honest, healthful rivalry carried it past the seventies and well on towards '80, the date of the present Association's establishment. Thus far have previous chapters taken us.

During these, the halcyon days of English athletics, men competed for sport; "amateur" was applied in truth and with significance, and the skirmishers of the great unwashed had not put themselves in evidence to sneer

LONDON ATHLETIC CLUB GROUNDS, AT STAMFORD BRIDGE

W. H. Grove

at the laurel wreath and demand expenses, compensation for loss of time, and extravagant prizes.

How many an English sportsman—how many a one in America, for here, too, we have run foul of the pot-hunter — fervently wishes he had answered the first challenge by fighting it out on the every-man-to-his-own-vine-and-fig-tree lines, if it had taken half a lifetime. Now there is nothing left for us but to abandon the bower planted in pride and nourished with such tender solicitude, and raise up another where experience will guard us against the vermin that have made this one uninhabitable.

Having reminded the reader that the very early epochs of English athletics have been elaborated for his edification in the preceding university chapters, it becomes my uncongenial task to bring him up to date in non-university athletics. It is not a pleasing journey, for the way is muddy and the resting-stones are few and far between.

The Amateur Athletic Association owes its existence to a dispute between university and non-university athletes over the time of year the championships should be held, and, thus born in strife, it has remained ever since a child of contention.

The recognition of their claims and the organization of an institution that would officially and conspicuously label them gentlemen — for it was argued that to be an amateur was to be a gentleman, and the latter distinction rather than the former was the dearer ambition — gave great zest to the sport of the people, and athletic contests throughout Great Britain multiplied extraordinarily. But as the spirit expanded, and the meetings grew and became prosperous, the element of greed replaced what there had been of sport. That class which had in times past popularized such brutish spectacles as cock-fighting, rat-killing, and the like, recognizing the rare chance at one and the same time of becoming "gentlemen" and winning prizes that could be turned to a pretty penny, threw itself bodily into the more lucrative field of athletics, and book-making, "roping," and every manner of swindling crushed all semblance of honesty out of the sport that had been inaugurated under such happy auspices.

With the ascendency of this element decency withdrew from active participation. Oxford and Cambridge sent no entries to games, and affairs went from bad to worse, until to-day, of the two hundred and fifty clubs composing the Association, not more than a score may be called honestly amateur, of which number the three government military colleges and Oxford and Cambridge constitute five.

The Association has striven hard enough to steer a straight course, but its earnest laborers are so few, and the task so huge, that their efforts have been about as effective as would be the tiny stream of a Babcock fire-extinguisher on a roaring bonfire.

American readers will the better appreciate the predicament of the minority in the English Association when I tell them it is identical with that of the few honestly amateur sport-caring members of the Metropolitan branch of our own Amateur Athletic Union. The Metropolitan Association is a growth of the last few years, membered and controlled by a precisely similar element to that which forms an overwhelming majority in English athletics. We know perfectly well what a farce is amateurism in a large percentage of the Metropolitan clubs, certainly in all of the boxing clubs. If, now, instead of swaying only the Metropolitan Association, this element should extend its control to the very Union itself, and dominate national athletics, then should we have such a condition as obtains in England.

I hope no one will understand me as disparaging ath-

QUEEN'S CLUB—RACQUET AND TENNIS COURTS

W. H. Grove

leticism among the lower classes, for I should not wish to be so interpreted. As I began, so I desire to end this pilgrimage with a sincere expression of unfeigned admiration for the universal sporting spirit in Great Britain, and an unshaken belief in the incalculable benefit it has been to the national manhood.

The value of athletics cannot be overestimated. It makes manly, enduring, and ready men. It cultivates the best vitality in the human form, and it must, in proportion, develop a certain precision and decision in cases of emergency. It has invariably an influence towards the improvement of one's self, for of a given number of participants a certain percentage must always be the better men for it, morally as well as physically; and who will deny that these qualities bespeak a purer heredity?

I should therefore be the veriest dolt to advise against athletics in all stations of every race of people on earth. It is not the wide-spread athletic activity I would inveigh against, but the dissimulation and swindling which have been drawn into it by the effort to harmonize what may be called the university element with men who, by instinct and education, are unfitted to live up to or appreciate the standard of those nurtured in more cultured surroundings. Only after generations of refining influence can be accomplished what these athletic associations, nothing daunted, set out to do off-hand. Nor do I wish what I say on the only practicable definition of an amateur to be set down to snobbishness; few who follow my writings will so misjudge me, I fancy. I fully appreciate how very difficult and many-sided a problem it is, but surely England's nearly thirty years of experience counts for something, and it may be safely asserted that mankind averages about the same, whether under the reign of a Queen or a President.

I am dwelling on this situation probably at greater length than the average reader will consider it warrants, because I wish to hold it up as a warning to America and to our own Amateur Athletic Union.

England's experience in letting down the bars to the class of men that formerly did, and naturally always would, fill the professional ranks teaches a lesson we cannot ignore if we would steer between the rocks that have wrecked amateur athletics in Great Britain. Theorists will argue that bringing this class of men in contact with that of higher conceptions and purer sentiments should have a refining and elevating influence on the former; perhaps it should, but the plain fact is that it has not.

Such an education must have its beginning in the home, or under the wise system that obtains in the Young Men's Christian Association, and extends through all its branches in the United States and Great Britain. Properly applied, athletics do have an unquestioned refining influence, but the desired result is not brought about by bringing together on the track two elements that are not in sympathy, and where the wish to win is likely to be the dominating motive. The educational process must be slow and most carefully undertaken in a class that, as a rule, is wanting in the true amateur instinct of sport for sport's sake; and it is comment enough on the folly of the experiment in England to say that at the last meeting of the Amateur Athletic Association an appropriation was made to bear the legal expenses being constantly incurred by the prosecution of these candidates for ethical reform. The A. A. A. is squandering its money in an attempt to retain the fealty of men who yielded allegiance in the first place only because they saw an opportunity of making amateur athletics more lucrative than open professionalism, and who recognize the laws merely as so

BRADFORD A. C. CLUB-HOUSE AND GROUNDS

many obstacles to be evaded. Thus, while this masquerading creature flourishes, the *bona fide* amateur languishes, and, meanwhile, athletics remain in a scandalous condition—a situation, too, that occasions a loss hard to estimate; for of the hundreds of men graduated annually from the universities and the public schools, who would naturally infuse athletics with a wholesome spirit, but very few, almost none, maintain an active interest, and in all of England, with its ever-apparent sporting spirit, only one athletic club (the London A. C.) attracts entries to its games from Oxford and Cambridge!

Such a state of affairs in any other country than England would, I have little doubt, eventually lead to a decadence of amateur sport generally, but the sporting spirit and the love of out-doors are too thoroughly imbued in the Englishman to suffer that dire extreme; he is safe from intrusion at his school and college, and when he has gone down from his university there is hunting, boating, cricket, or golf, all of which have thus far escaped the taint of the athletic, cycling, and football "amachoor."

What will be the outcome of this maddening problem few Englishmen care to hint, but my own observations lead me to believe the day not far distant when the mask (which deceives none but the officers of the Amateur Athletic Association) will be torn from this class of "amachoors," and they will be branded professionals, which, in plain fact, they have always been. To attempt to cleanse so-called amateur athletics in England by any other method would be simply an utter impossibility. The decay that was has advanced to putrefaction; it is no longer a case for the physician, but for the surgeon, and nothing short of complete amputation will save the parent body. Indeed, it is my opinion that the latter is already impregnated beyond recovery, and that only by separation immediate and complete may the remaining healthful ones be saved from the approaching wreck. Let these survivors abandon the present Association to the class which is now in the majority, and form another where sportsmen only may gain entrance, and in which an amateur shall be defined as in rowing.

Rather a drastic remedy, to be sure, but the condition is extreme, and entirely impervious to milder measures.

The Amateur Athletic Association is divided into the Northern, Midland, and Southern counties of England, which are given votes and send representation to the general meeting in proportion to their numerical strength. In the matter of geographical divisions these are to the A. A. A. as the Atlantic, Central, Metropolitan, and Pacific associations are to our Amateur Athletic Union, but differ in the method and number of votes. Thus, the Northern counties, comprising 101 clubs, are entitled to 30 votes; the Midland, 43 clubs, and 15 votes; and in the Southern district, Cambridge, Oxford, and the London Athletic Club are allowed 6 votes each; the Blackheath Harriers, Civil Service, and a few others, 3; while a large number in London have 1 vote, and some none at all.

Matters of purely local significance are administered by the sectional legislators, but the A. A. A. general committee is always composed of one representative each from

Oxford, Cambridge, London Athletic Club, Civil Service, Amateur Athletic Association, Blackheath Harriers, Finchley Harriers, German Gymnastic Society, Highgate Harriers, National Cross-Country Union, Polytechnic Harriers, Ranelagh Harriers, South London Harriers, Spartan Harriers, United Hospitals Athletic Club, Midland Counties Amateur Athletic Association, Northern Counties Amateur Athletic Association, and one from a West of England Club. These, with "thirty members equally apportioned between the North, South, and Midland, to be elected by the association or governing bodies of the representative divisions," govern the athletics of England, and in the voting each delegate casts the number to which his club or association is entitled, as, for instance, Oxford's opinion would go for six votes, the Civil Service for three, while the Midland Counties' representative would place fifteen to the credit of whichever side of the question he upheld. One each from the sections, the two universities, and the London Athletic Club usually complete the number of vice-presidents. The A. A. A. amateur definition reads:

"An amateur is one who has never competed for a money prize or staked bet, or with or against a professional for any prize, or who has

Edward Alroy

BRADFORD CRICKET CREASE AND HOUSE

never taught, pursued, or assisted in the practice of athletic exercises as a means of obtaining a livelihood.

"The following exceptions shall be made to this rule—

"(*a.*) That amateur athletes shall not lose their amateur status by competing with or against professional football-players in ordinary club matches for which no prizes are given, or in cup competitions permitted by the National Football Associations or Rugby Unions of England, Ireland, Scotland, or Wales, providing that such competitions or matches form no part of, nor have connection with, any athletic meeting.

"(*b.*) That competitions at arms between volunteers and regulars shall not be considered as coming within the scope of the A. A. A. laws.

"(*c.*) That competitors in officers' races at naval and military athletic meetings (such races being for officers only, and for which money prizes are not given) shall be exempt from any of the laws of the A. A. A. disqualifying runners for competing at mixed meetings.

"(*d.*) That the 'Championship of the Army' race at the Aldershot sports be exempt from the effect of this rule.

"(*e.*) That a paid handicapper is not a professional."

Each section elects a handicapper, who may not go out of his province or his class, permits being granted as follows:

Class 1. Open handicaps, any distance up to 880 yards.
Class 2. Open handicaps, 880 yards and upwards.
Class 3. Walking races.

Penalties for attempts to beat the pistol are, "one yard for distances up to and including 220 yards, two yards up to and including 440 yards, three yards up to and including 880 yards, and five yards up to one mile; the sum of these penalties to be doubled for second offences, and disqualification on the third."

There are similar athletic organizations in Scotland and Ireland, which work in harmony with the English Association, the sentences of disqualification and suspension of each one being binding on the other. This latter is true also of the Amateur Swimming Association, the National Cyclists' Union, and the Amateur Gymnastic Association.

Challenge cups are offered at championship competitions, together with gold medals for firsts and silver

RICHMOND ATHLETIC FIELD AND CLUB-HOUSE

W. H. Grove

medals for seconds, besides which a gold medal is given for a record performance, and a bronze medal to those reaching a standard fixed by the committee. Prizes in handicaps may not be of greater value than £10 10s. ($52.50), but in a scratch race there is no limit.

Competitors are allowed three trials in the broad jump and three at each height in the high, at which, as with us, no diving or somersaulting is permitted. I have already commented to some length in the university chapter on the method of measuring the broad jump, which is totally at fault, and the length of pegs allowed in the uprights for the high jump, likewise open to criticism. All tracks are measured twelve inches from the inner side of the path, instead of eighteen as with us, and the men run with their right arm to the pole, instead of the left as in America.

The 16-pound hammer, total length, including the handle, not exceeding four feet, is thrown from a 9-foot circle. The 16-pound shot is put from a 7-foot square, each competitor having three trials, and the best three of the first rounds having three more each for the final, as in the hammer. In both events crossing the scratch counts as a try. The 56-pound weight is not an event on the English programme; neither is the 220-yard hurdle.

In its constitution the Association proclaims "all open betting must be suppressed at athletic meetings," notwithstanding which, however, it flourishes to an extraordinary degree, despite the vigilance of officials at games, and the thorough placarding of grand-stands, warning book-makers that they will be "ejected" from the grounds. It seemed to me at some of the meetings I attended as if every other man was a book-maker, for whenever I stopped in my sauntering about the grounds the refrain of "Five to three on the field bar one," "Two to one on Smith," "Evens on Jones," etc., were sung in my ear to the accompaniment of jingling shillings.

As a matter of fact, book-makers are scattered throughout the spectators, and carry on their business in defiance of the placards and the officials, who do make honest attempts to stop the betting, and are thoroughly in earnest, for I saw several detected offenders put outside the gates in a hurry and *sans ceremonie*.

Athletic meetings promoted by companies or as private enterprises are not recognized by the Association, so they advertise; but it is a fact, none the less, that the most flourishing athletic institutions in England, and those which give the largest meetings, are "limited liability" companies devoted to athletics, cricket, and other sports (separate committees managing the different branches), and organized for business quite as much as if the venture were dry-goods instead of athletics. Such, for instance, are the Huddersfield Cricket, Football, and Athletic Club, the Bradford Cricket, Athletic, and Football Club, and the Leeds Cricket, Football, and Athletic Club—three of the largest, I believe, in Great Britain.

The Amateur Athletic Association championship is given during the summer in each of its sectional districts alternately. When held in the Southern counties the London Athletic Club grounds at Stamford Bridge are invariably chosen; in the North: Crewe, Manchester, Southport, and Huddersfield; in the Midlands: Birmingham or Northampton. In addition, the local organizations in the North and Midland farm out several championship events to different clubs, as, for instance, a hurdle-race to one, a quarter-mile to another, etc., which add much to the sectional prestige of the favored club.

Although there are a great many meetings throughout Great Britian during the season, the best, aside from the

Edward Airey
POLE VAULTING ON A MATTRESS AT BRADFORD

A. A. A. championships, held in July, are the spring and autumn games of the London Athletic Club—the L. A. C.-Oxford in the spring, and the L. A. C.-Cambridge in the autumn—and those of the Civil Service and the United Hospitals clubs. These, which are the choice—and there are few others that are good (for most athletic clubs in England consist of a name only, under which a few men compete)—are beginning to hold strictly invitation meetings. In fact, the unclean condition of athletics, and the hopelessness of anything being done by the Association towards purifying the situation, have created a feeling of abhorrence among the few respectable clubs, and a determination, by restricting their games to invitation entries, to take the law into their own hands.

The National Cross-Country Association is a distinct body from the Amateur Athletic Association, likewise divided into Northern, Midland, and Southern counties, in each of which a junior and a senior championship is held, but, unlike the A. A. A., there is, strange enough, no general meeting to decide the English championship. It is different in Ireland and Scotland, where, as in athletics, there is a general championship for the entire country.

Cross-country running, as everybody knows, is extremely popular in England, there being no end to the number of clubs devoted to one form or another of this sport, including paper and rabbit chasing. At the Southern championships I attended, at least 130 men finished out of 150 starters, notwithstanding it was as heavy going as I ever saw; and although the rain came down in torrents, about 2000 spectators remained to the end.

It is too bad to dispel the illusion, however, by adding that the amateur status in cross-country running is just about the same as it is in athletics under the A. A. A., and that betting, "roping," and all other little devices peculiar to the English athletic club "amachoor" are quite as prevalent at their meetings.

Allied to the A. A. A. is the Amateur Swimming Association, which has united with the National Life-Saving Society in making natation recognized in schools as a necessary part of a boy's education; and a great and good work have they succeeded in accomplishing throughout the British Kingdom. Nor are the benefits restricted to mankind, for the women have not been neglected in the general movement. Swimming matches are held wherever there is water, and the average Englishman seems to be as much at home in that element as on land. The Swimming Association does not recognize professionalism, but the members of the water-polo teams, which are legion, are just about of the type that distinguishes general athletics.

These polo clubs hold a series of matches in the North-

POLO-FIELD AND RACE-TRACK, RANELAGH CLUB

W. H. Grove

ern, Midland, and Southern counties of England, which culminate in an English championship tournament, followed by international games with the teams of Scotland and Ireland. It is a rather unsavory lot one sees in this sport, from an amateur point of view, but it is a fine work that is being done for the English nation.

Altogether the athletic outlook of Great Britain, from a popular point of view, is brilliant; but from an amateur point of view it is discouraging, and the question just at present on the other side is whether the dog will wag the tail or the tail wag the dog; whether, indeed, the vexing problem could not be solved by permitting the discordant element to go its way rejoicing, while the few representative sportsmen's clubs withdraw from the Amateur Athletic Association to reorganize in the interest of honest amateur athletics.

COMPARATIVE TABLE OF ENGLISH AND AMERICAN AMATEUR TRACK AND FIELD ATHLETIC RECORDS.

Event.	English.		American.		
	Performance.	Holder.	Performance.	Holder.	
100 yards	10 s.	A. Wharton.	*9.4-5 s.	John Owen, Jun.	
220 "	21 4-5 "	C. A. Bradley.	*21 4-5	Luther Cary.	
440 "	44 1-2 "	C. G. Wood.	49 3-4	Wendell Baker.	
880 "	54 2-5 "	H. C. L. Tindall.	1 m. 54 1-2	W. C. Dohm.	
1-mile run	*1 m. 54 1-5 "	F. J. K. Cross.	4 23 1-5	T. P. Conneff.	
2 "	4 14 1-5 "	F. E. Bacon.	9 42	W. D. Day.	
3 "	*14 24 "	Sidney Thomas.	14 39 1-5	E. C. Carter.	
5 "	*24 53 3-5 "		25 23 3-5	W. D. Day.	
10 "	*51 20 "	W. G. George.	52 38 2-5		
120-yard hurdle	turf 16 "	W. G. George, C. N. Jackson, W. R. Pollock, C. F. Daft, S. Jagrs, D. D. Bulger, G. Shaw.	*15 3-5	Stephen Chase.	
220 "	6 " 36 "	H. Curtis.	*6 4-5	J. P. Lee.	
1-mile walk	21 " 25 2-5 "		99 3-4	F. P. Murray.	
3 "	*52 " 29 3-5 "		64 7	E. E. Merrill.	
10 "	1 h. 19 " 47 2-5 "		†1 h. 17 40 3-4		
Running high jump	*6 ft. 31-4 in.	W. B. Page (American).	*6 ft. 4 1-4 in.	M. F. Sweeney.	
Standing " "	4 " 10 "	J. M. Ryan (Irishman).	*5 " 3 1-4	A. P. Schwaner.	
Running broad jump	†23 " 6 1-2 "	F. Hargreaves, E. Moore.	*23 " 6 1-2	C. S. Reber.	
Standing " "	10 " 5 "	C. H. Fry.	*10 " 9 3-4	A. P. Schwaner.	
Running hop, step, and jump	44 " 6 "	J. J. Pickel.	48 " 6	E. B. Bloss.	
Pole vault	11 " 2 "	R. D. Dickenson.	*11 " 5	George R. Gray	
16-lb. shot	44 " 10 1-2 "	J. O'Brien.	*45 " 3 4	J. S. Mitchell.	
" hammer	†138 " 11 "	T. F. Kiely.	†35 " 10		
1-mile bicycle	2 m. 41-5 s.	G. M. Ross.	2 m.		Handle, 4 ft.; 7-ft. circle.
2 "	4 " 90 "	A. W. Harris.	4 " 11 3-5 s.	J. P. Bliss.	7-foot circle.
3 "	6 " 53 2-5 "	F. Pope.	*6 " 43	H. C. Tyler.	Safety
4 "	8 " 14 2-5 "	J. W. Stocks.	*8 " 61 3-4	W. W. Windle.	"
5 "	11 " 33 1-5 "	F. Pope.	11 " 34 3-4	L. S. Mehjes.	"
10 "	23 " 20 "	J. W. Stocks.	*†23 " 4 3-4		"
15 "	35 " 20 3-5 "		*34 " 27		"
25 "	59 " 6 4-5 "		*57 " 40 3-5		"
50 "	*2 h. 5 " 45 4-5 "		2 h. 11 " 6 4-5		"
100 "	*5 " 12 " 2 "	E. Hale.	5 " 37 " 15		Road record

Note.—It is very difficult to compile authentic cycling records with the division of class riders and the frequency of record breaking under so many varying conditions. Those above are from a standing start.

COMPARATIVE TABLE OF ENGLISH AND AMERICAN AMATEUR SWIMMING RECORDS.

100 yards	*1 m. 2 2-5 s.	W. J. Gormley.	1 m. 9 3-5 s.	A. T. Kenney.	Still water, 2 turns. Straightaway, still water.
220 "	*2 " 41 3-5 "	J. H. Tyers.	3 " 33 2-5	A. McBirt.	Still water, 7 turns. Straightaway, 7 turns.
440 "	*5 " 53 2-5 "	"	6 " 24 3-5	A. T. Kenney.	Still water, 11 turns. Still water, 1 turn.
880 "	*12 " 3 "	"	12 " 47	Dana Thompson.	Still water, 3 turns. Still water, 21 turns.
1 mile	*27 " 31-3 "	W. J. Gormley.	28 " 55 2-3	G. Whitaker.	Still water by turn. Still water, 7 turns.

* World's record.   † English measurement.   ‡ Unlimited run and length of handle.   § Straightaway against time.

XI

CLUBS

VERY few clubs in England own grounds, still fewer have houses; pavilions for spectators and dressing-rooms for contestants being the extent to which building is carried. Such athletic club-houses as we have in the United States, with their completely equipped gymnasia, Turkish baths, swimming-pools, billiard, dining, and smoking rooms, that cost from $100,000 up to $800,000, exist only in dreamland on the other side. There is not one in all England (so far as I could hear) that has even a restaurant or sleeping accommodations. The London A. C., the oldest and by all odds the first athletic club in Great Britain, has no club-house either in town or at its excellent grounds at Stamford Bridge.

There are, however, several clubs in England devoted to sport that have extensive grounds and club-houses, though even these fail of having the elaborate and modern living and dining facilities of our athletic clubs, while they are not to be compared at all with our country clubs, to which the class of membership may be likened.

Of these there are, in London: Lord's, headquarters of the Marylebone Club, the cricket authority of the world; it has racquet, tennis, and lawn-tennis courts, and a cricket crease, which has been and continues to be the scene of all the great matches in England. Hurlingham, which occupies the position in polo that Marylebone does in cricket, has a club-house and a field like a billiard-

INTERIOR OF PRINCE'S CLUB
Showing the position of racquet-courts

W. H. Grove

table. Queen's Club ground is the one on which are played the football and athletic games of Oxford and Cambridge, and in the courts of which the university, public-school, and army racquet championships are decided; it has an open skating-rink, tennis and covered lawn-tennis courts. Ranelagh has a picturesque old house, the most beautiful grounds of them all, and an equipment for golf, polo, and pony-racing; and Kennington Oval, with its cricket crease and cycling track, has been the scene of many a memorable contest.

Prince's Club is the swell racquet and tennis club of England, with courts in London and at Brighton, and corresponds in class of membership and in social position to our Racquet and Tennis Club of New York, but it has no such home. In fact, it is used for play only, and is closed every evening at eight o'clock. Its courts, two for racquets and two for tennis, are very fine, with limestone instead of cement floors. The gallery for spectators is so very happily arranged that a view of both racquet and one tennis court may be had without leaving the one floor or the electric button which summons the native beverage. There are no dining facilities, and one may get merely a bite of luncheon; but the bathing department is thoroughly and elaborately equipped, and the

W. H. Grove

PRINCE'S CLUB-HOUSE

plunge one of the handsomest, though not the largest, in any club on either side of the Atlantic.

The one club in London with sport as a *raison d'être* which pretends to have club features is the recently organized Sports' Club. When the defunct Pelican Club dissolved, the boxing contingent went over to the National Sporting Club, and the better element, headed by Sir John Astley, formed the Sports' Club, one of the rules of which, to show their sentiment on the subject, being that there shall be no sparring matches given under the club's auspices. Membership is less exclusive than that of Lord's, Queen's, Isthmian, or Prince's, nor does it fill such a place in college sports as our University Athletic Club of New York, but it does entertain university football teams, and aims to do what it can to perpetuate a thoroughly good sporting feeling—rather an easy lot in England.

How well off we are in the matter of clubs, the following partial list will show:

Clubs.	Members.	Towns.	Value of Property.
New York Athletic Club	2500	New York	$650,000
Racquet and Tennis "	800	" "	400,000
New Jersey Athletic "	1000	Bayonne, New Jersey	80,000
Boston Athletic Association	1800	Boston	400,000
Chicago "	2000	Chicago	800,000
Olympic Athletic Club	1500	San Francisco	250,000
A. C. Schuylkill Navy	1500	Philadelphia	150,000
Detroit Athletic Club	600	Detroit, Michigan	75,000
Louisville " "	700	Louisville, Kentucky	60,000
Orange " "	500	Orange, New Jersey	75,000
Columbia " "	700	Washington, D. C.	100,000
Crescent " "	1000	Brooklyn, New York	125,000
Southern " "	1000	New Orleans, Louisiana	50,000
Young Men Gymnasium Club	1200	" " "	80,000
Denver Athletic Club	1200	Denver, Colorado	200,000
University " "	1600	New York	50,000
Cleveland " "	1200	Cleveland, Ohio	50,000
Michigan Athletic Association	500	Detroit	50,000
Buffalo Athletic Club	1500	Buffalo, New York	75,000

The Isthmian Club has a very handsome house, and formerly preserved the relationship to college athletics that the Sports' Club is now endeavoring to establish. Like our University Club, none but college men are eligible (really

HAMPTON COURT, FROM GARDEN—SITE OF ONE OF THE OLDEST TENNIS-COURTS

W. H. Grove

university, public-school, army or navy men, though a very few who possess none of these qualifications are annually elected), which is not a *sine qua non* of membership in the Sports' Club. Though gradually losing active interest in college sport, university men invariably join the Isthmian, if for no other reason than to gain admittance to its enclosure at Henley, where an elaborate collation and an orchestra are provided, and which is altogether the swagger place from which to view the regatta.

Aside from racquets and tennis, there is practically no in-door exercise among English sportsmen, fencing or boxing at either Oxford or Cambridge not having enough popularity to give it a name; one is supposed to leave boxing at Eton and Harrow when one goes up to the universities. There is no boxing or fencing at Prince's or any other of that sort of club, though a fencing club does exist (in rented quarters) in London, with a *maître d'armes* and a membership of gentlemen, but it leads an indifferent sort of life. Fencing in England is not in a flourishing condition.

There is really very little in-door sport in England, and, consequently, no occasion for the elaborate club-houses erected in the United States. The English climate permits of out-door play at one game or another the year round. The hospitable and innumerable handsome country-homes of English sportsmen give country clubs as we know them no excuse for existence. Golf has its club-house, usually a modest home with plenty of cheer within, a few bicycle and three or four athletic clubs have unpretentious homes, but, as a rule, the club-house is the last consideration in Great Britain, except, of course, where it is essential to the game.

Of boxing there is no lack among the lower element; and one may see half a dozen "slugging matches," if one cares for that sort of thing, almost every night of the season in London, the contestants being the same "great unwashed" breed with which we are familiar in New York. The Amateur Boxing Association exists, though apparently more as a professional nursery than as amateur guardian; and it is pretty safe to say there is little, if any, honest amateur competitive boxing in London.

There is no excuse for the young men of London growing up with undeveloped muscles, for in no country is the physical condition of the laboring element given more attention. There are the Amateur Gymnastic Association, the National Physical Recreation Society, the Polytechnic, and the Young Men's Christian Association, all doing a splendid work in this direction, to say nothing

W. H. Grove

THE SPORTS' CLUB

of the public tennis-courts and innumerable opportunities for out-door games of every description.

It is not hard to see why there is so far-reaching a sporting spirit in Great Britain.

XII

CYCLING

So far as the racing side of cycling is concerned, this article might be dismissed very briefly by dittoing the foregoing chapter on athletics.

The National Cyclists' Union of Great Britain, like unto our own League of American Wheelmen, lacks discernment, courage, and, to all appearances, sympathy with the better side of the sport, making a veritable mockery of their mission to keep it honest and healthful. Were the results not so serious, the legislative meetings of these two bodies would furnish the plot for a screaming farce—the perfunctory assemblies, the grave discussions over amateur definitions—as though there were more than one definition of an amateur—the solemn consideration of pleas for reinstatement to the fold, the self-congratulations on none of the inner circle having broken the thirteenth commandment, and, finally, after the greatest apparent labor, the tiny little mouse put forth by the mountain, and caught up again, once the lights are out, for future exploitation.

It's huge sport; like the story of the little boys throwing stones into the frog-pond, it is great fun for the boys if death to the frogs.

One must go to England and see with his own eyes the rottenness of cycle-racing to appreciate just how merry a joke this Union perpetrated when it withheld A. A. Zimmerman's license last year. Not that Zimmerman's amateur status was above question, or that the National Cyclists' Union loved him less, but its whitewashed amateurs more; it was the most delicious instance I have ever known of the pot calling the kettle black.

The Union began the year of '93 by passing a rule that all riders should be licensed, ostensibly for the sole purpose of protecting amateur bicycling from the invasions of the makers' amateurs, the men who are hired to ride by the manufacturer, and well paid for it. This was the beautiful bubble the Union floated before the dear public, but it was only another frolicsome gambol of the little trained mouse which popped into its cage once the exhibition was over. Not a single maker's amateur of any especial speed failed to secure his license, and one might almost believe it to have been a tidy little business scheme on the part of the Union to levy an assessment of 2*s*. 6*d. per capita*.

This license scheme has not purified English racing cycling; nobody who gave the subject careful consideration thought it would, any more than they believe the inconsistencies of Class A and B will cleanse the track in America. Nothing short of a rigid adherence to the amateur definition that obtains in other branches of sport, and the election of officials who really know an amateur when they see one, and have the courage of their convictions, will ever purify racing bicycling. There is no occasion to instance special cases of professionalism; they are patent to everybody — even to the most indifferent onlooker; and sportsmen in England as in the United States are thoroughly disgusted with the existing condition of affairs.

The history of the National Cyclists' Union does not make very agreeable reading. It seems almost as though they had set to work to swell the numbers of their association, regardless of the means to the end, or the status of the amateur. Founded in 1878, they immediately began to legislate for riders who previously had quite capably managed their own affairs, and had not the slightest desire to be ruled. That they were in touch neither with *bona fide* amateurs nor with honest professionals is evidenced by the fact that out-and-out professional racing is dead, whereas it flourished, and that amateurs dropped out of the sport once the National Cyclists' Union had firmly established itself.

The latest departure of this body is the adoption of a series of rules somewhat similar to the Class A and Class B distinctions of our League of American Wheelmen, which follow:

> In the League of American Wheelmen, Class A is one "who shall not have engaged in nor assisted in nor taught cycling or any other recognized athletic exercise for money or other remuneration, nor knowingly competed with or against a professional for a prize of any description, or who, after having forfeited the amateur status, has had the same restored by unanimous vote of the National Assembly, L. A. W."
>
> "He forfeits his standing when he engages in cycling or other recognized athletic exercises, or personally teaches, trains, or coaches any person therein, either as a means of obtaining a livelihood, or for a wager, money prize, or gate money; or if he competes with a professional or an amateur of Class B, or makes a pace for or has a pace made by such in public or for a prize; or if he accepts, directly or indirectly, for cycling, any remuneration, compensation, or expense whatsoever."
>
> Class B is one "who may be in the employ of, and have his travelling and training expenses paid by, a manufacturer of cycles, club, or other parties interested in cycling; but shall not compete for a cash or a divisible prize, nor realize upon any prize won by him, except that prizes may be exchanged or bartered, provided that in no case a cash bonus is received. He will not forfeit his status by teaching the elements of cycling, but he will cease to be a member by competing with a professional, or making pace for or having pace made for himself by such in public or for a prize; by selling, pawning, or otherwise turning into cash, or in any manner realizing cash, upon any prize won by him, except that they may be exchanged or bartered, as provided above."

With the National Cyclists' Union, which has made

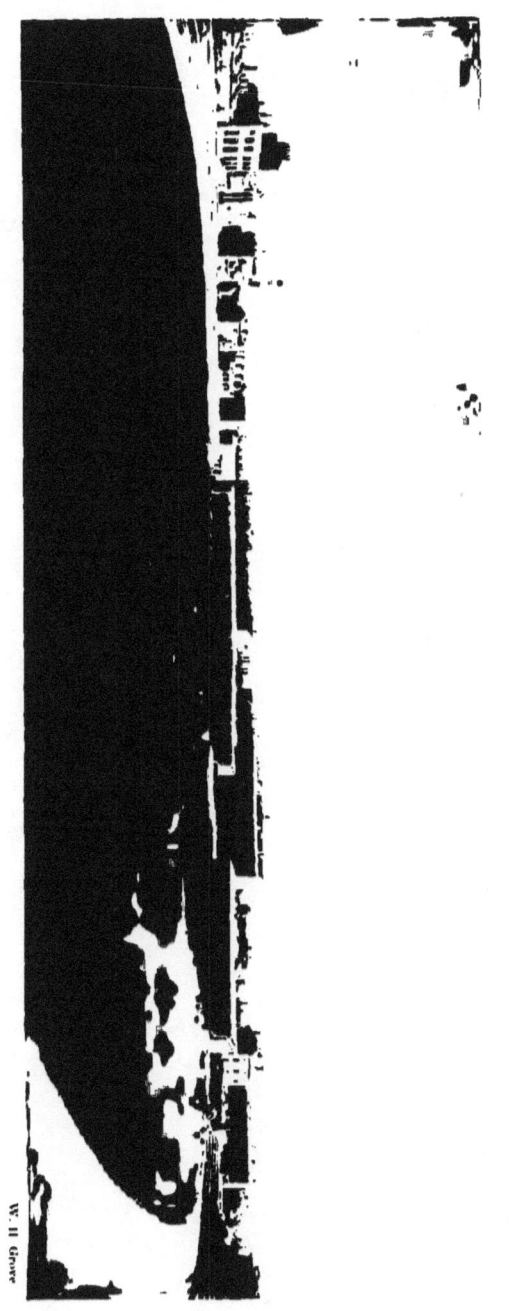

three legislators of the Union into a professional licensing committee, the definition reads:

> "A professional is a rider engaged in connection with a ground or track as trainer, who is engaged by a manufacturer solely for the purpose of riding; or who acts as a paid pace-maker in record trials or pace-races; or who takes parts in matches for stake bets with other riders. A cash-prize rider is one who races for cash prizes, and who may be connected with the trade, or riding the machines or goods of the firm he is engaged with in his races; being engaged partly but not solely for racing purposes."

Both these class distinctions of the League of American Wheelmen and the National Cyclists' Union are filled with absurd inconsistencies, but none equal to that of the English Union, which permits both classes of riders to meet in the same race.

In an attempt to explain its position on this question the National Union is befuddled in diffuse theorizing on the difference between the cash-prize rider and the professional, making preposterous statements, which, analyzed, mean simply that the manufacturer is prodding it into creating more business. It proclaims its object to be that of popularizing bicycling by raising up a new class of riders, professional only in name, but really amateurs not rich enough to race for anything but cash prizes — another case of Coxeyism in sport; but the Union is nothing if not optimistic, as may be judged by the rhetorical gem in its prospectus, which tells us the scheme will prove "a workable and satisfactory system upon which to work." The National Cyclists' Union in its dual rôle of impresario and general popularizer of cycling, fathering both amateur and money-prize riders, is assuredly an imposing spectacle.

If professional riding was moribund before, it is certainly as dead as the proverbial door-nail now, since the Union will permit its riders to compete for money, protecting them by arbitrary rules against all challengers, unless the latter become dutiful subjects, paying tribute to that hocus-pocus of a licensing committee that guards the purity of cycling in England forsooth.

It is little else than a scheme, and a corrupt one at that, to absolutely control, and for no good purpose, racing cycling in Great Britain; protecting and whitewashing the cycle manufacturers' hirelings, who, but for the speed which enhances their advertising qualifications, would have been cast into outer darkness long since. They may now race for cash, and snap their fingers at less favored riders who are not fast enough to be granted similar privileges.

So in America the League of American Wheelmen, finding itself unable or unwilling, or both, to put these riders in the professional ranks, where they belong, made Class B for their particular emolument, legalizing, in fact, that which they had not the courage or sportsmanship to penalize.

In all the long history of amateur sport, nothing has ever transpired of such a temporizing nature as the workings of these two bodies that pretend to govern racing cycling on both sides of the Atlantic.

It remains to be seen now how long the Amateur Athletic Association of Great Britain and the Amateur Athletic Union of the United States will play the rôle of accomplice; for that is precisely their position if this joblot of "amateurs" is permitted to race at athletic meetings given under their auspices. If such were the case, then, indeed, might we as well give over all track cycling to the professional, and look only to the universities for honest racing. But I expect the best clubs in the A. A. A. and A. A. U. to reject Class B and its ilk, and a revulsion of feeling against the present wretched condition of cycling.

The first cycle races in England, I believe, were given in the Crystal Palace, in 1869, in conjunction with an exhibition of wheels, and both created general interest. The popular wave may be said to have been set in motion about '75, and the early meetings and the cycle championship were peaceably held under the auspices of the old Amateur Athletic Club.

From the hour the National Cyclists' Union came into the field, however, an era of strife, internal as well as external, was entered upon. At first the Union attempted to supervise all cycling in England from its headquarters, but the sport grew so widely that in '80 local centres were found necessary and formed, thereby relieving the Council of much labor. The Council is composed of members of affiliated clubs and the secretary and chairman of the various local centres. Each local centre is really a local union, banded with other local unions for the more thorough supervision of cycling.

In '85 war was declared between the National Cyclists' Union and the Amateur Athletic Association, and a vituperative and florid campaign entered upon that has been equalled in athletic history only by the battle royal between our Amateur Athletic Union and League of American Wheelmen a few years ago.

To view general wheeling in Great Britain is a much pleasanter picture, for England is a veritable home of cycling, with its splendid roads, its shady lanes, and its closely located little towns picturesquely nestled along the winding highways. What a country for the touring wheelman, with its historic associations, its fascinating and soothing rural beauty, its vigor-imparting climate! Here he may, indeed, gratify all the senses and exercise his muscles simultaneously in one of the choicest garden spots of the Old World.

One fancies all England must be awheel; in London the tradespeople utilize the machine for the delivery of orders, and you may see the butcher's boy or the milkman scudding through the streets on the tricycle, while in the country the artisan, with tools trapped on his back, pedals his way to the scene of his daily labors.

The Touring Club of England, formed in '78, has done a great deal in bringing about road improvement, which began in '86, while the sleepy little inns that were fast falling into decay from lack of patronage have been revivified by the thousands of touring cyclists that in season trail the kingdom from end to end. Indeed, if you pick up a hotel directory, you will find particular advertising and especial inducements offered for cyclists as a result of this Touring Club's influence. It publishes a complete directory for members, in which are given detailed road direction, the most desirable hotels, and the shops to patronize if you are unfortunate enough to break down; at all of these members of the club are given a reduced tariff, arranged for by the councils which are in residence throughout England.

The oldest club—the Pickwick B. C.—was formed in '70, the London B. C. being the next, in '74, and these, with members of the Surrey and Temple B. clubs, formed the National Union, but the sportsmen who gave it birth have long since withdrawn from active service.

Oxford and Cambridge had cycling from '74 to '85, but since the beginning of the present era of corruption they have dropped out of it altogether, and the event is not now to be found on any of their athletic programmes.

The year of '93 in England, as with us, saw better tires, improved gearing, and consequently an advance of records. In fact, '93 was a year of pace-making records, for on both sides the ocean these racers lived about the track, ready to seize upon the most favorable opportunity to ride against time. Such records are, undoubtedly, of little real value, and it is an extremely difficult matter now to compile a bicycling table that shows genuine performances, the English Union having gone to the extreme of recently passing a rule allowing pace-makers in championships.

Racing cycling under present methods is going the way of all sport where professionals and dishonesty secure a foothold. Already the better elements have dropped out of it, and dissolution is only a question of time. These makers' hirelings, who are paid to keep in training, must of a necessity excel the men who ride because of the pleasure it affords them, and give but a percentage of their time to getting fit. One looks upon it as giving him exercise and recreation; the other, as a means of livelihood. With one it is sport; with the other it is business.

XIII

CRICKET

I have left cricket among the last, because there is not a great deal I can write about it that will interest the average American, and because I want to close my pilgrimage with that which is free from scandal and corruption, and cricket gives me the desired opportunity. It is the only one—always excepting golf, where his duties are tutorial, as indeed they are to a considerable extent in cricket—the professional has entered without lowering the tone, reason for which may be found in the fact that there has been no sailing under false colors. In America the national patience seems intolerant of a game that requires three days of play to determine the winner, and it has on that account alone, I have no doubt, failed of popularity, except in a very few sections.

It may be said, in fact, that the American game thrives only in Philadelphia. Elevens are maintained in New York, Boston, Baltimore, Detroit, Chicago, and in San Francisco, but they are almost wholly composed of Englishmen. Nevertheless the last two years have shown a slight increased interest and improved form; but Philadelphia remains the American cricket centre, and the only one that can turn out an all-gentleman team of "county" class. In England, however, cricket is considered almost part of the school-boy's education. It has been called the national game, and perhaps rightly so; yet, in truth, my investigations led me to conclude that both in point

LORD'S—SHOWING PUBLIC STAND ON THE RIGHT

of spectators and players cricket had dropped into second place in popularity since the tremendous football wave spread over the British Isles.

But cricket, however, has the advantage of being played everywhere by gentlemen, and its matches therefore attract the largest percentage of fashion of any sporting events in England. That the game really has a refining influence was impressed upon me by a prominent member of the Athletic Association, who said that when invited to officiate at athletic sports in provincial England he never felt disturbed over his reception if the games happened to be under the auspices of a club with a cricket department; but if given by an athletic club pure and simple, he invariably made arrangements to return by the first train after the games.

Cricket was first mentioned in the sixteenth century, chiefly as a boy's game, and as such continued to be considered in the seventeenth, nor did it attain the dignity of man's estate, so to speak, until the formation of the Hambledon Club, at the opening of the eighteenth century.

Originally — so the historians tell us — the game was called stoolball, and consisted of a batsman defending a stool with his hand against the tossing of the ball by a player, who tried to bowl the primitive stumps, and when successful took his turn at the thrilling defence. Evidently the game was nearly as exciting then as now. At the beginning of the seventeenth century the bat was crooked, a form which continued until the middle of the eighteenth century, when for the first time, too, cricket was mentioned in literature.

It shows that there are always some disgruntled mortals in the world to find fault with whatever attains popularity, for even this gentle game found detractors, who bemoaned its existence in the eighteenth century, proclaiming that it "propagates a spirit of idleness."

The world-famed Marylebone Club, the parliament of cricket, was formed about 1787 (Eton had played cricket in 1750) by some of the members of the White Conduit Club, which had just been dissolved. No one thinks of questioning its prerogatives, and although there is no association and no law compelling clubs to abide by the Marylebone rulings, yet they all choose, and are glad to do so.

The historic Lord's, headquarters of the Marylebone Club, was originally a plot of ground laid out by Thomas Lord and some other members of the White Conduit Club in what is now known as Dorset's Square, London. It was moved once, and again in 1814 to the present ground, where the first match — Marylebone Cricket Club vs. Hertfordshire — was played the same year. It is the scene of all the Marylebone Cricket Club - Middlesex, Eton - Harrow, Oxford-Cambridge, and Gentlemen-Players' matches, though some of the latter are also decided at Kennington Oval. Oxford and Cambridge played their first inter-'varsity match in 1827; the Gentlemen-Players' their first in 1806; Eton and Harrow in 1805.

A cricket match at Lord's is a sight worth crossing the ocean to witness, for it brings out all classes, and one may see every type of England's social fabric represented in the pavilion and in the immense public stands.

Cricket England is divided into counties which play off a championship series, and from the leaders are chosen the players for the All-England eleven.

The first-class counties, as decided by the season of '93 play, were Yorkshire, Lancashire, Middlesex, Kent, Surrey, Nottinghamshire, Sussex, Somerset, and Gloucestershire.

The second class, Derbyshire, Warwickshire, Essex, Leicestershire, Cheshire, Hampshire, and Staffordshire.

W. H. Grove

THE PAVILION AT LORD'S

The first have an organized inter-county competition, but not so with the second, which seems like ignoring teams that furnish unqualifiedly good sport, and that could be greatly improved by the institution of a regular championship series. There has been some agitation of doing away with the first and second class county distinction, but nothing has come of it thus far.

The batting and bowling averages of the first-class elevens are carefully compiled at the end of the season, and an annual list of the highest published. That these averages of skill are high the following records of '93 will show:

Fourteen batsmen made over 1000 runs.

Two batsmen (one a professional—Gunn) made over 2000 runs.

Sixty-nine made individual innings of over 100, and the highest of these were 195, 191, 186, 180, 171, 169, 164, 159, 156, 154, 150.

The best averages (amateurs):

A. E. Stoddart, 50 innings, 2072 runs; average, 42.14.

F. S. Jackson, 36 innings, 1328 runs; average, 41.16.

Rev. W. Rahleigh, 14 innings, 482 runs; average, 37.1.

W. G. Grace, 50 innings, 1609 runs; average, 35.34.

Gunn, the professional, made in 51 innings 2057 runs, an average of 42.41.

Bowling averages (amateur):

C. M. Wells, overs, 453.3; runs, 1049; wickets, 73; average, 14.27.

C. J. Kortwright, overs, 82.3; runs, 269; wickets, 17; average, 15.14.

H. R. B. Davenport, overs, 228.1; runs, 560; wickets, 32; average, 17.16.

J. T. Hearne made the highest professional bowling average with overs, 1741.4; runs, 3492; wickets, 2.12; average, 16.100; the next highest professional being Mr. Peel, overs, 1060.3; runs, 1722; wickets, 121; average, 14.28.

Thus it will be seen that the amateurs hold their own well with the professionals in both batting and in bowling, though more particularly in the batting, for in neither case did the latter, beyond Hearne and Peel, average so high.

Until the famous W. G. Grace began his wonderful career along in the latter part of the sixties, and that has lasted up to date despite his age, the batting of the professionals averaged very much higher than that of the amateurs; but nowadays there is very little difference, or, if any, it is in favor of the amateurs. In bowling the predominance of skill still rests with the professionals.

No game shows so little difference between the skill of amateurs and professionals—the latter doing the bowling and coaching for practically all the elevens in England—for there is none to which the former give so much time. A very large majority of cricketers do little else but play cricket during season, and therefore the two classes contend on more even terms than in any other sport.

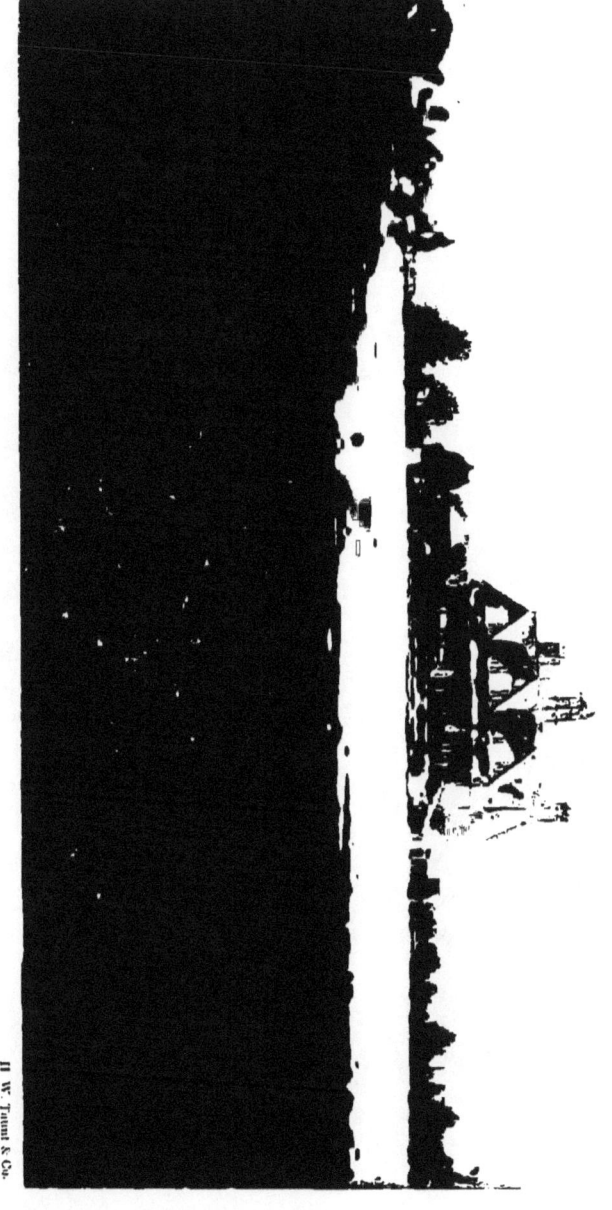

OXFORD CRICKET-GROUND AND CLUB-HOUSE

H. W. Taunt & Co.

The fact that in England cricket is largely a game of the leisure class, which has the advantage of playing against and under the instruction of the most skilled professionals in the world, explains also their much higher standard of play as compared with the American game.

A great deal of rivalry exists between the counties, which creates a careful scrutiny of all the clever players within the county boundaries, and sometimes the base of residence is changed in a hurried manner altogether unseemly in the dignified Britisher. As a result of these efforts by counties to outdo one another, and the consequent struggle to get men of known ability, the amateur question was once raised, and led to a situation so strained that the Marylebone Club, which is not easy to move, was obliged to take cognizance of the disturbance, and ruled that players might be paid their expenses if clubs chose to do so.

Men sometimes take up their residence in a county simply to play on the eleven; but it has never been carried to a harmful point, and cricket has remained untouched by scandal and is undeniably honest sport.

County play is, after all, the most pleasing feature of English cricket.

At Oxford and Cambridge each college has an eleven, from which the 'varsity is chosen in a manner similar to that which rules in football and others, and here, as at Eton and Harrow, the Marylebone Club is, of course, the high court of appeal.

There are no other games on at the time of the cricket season at either the public schools or the colleges, and it is therefore very generally played, and without any training whatsoever—not even so much as maintained in football.

Every town in England has a green common to its inhabitants, and with usually a cricket history of its own.

Here the matches are played, and here the great mass of players receive their first schooling. It is astonishing what a number of youngsters play cricket throughout the country, and what an interest is taken in the game by the villagers. The following high score records will show what has been done where cricket has reached its highest development:

803, Non-Smokers *vs.* Smokers, at East Melbourne, March 17, 1887; 775, New South Wales *vs.* Victoria, at Sydney, February 10, 1882; 703 (for nine wickets, innings declared closed), Cambridge University *vs.* Sussex, at Brighton, June 19, 1890 (highest in England); 698, Surrey *vs.* Sussex, at Kennington Oval, August 9, 1888 (highest score in a county match); 650, Surrey *vs.* Oxford University, at Kennington Oval, June 24, 1888; 650, Surrey *vs.* Hampshire, at the Oval, May 24, 1883; 643, Australians *vs.* Sussex, at Brighton, May 18, 1882 (highest by an Australian team in England); 635, Surrey *vs.* Somersetshire, at the Oval, August 10, 1885; 614, Surrey *vs.* Oxford University, at the Oval, June 24, 1889; 612, Oxford *vs.* Middlesex, at Prince's, June 19, 1876.

XIV

GOLF

NEVER was sporting England more seriously afflicted than it is to-day by golfiana. Never was a situation so incongruous with our orthodox preconception as that of the Britisher in the throes of this disease, for disease it certainly is, and not the less deeply seated for failing to disclose its symptoms.

To the occasional or casual observer there appears in the Englishman's demeanor on the links no departure from his usual placidity. He stalks upon the grounds with habitual solemnity, and takes up the game in the same seriousness that has been associated with him at play. If the on-looker follows the player around the course, he seeks in vain for any visible sign of that joyous spirit which he, likely as not, has imagined fitting accompaniment to athletic contest.

But in golf the Briton is a contradiction. He gives no outward evidence of perturbation, though, to borrow topical opera slang, he boils within. It is only to his familiars in the club-house and around his own board that the Englishman reveals himself, and there, by the softening influences of good cheer, may you discover how hopeless a victim he is to the ancient and royal game.

Before he has finished his Scotch and soda he will play over again every stroke of that last round in which he was beaten a single hole, and then take up in elaborate detail certainly every bunker and almost every brae on the course, until he has at length decided to his complete satisfaction on the identical stroke and spot that caused his downfall. I should be willing to give long odds in a wager on every golfing enthusiast in Great Britain being able to find, blindfolded, any given hazard on his home links, and the great majority of hazards on every course in England or Scotland. To hear them discuss strokes to evade, I was near saying, almost every bit of whin, and locate every sand dune, is to gain some idea of the range and strength of golf-mania.

ALMOST AS EXCITING AS SALMON FISHING

I was prepared to find the country gone golf-crazy, but I found instead a condition bordering on what I have called golf-insomnia, though I should add that my observations were made from esoteric vantage-ground. At first I was disappointed, and ascribed the stories I had heard of the golf-furor to newspaper license; I had looked for some familiar token by which I might recognize the craze—signs such as in America indicate unmistakably that a boom is on. But my first visit to links so depressed me that I

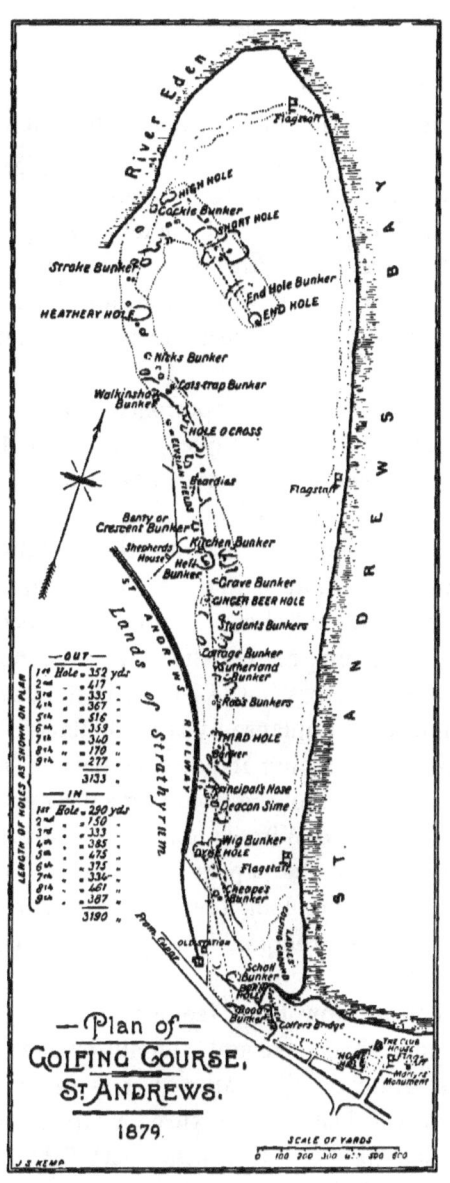

nearly reached a determination to pass by golf altogether in my pilgrimage — in the eventual failure of which resolution my readers have my heartfelt sympathy.

I had but just returned to London after an exciting day's sport with the Devon and Somerset stag-hounds, and concluded to devote an afternoon to golf at Wimbledon, which is in the suburbs of London, and will be remembered by Americans as the scene of the international rifle matches.

It was a disillusionizing experience, that first sight of the much-heralded and antique game. Speaking retrospectively, I am not sure I have a very distinct recollection of just what I reckoned on viewing; I do not believe I expected to see players astride their clubs prancing about the teeing-ground in ill-concealed eagerness for the affray, nor a dense and cheering throng of spectators surrounding the putting-green of the home hole, nor triumphantly shouldered victors borne from the field amid hosannas and tumultuous applause by the populace. We Americans, I know, are nothing if not speculative, but I really question if such a will-o'-the-wisp danced to my seduction on the journey out to Wimbledon. Yet I do remember I had read so much in the papers and heard so much in the clubs that I was led to look for a certain amount of animation on the links, tempered, of course, by the national disposition.

Even as I write now I can feel again the dejection that came over me in successive and widening waves as I looked for the first time on the game that is reported to have converted in the last two or three years more disciples than any other in the old country. At first I thought I had gone on the links during a lull in the play. Then I persuaded myself that I had arrived on a day set apart for the convalescents of some near-by sanitarium, but as I dis-

A VIEW OF THE ST. ANDREWS LINKS

covered my error in the ruddy imprint of health on their cheeks, my wonder grew that so many vigorous young and middle-aged men could find amusement in what appeared to me to be a melancholy and systematized "constitutional." Once recovered from the initial shock, I found amusement in the awful solemnity that enveloped the on-lookers about the putting-green, every mother's son of whom watched the holing out with bated breath. One, standing next to me in the crowd, and whose pleasing face gave encouragement, while the frequency with which he had trod on my toes seemed to me to have established a sufficient *entente cordiale* between us, bestowed upon me, when I asked why no one called the number of strokes each player had taken, so we would all know how they stood, such a look of righteous horror as I am sure would have caused any but an irrepressible American to wish the earth might open and swallow him. But being an American it simply increased my thirst for knowledge, and at the next sally I upset him completely by asking why a player, who was executing the "waggle" with all the deliberate nicety of one thoroughly appreciative of that important prelude to the flight of the ball, did not hit it instead of wasting so much time and energy flourishing his "stick" above it.

To have alluded with levity to one of the rudimentary functions of the game was appalling enough in all conscience, but to have called a club a stick was too much for my neighbor, and he of the aggressive feet moved away from the tee with a pained expression clouding the open countenance that had tempted my golfing innocence.

Subsequent and solitary wanderings about the links brought but little solace to my joyless sporting soul, for it seemed that at every turning I was challenged by loud and emphatic cries of "fore," the significance of which I did not understand, while the air appeared to be filled with flying balls that whizzed past at uncomfortable proximity, or alighted just behind me, after a flight of a hundred and fifty yards or so, with a thud far from reassuring. It does not seem probable such a situation could under any circumstances have a humorous side; but it may, and I have laughed until my head ached over the comical consternation of some luckless and obstinate duffer, who, instead of permitting, as courtesy and tradition teach, more skilful following players to pass him, continued on his laborious and turf-bruising way, driven into by those immediately back of him, and damned by every golfer on the links. Given an irascible and stubborn and indifferent (a combination that has been known to exist) leading player, with following balls dropping around him, and I fancy even an Englishman, if he is not playing, will acknowledge the picture mirth-provoking. At Wimbledon I was the hapless but by no means adjectived victim, for though I was looking for animation, it was in the rôle of spectator rather than that of participant.

"BUNKERED"

What broke the gloom of that first day of my experience, and turned indifference to a desire for knowledge, were the individual manœuvres on the putting-green, which, sometimes grotesque, frequently picturesque, and invariably fraught with the weightiest meditation, convinced me that any game requiring such earnest play must improve on acquaintance. The putting-green presents a scene for the student of human nature, with its exhibitions of temperaments and varied styles of play; one will make a minute and lengthy survey over the few yards of turf that separate his ball from the hole, and attain the climax of his joy or woe by a short, sharp tap with the club; another devotes his critical attention to the lie of the ball, followed by a painfully deliberate aim that seems never to quite reach the explosive-point; some appear to acquire confidence by the narrowing of the human circle around the hole; others wave all back save their caddie, who, like a father confessor, remains at their side administering unction of more or less extremity to the last.

The duties of the caddie are manifold, including the responsibilities of preceptor, doctor, and lawyer. He will be called upon to devise means of escape from soul-trying bunkers, administer to the wounded pride of the unsuccessful, and turn legislator at a crowded teeing-ground; he must even at times serve as a foil to the wrath of the

CLUB-HOUSE AND HOME HOLE, ST. ANDREWS

disconsolate player who has "foozled" a drive that was confidently expected to carry him safely beyond a formidable hazard. There are caddies and caddies, to be sure, but when of the right sort, no servants, I fancy, receive such marked evidence of their master's regard. Most of them are Scotch, and some of them the most picturesque figures on the golfing-green.

I was shortly to have my wish for knowledge fulfilled, for not a week after my Wimbledon experience a Good Samaritan, in the guise of a handsome type of the beau-ideal Briton — six feet in height, and with cheeks that bloomed as rosy as a girl's — introduced me to the Ranelagh links, and so let his good-nature get the better of his judgment as to undertake the direction of my golfing education. I dare say he was misled into this rash undertaking by my evident confidence in myself, which was really supreme. I had previously gone around the links a couple of times with a very respectable score for a duffer, and grown thoroughly convinced of my ability to master the game very shortly. I did not know it at that time, but I was just in prime condition to become a convert.

To obtain a full appreciation of the charms and difficulties of golf you must have acquired a settled conviction of its inferiority as a game requiring either skill or experience; you must have looked upon it with supreme contempt, and catalogued it as a sport for invalids and old men. When you have reached this frame of mind go out on to the links and try it. I never believed a club could be held in so many different ways but the right one until I essayed golf, nor dreamed it so difficult to drive a ball in a given direction. The devotion of the golfer to his game is only equalled by the contempt of him who looks upon it for the first time. You wonder at a great many things when you first see it played, but your wonderment is greatest that a game which appears so simple should have created such a furor.

The secret of its fascination rests largely in the fact that it beats the player, and he, in his perversity, strives the harder to secure the unattainable.

A LOST BALL

The game is by no means easy; in fact, one of England's foremost players asserts that it takes six months of steady play to acquire consistent form. You must hit the ball properly to send it in the desired direction, and you must deal with it as you find it; you cannot arrange the ball to suit your better advantage, nor await a more satisfactory one, as in baseball and cricket. The club must be held correctly and swung accurately in order to properly address the ball, from which the player should never take his eye, while at the same time he must move absolutely freely, and yet maintain an exact balance. Besides which, it demands judgment and good temper, and if you fail in the latter your play will be weakened on the many trying occasions that arise.

It is a selfish game, where each man fights for himself, seizing every technicality for his own advantage, and there is no doubt that to this fact its popularity may in a large measure be attributed. Unlike cricket, baseball, or football, one is not dependent on others for play. You can usually find some one to make up a match, or you may go over the course alone, getting the best of practice and fairly good sport, or at least there is always a caddie to be had for the asking and the usual small fee.

The exercise may be gentle, but whosoever fancies golf does not test the nerves should play a round on popular links. Unless he is a veteran of tried experience he cannot be indifferent to the scrutiny to which his form is subjected at the tee, nor does it make him more certain

HOLE O' CROSS, HEATHERY HOLE, HIGH HOLE, AND THE RIVER EDEN, ST. ANDREWS

of his swing to know that he is being mentally criticised by the most skilled players in the world. If he is a novice, he is pretty apt to top his ball on the drive, and fancy all kinds of maledictions heaped upon his duffer play by those awaiting their turn at the tee. I should advise a beginner to serve his novitiate on little-frequented links, if such are to be found in Great Britain, for on popular ones both his pleasure and form are likely to suffer. He is sure to make wild drives and erratic iron shots in his anxiety to play hurriedly and keep out of the way of following golfers, and it is not calculated to increase his accuracy to hear balls dropping around him, and to know he is delaying the game of a dozen or more back of him. But the duffer's trials are suspended for the time being once he has reached the putting-green, since tradition rules that here on this golfing sanctuary no man may drive into or molest him. And yet his respite is but half enjoyed, and not at all shared by his partner, if it be a four-some match, for the desirability of always being "up" in his putts having been vigorously impressed upon him, he is likely, in his zeal and wish to win a look of approval from that patient individual, to entirely overshoot the hole.

It would take all my space were I to attempt a list of the golfing clubs of Great Britain; but the publication

W H Puddicombe

ROYAL NORTH DEVON CLUB-HOUSE AND FIRST TEEING-GROUND, WESTWARD HO

of a 350-page annual compendium, which devotes itself mainly to the subject, rather suggests what that number may be, and gives, too, a good idea of the game's popularity. I do not know of another sport on either side of the Atlantic that is similarly treated by the publisher. But one need not resort to literature to catch the popular trend, which in England has spread at such a pace that nowadays you need only lay out links, build a hotel, and you have founded a town. As for Scotland — well, one expects golf up there, and one gets it. The coast is simply a succession of links, and the vision of beknickerbockered, begaitered, and beclubbed men is a never-fading one. There is a certain indefinable charm in the golfing atmosphere of Scotland one does not find in England, and not altogether explained by the more picturesque surroundings of the northern links, that wooes you irresistibly; an unobtrusive assumption of superiority by its players, that evinces itself in kindly suggestion rather than arrogant admonition, and caddies that seem to be following on in a line of hereditary dignity.

I know my greatest enjoyment was obtained by wandering over the St. Andrews links with a gray-haired old caddie, who told me, among a chapter of picturesque bits, that he had many a time carried Mr. George Glennie's clubs, and similarly officiated for Tom Morris. I do not believe I know anything quite so delicious, not even the ancient angler, as a talkative and reminiscent caddie. Of course, on sober reflection, you realize he is drawing on his vivid imagination; but the difference and the charm is that while the fisherman only half convinces, somehow there is such an earnestness about the caddie as he recounts the most unheard-of shots, and the air is so charged with golfing intoxicant, that your credulity is up to any tale, and you fall a willing victim to the blandish-

LOOKING TOWARDS THE SEA, WESTWARD HO

W. H. Prible, ph.

ments of the insinuating servant of the ancient and royal game. But do not get the impression that all caddies are so picturesque or entertaining; their imaginations may be and undoubtedly are quite as productive, but it is only the rare few that lend so fetching a setting to their garrulity.

The caddie pure and simple occupies the lowest stratum of professional golf; he may earn his way to the ranks of the professional players, if he is capable and provident, or, if he is shiftless, he will supplement his work on the links by odd jobs here and there, with no ambition for a professional career. The latter specimen can make about a dollar a day carrying clubs, or twice that amount if he plays a couple of rounds, and he usually divides his time between the links and the dram-shop. Some of the more trustworthy of this class serve additionally as rough-and-ready valets at about twenty dollars a month, and the more thrifty, again, earn an extra few pence by commissions on the clubs they sell. All must be capable on the links or they cannot earn their salt. Nothing is more exasperating than a poor caddie, and he is not tolerated, while, on the other hand, he may make himself invaluable, and his services always in demand.

The autocrat of all golf professionals is the green-keeper, employed by a club on salary to officiate as general custodian, and who usually has under him several lesser lights in the professional world, that, differing from the caddie class, invariably follow golf as a means of livelihood, by either teaching or making up four-somes with amateurs; they may and frequently do have an interest in a club-manufacturer's shop, or, failing of such consequence, take a turn at the bench at day's wages.

I cannot say if the native views it in the same light, but I concluded before I had half finished my tour that the attraction of golf was as much due to the atmosphere

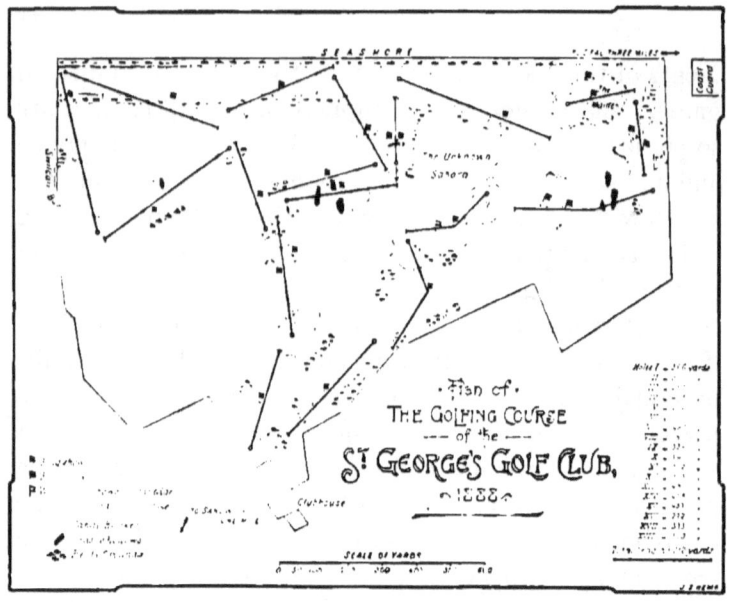

of tradition on the links and good-fellowship in the clubs as to the qualities of the game itself. I doubt if we in America will ever be able to extract so much pleasure from it. Our dispositions, our temperaments, are not golf-like; we hurry through life at too rapid a gait; we have not the time to give golf in order to gain that responsive charm the game holds for the leisurely suitor. Before I sailed for the other side I had played on the St. Andrews course at Yonkers (New York), the oldest in America, but it required a day on links in the old country to bring me under the influence; on this side I had thought it an entertaining way of taking gentle exercise in agreeable company; on the other side the associations of the green, the memories, constantly recalled, of famous players, the enthusiastic discussion of strokes around the hospitable board of the club, combine to your final unconditional surrender to the golfing spirit.

The omnipresent memories of the game that salute you everywhere are what entrance you; and where will you find them so dear or so abounding as at St. Andrews? Not to have been to St. Andrews is not to have seen golf at home, for despite the greater age of Blackheath in England, the Scottish green is universally regarded as the *alma mater* of the game. It is a connecting link with the past, from the collection of queer old clubs in the club-house, to "Old Tom" Morris, the venerable and revered keeper, out on the links. Royal blood has golfed on its green, and matches that will live longest in history have been won and lost over its eighteen holes. It was here that Allan Robertson some sixty years ago showed the wonderful play that earned him the right to be considered the most skilled of professionals, and gave him a 79 record, which remained unequalled until a few years

A. C. Hawkins

THE "SAHARA"

ago. It was here that Robertson, "Old Tom" Morris, and the Parks and the Dunns decided many a hard-fought match, and where "Old Tom" learned the golf that has made him famous, and left him, even now with his seventy-two years, among the best in the land.

Small wonder the memories are kept alive, for those must have been great days along in the middle of the present century. The professional golf-player as he exists to-day was not known at that time; and the few like those mentioned were constantly being matched against one another by the several clubs to which they belonged. Allan Robertson's 79 stood until "Young Tom" Morris, who gave promise, had he lived to fulfil it, of being a more brilliant performer than even his skilled father, made it 77, which continued the St. Andrews' record up to October, 1888, when the professional Hugh Kirkaldy made it 74, and a year later established the present remarkable record of 73, taking 35 strokes out, and 38 on the return.

Aside from Mr. George Glennie, we do not hear so much of the amateurs of the old days, and must conclude that amateur golfing skill has increased a long way beyond what it was even twenty-five years ago, and improved at a much greater proportion than that of the professional. Mr. Glennie established a St. Andrews record of 88 in 1855, and it was not bettered until 1884, when Mr. Horace G. Hutchinson went the round in 87. It has been claimed that the links is not so difficult by several strokes as before the present craze set in, and true it is that the wearing down of the whin has broadened the course, and exacted less accuracy in placing. It is a fact, too, that the driving, which is a great feature of to-day's game, is of comparatively modern development, the old players being celebrated more for skilful placing than far driving. However, there is no doubt that not only has there been an extraordinary increase of good scores, but a widening of the class that establish records. To cite, for instance, simply those that may be said to compose the championship class, and who have a St. Andrews record: Mr. H. G. Hutchinson, who cut down Mr. Glennie's 88 to 87, has gone the round since then in 84; Messrs. William Mure, 85; Alexander Stuart, 83; Leslie Melville Balfour, 85; Ed. R. H. Blackwell, 82; A. F. Maclie,

A. C. Hawkins

ST. GEORGE'S CLUB-HOUSE, SANDWICH

82; J. E. Laidley, 83; F. G. Tait, 80; F. A. Fairlie, 86; and last September ('93) Mr. Mure Fergusson made the present record by holing out in 79. John Ball, Jun., Esq., has no St. Andrews record, but his prowess may be judged by his average of 83 in winning 48 scratch medals. Mr. H. Hilton likewise has not made a record on the Scottish links, but has done Hoylake in 75 and Sandwich in 82. Probably the improvement in amateur form is

Rogers

"WALKINSHAW'S GRAVE"

best exampled by the statement that twenty-five entries returned scores of 90 and under in the championship of 1893.

There are many other players, some of them very little inferior, a few of them perhaps as good as those here named, but I have simply picked out the best-known to instance present skill, and made no attempt at a graduated and authentic list. Apropos of average skill, it is the popular conception that a 300 or 400 yard drive is an every-day occurrence, and like many other popular conceptions, this one is a fallacy. On looking it up carefully, I found that the average player will loft his ball from 120 to 140 yards, a thoroughly good player from 140 to 160, and an exceptional driver 170 to 180. Men have driven farther, of course, but the everyday average is about what I give it. 70 to 100 yards represents the average drive of a good golfer of the gentle sex.

The delight of play on the St. Andrews links is largely due to the golfing atmosphere that here more than anywhere else envelops you at every turning. The town seems almost to exist by golf and for golf. The streets are called after the game, the taverns greet you in its name, every urchin on the street appears to have connection with it one way or another, and when you play upon the green, all the world—all the golfing world, for of course you care for no other—sees you. You follow the white flags out and the red flags in over the full eighteen holes, with the Eden River on one side and the German Ocean on the other, to awaken you to the beauties of the old university town, revealing its gray towers in the background. You tread the hallowed ground, brightened here and there by blossoming whin or heather, every moment a pleasurable one; and finally, when you have made the home hole, with "Old Tom" Morris likely as not officiating as high-priest of the ceremony, you go into the handsomest golf club-house in Great Britain, and sit down before the wide windows to watch others tee off, while you devour a simple luncheon with more relish than ever elaborate *menu* occasioned.

"HELL" BUNKER

Despite the widening of the course and the wearing of the soil, the all-round quality of the links of the Royal and Ancient Golf Club of St. Andrews continues unsurpassed, indeed unequalled. Westward Ho demands more accurate placing, Sandwich mightier carries, and Hoylake affords finer putting-greens, but a round at no one of these will give you the golf to be had at St. Andrews. Unprejudiced golfers (and, by-the-way, let it be understood that there is a wide distinction drawn between the golfer and the golf-player) that have played on them all declare the Scottish links to be the most sport-giving. And its unquestioned superiority is in the rare judgment with which the holes are placed. Though there are no such immense carries to make from the tee as at Sandwich, one must needs be a long and skilful driver, for no "levellers" are found, and poor drives do not go unpunished at St. Andrews. It is a hard links for the duffer, for the distances are ideal, and whoso "foozles" suffers dire consequences; he may not, as on most other links, atone for a poor drive by an extra good one. If two drives measure the distance, it will take two of the best he can make; failing, he loses a full stroke.

The bunkers, most of them natural, but many artificial, are sunken, and do not always show from the tee, but they are very good, and well distributed about the holes to try the approaching golfer's soul and skill, none being more famous anywhere than the suggestively named "Hell" and "Walkinshaw's Grave." All the putting-greens are good, but the one at hole No. 5 is notable.

The hardness of soil usually assures you a good lie, unless you happen to fall behind a brae, even at the bottom of a bunker. Indeed, this toughness has been the salvation of the links; otherwise it would have gone the way of the forsaken but always famous Musselburgh,

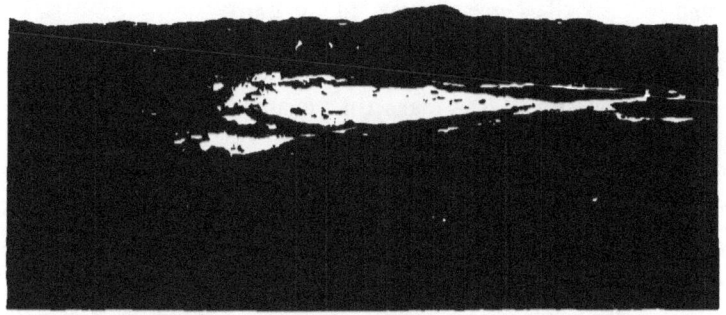

A. D. Hawkins

THE "MAIDEN"

and been worn out long ago. It is more played upon twice over than any other in the world, and in such continuous demand that a second course of eighteen holes is being added. The ground belongs to Mr. Cheape, of Strathtyrum, although the club has always paid for keeping up the green. The public has a prescriptive right of golfing over it through license by the city of St. Andrews to John, Archbishop of St. Andrews, dated 1552. The famous club prizes are the silver cross of St. Andrew and the Bombay Medal, played for on the first Wednesday in May; the Royal or King William IV. Medal, and Gold Medal, last Wednesday in September; George Glennie Medal (lowest combined scores at the two meetings). All these are scratch. The handicap events are Calcutta Cup, first week in August; Queen Victoria Jubilee Vase, first week in September.

These are the times to see St. Andrews at its best, the black-collared, brass-buttoned scarlet coats of the members making a brilliant foreground against the more sombre setting of the mass that crowds as near the holes as their reverence will permit.

Next to St. Andrews, I believe I prefer Westward Ho, of the Royal North Devon Club, though the four best-known courses are all so good one's choice might be ascribed to personal prejudice. Westward Ho appealed to me, first, by reason of its being down in that home of sportsmen, the Devon and Somerset country; second, by its picturesque surroundings, resembling somewhat in its broken character the North Berwick and Prestwick environment; and last, by the sport-giving quality of its links, all of which goes to prove, I suppose, that I am not yet a true golfer. No links in Great Britain requires greater accuracy, for the course is covered with innumerable rushes, and you must not only drive in a given direction, but drop your ball almost at a certain spot. Really the links is ideal, the drives are magnificent, the bunkers difficult, the putting-greens large and excellent, and your ball seems always to be teed.

Many assert Sandwich, the course of the St. George's Club, to be the most difficult one in Great Britain, a claim that certainly impresses you on first playing over the links as entirely justifiable. The surface of the ground looks like one vast irregular succession of congealed sand waves, one stretch of it being most appropriately called the "Sahara." There are tremendous carries, the tees being so far away from the hazards as to require a strong driver to get his ball over safely; the sand-hills are mountainous, the bunkers formidable, and the penalties severe. The short driver may circumvent some of the terrific obstacles through roundabout ways, but he is never on level terms with him who can carry them from the tee. The greens are excellent, though not equal to those of St. Andrews, Westward Ho, or Hoylake. The Maiden, a lofty sand-hill, with a veritable yawning chasm for a bunker, is one of the most famous hazards in golfing Great Britain, while the fourteenth hole, requiring three long drives, with a hazard in each one, is probably the best of England.

Hoylake, where the Royal Liverpool Club golfs, is famed for its putting-greens, which are the finest in the old country. The character of the course is flat, somewhat like St. Andrews and Musselburgh, and abounding

A VIEW OF HOYLAKE

in hedges that require straight and accurate driving, or else you pay dearly. At the same time the penalties are not so severe nor so frequent as at St. Andrews, Sandwich, or Westward Ho. While it does not present the difficulties of these, it is a thoroughly sporting links, and the fact of its having evolved Messrs. John Ball, Jun., and H. Hilton, two of the best players of the day, and been once chosen as the championship site, answers for its merit.

Musselburgh, formerly one of the championship courses, recently deserted in favor of Muirfield, is one of the oldest and most celebrated of all Scotland's links. It was the original home of the Honorable Company of Edinburgh Golfers, next oldest club to St. Andrews, whose dinner matches have long since become treasured history, and whose quaint and venerable cup, presented to the club by Thomas McMillan in 1774, is still played for every autumn. On its links, too, some of the famous players of to-day learned their first golf, and in times gone by it was the scene of several of the keenest contests between Allan Robertson, " Old Tom " Morris, Park, Jun. and Sen., and " Old Man " and " Young Man " Dunn. Being open to the public, and so near Edinburgh, its popularity has been its downfall; its whins are literally trodden out of sight, and though its nine holes still call for fine golfing, and its bunkers are good, as those that have run foul of " Pandemonium " and " Lord Shands " will testify, yet it has fallen below the distinction of a championship links.

Muirfield, despite its good greens, seems tame beside the old course, and its eighteen holes fail of giving so much sport as Musselburgh's nine.

Prestwick, on the west of Scotland, fortunately for its preservation, for it would never stand the wear and tear of publicity, is a private club course, with soil of a sandy

ROYAL LIVERPOOL CLUB-HOUSE, HOYLAKE

nature covered by turf, very much like our Shinnecock Hills on Long Island, and much softer than St. Andrews. The character of the ground is undulating, with regions of sand-hills, the most formidable being called the Himalayas, which runs between two fairly level fields, and calls for a tremendous drive. The bunkers are difficult, but the most famous is the Cardinal's Nob, which is stiff and steep, coming in your second shot instead of from the tee, and is said to have buried more ambitions than any other bunker in Scotland or England. The putting-greens are all in hollows between sand-hills, and British dignity is sorely taxed to keep from incontinently rushing up one side of the elevation to see how near the hole the ball has rolled on the other side.

North Berwick, although short, is another of Scotland's famous links. There are eighteen holes, small ones, but no eighteen in Christendom are so filled with hazards of every description—stone walls, gardens, woods, and cultivated fields. It is a fine school for learning to approach; you have small need for a driver. The putting-greens are excellent, and though they are generally blocked, the links furnishes the best of sport, and the neighborhood the most pleasing of scenery. What more can any man want? Good sport to stir his blood, and nature's loveliness to soothe him into forgetfulness of the world with its vanities and deceits.

You hardly wonder that golf did not make its way in England from the Blackheath links once you have been there, for although the oldest, it is among the poorest, and no one should think of a visit unless attracted, as I was, by the antiquity of the club.

It is the only course I heard of where a fore caddie is used; but here he really is needed, for one of the seven holes is so long that it requires three big drives and the caddie's red flag to reach it. The soil is very hard, the lies not good, and the hazards few and not difficult. It seemed to me, on the day of my visit, they consisted chiefly of nurse-maids and bench seats.

I have commented on those links only that are world-renowned; that there are many excellent and sporting ones besides may be imagined. Great Yarmouth, for instance, is a full eighteen-hole course with a fine sandy turf, stiff bunkers, level putting-greens, and requires good golf; then there are excellent links at Little Stone, Felixstow, Dornoch, Montrose, and Carnoustie, the last being especially good, and Brancaster, one of the newest, and said to be one of the finest natural courses in Great Britain. Of the many about London, Wimbledon probably ranks first (though Ranelagh, with its two ponds and better putting-greens, yields good sport), has good hazards, some whins left, a pond, uneven greens, and gives the best golf near the city.

Ireland and Wales both have their clubs, and in the former, Portrush, where the Irish championship is held, has links with sand-hills, good though somewhat heavy greens, and one big drive over a flower-lined ravine.

Across the Channel, in France, Pau boasts the oldest club in the Old World next to Blackheath, though the course is a tame one. Biarritz, on the coast, has a links better adapted to the sport, and though its greens are not

Barraud

A HOYLAKE PUTTING-GREEN

so good as those at Pau, and the holes shorter, the penalties are more frequent and severe.

That the game has history and literature to no end has been evidenced by the abundant articles, descriptive and educational, that have been finding their way into magazines since the golfing wave swept over the country. When I set out on my pilgrimage to St. Andrews, the Mecca of all golfing enthusiasts, I determined to supplement my impressions by a bit of early history, but when I looked upon those antique clubs in the home of the ancient and royal organization, relics of a game which existed before sporting history began, I decided to delay the task.

What I have endeavored to show here is the breadth and depth of the spirit which has made the golfing widow an accepted national institution, seized the usually serene Briton by the ears, and set him putting into tumblers and whisking off the heads of daisies overnight, that in the morrow's play his aim may be the truer and his swing the deadlier.

XV

A BIT OF HISTORY

In the several papers I have prepared as a result of my studies in English sport, I have thought it advisable to incorporate something of the early history of each; but I throw down the historian's pen instantly on touching golf. It already has too many chroniclers. If one really wants a history of the ancient and royal game, I advise the purchase of Clark's volume, published in Edinburgh in 1875. It is complete, authentic, and the task was entered upon by the author *con amore*.

It has often been said there is nothing new under the sun, and the revival of golf, which is flourishing with all the vigor of an entirely new game, fortifies the old saw. Curious it is, indeed, that golf, dating back into the shadowy past, should lie dormant for generations, suddenly to spring into new and enthusiastic life. Like hunting, its early history is scrappy and incomplete, but enough of the scraps have been gathered to fill chapter after chapter, and surely abundant proof of the historian's persistency has been given the public without my mite; therefore I shall touch the subject, if only to be consistent with my original purpose, but touch it gently.

Some claim German origin for the game, the word "golf" being akin to "kolbe" (club); again, "kulban" is Gothic for a stick with a thick knob; yet, further, the Dutch game "kolf" is dragged in as a prototype, which, however, is declared by those who delight in musty research to have borne no resemblance to golf of to-day, though being unquestionably analogous. One might with truth, indeed, say that much of all games in which a ball and club figure. Chole, still played in northern France, and a game of undoubted antiquity on the Continent, is also cited as a possible progenitor. It appears, however, to have been more of the type of American shinny or English hockey than golf, apparently having consisted merely of a wooden ball struck by a club, as in these modern survivors. None of the earlier manuscripts—and some go back to the middle of the fourteenth century—allude to the putting of the ball into holes.

In fact, the chole of to-day, like the earliest form of football, is played by sides, comprising as many as may be on hand to participate, without regard to numbers; and the play consists of batting the ball to a given mark, as was the idea in the very first football struggles—either a tree, house, or other goal, some distance away.

Dutch tiles record the story of a sort of golf on ice about the seventeenth century; and the ancient *jeu-de-mail* commands some consideration among the list of golfing forefathers, because it is played by a boxwood ball —said to be batted to extraordinary distances—and a club somewhat of a compromise between a croquet and polo mallet, but chiefly because the position and swing are similar to those which obtain in golf.

There seems, indeed, to be no end to the reported sources from which golf is said to have sprung, the most ingenious and amusing being that of Sir W. G. Simpson, whose *Art of Golf* is worth buying, if for no other reason than to read his chapter on the origin of the game. The attempt to trace golf through the derivation of its name has been made over and over again—*ad infinitum;* and I for one leave the task with great pleasure to the

A BIT OF HISTORY

philologists, to whom such delving properly belongs. It is enough for us to know that the similarity in origin which must always exist, to a greater or less extent, between games that are variations of balls to be batted, and clubs with which the batting is done, has furnished no end of material for argument and groundwork on which to build almost to suit the fancy of the architect.

En passant, I will venture to say one can take up any game of the present day in which a ball and bat (of varying form and size) are the essential features, and trace it,

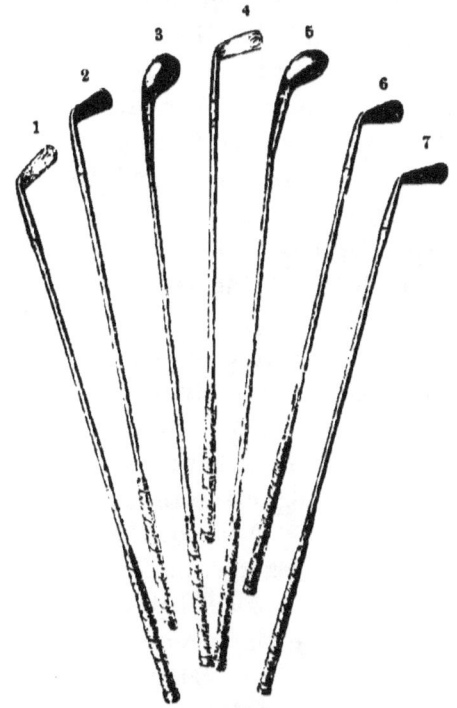

MODERN GOLF CLUBS

1. Cleek. 2. Mashie. 3. Brassy. 4. Putter. 5. Driver.
6. Lofter. 7. Iron.

by logical argument, to a common source. The early—*i.e.*, the primitive—history of nearly all such games is lost in the shrouded past, and some study, a little skill with the pen, and a vivid imagination paints many pictures that would likely as not fail of recognition in the days they portrayed. Every last one of us might write a history of golf before the fifteenth century; and who could question its authenticity?

Probably the original home of golf will never be settled upon; but certainly in James VI.'s reign Holland furnished the Scotch with their balls until a prohibitive tariff made them too expensive. Moreover, there is an old Flanders club in the Royal Wimbledon Golf Club-house, which is a very curious affair in its way, and looks for all the world like a hockey-club. Indeed, all my research into its history has led me to believe that the first golf was more like hockey than any other game, and it is very probable that both came from that good old-fashioned unpretentious sport called shinny in the United States. There seems always to be a striving after originals, and I am satisfied much time and paper has been wasted in quest of the golf prototype. There is no question whatever that the game was played in very early times—Biblical times, if you like; for may not David's strength of arm and accuracy of eye with the sling have been acquired by driving off the tee and holing out on the green?

Golf was undeniably a game of the people about the middle of the fifteenth century, and by the last of the sixteenth had grown so popular that the Edinburgh City Council forbade Sunday playing, and it was periodically frowned upon by the Crown, though never proscribed so thoroughly as football in its early days. When the Stuarts ascended the throne the restrictions of Sunday playing were modified to permit of games after church service; but mandates of this royal family were not relished by Scotchmen, and the privilege was not taken advantage of to any noticeable extent.

But the game at this time, nevertheless, was being played by the gentry and even by royalty. Clubs cost one shilling apiece, and balls, which, by-the-way, were stuffed with feathers (pressed in so tightly that, it is recorded, the contents of one would fill a hat), nine shillings a dozen. The gutta-percha balls of to-day did not come in until 1848. The game must have been making great strides; for James VI., in 1603, found it de-

HOLDING CLUB—CORRECT POSITION

sirable to appoint a royal club-maker, and fifteen years later a royal ball-maker; for which distinction players paid the usual penalty of fashion by giving four shillings apiece for balls instead of nine shillings a dozen. There has been no especial evolution in golfing implements: balls and clubs are about the same as at first, except as to material; the clubs are lighter, but practically not changed in shape.

Golfing historians delight in attaching different epochs of their game to royal personages; and thus we are told

Charles I. received news of the Irish rebellion while at play on the Leith Links, the most celebrated ones of that day; that Prince Charles introduced golf into history in 1738; and that it was during James II.'s reign a "forecaddie" (to run ahead and mark where the balls landed) became an institution.

The first record of a trophy being given is in the early part of the eighteenth century, when the Edinburgh Council directed its treasurer to offer a silver cup, valued at fifteen pounds, to be played for annually, the victor being styled "Captain of the Goff" and "that he append a piece of gold or silver to the club, and have sole disposal of the booking money (entrance fees), at five shillings a head, the settlement of disputes, and the superintendency of the links." It is noteworthy that while it may not have taken an exceptional man to win the club, it must have required an unusual one to fulfil all the requirements of the captaincy.

Heaven only knows when golf was first played in Scotland; but St. Andrews, founded in 1754, has the undisputed honor of age among clubs, though in point of fact the Royal Blackheath Club, in England, dates as far back as 1608, and was undoubtedly instituted by the Scottish court during its sojourn in that neighborhood. It was during James VI.'s reign known as the Knuckle Club, a name it retained until 1822, when the present one was adopted.

The Honorable Company of Edinburgh Golfers, established in 1774, with links at Musselburgh, was most active in popularizing the game, presenting school-boys with golf balls, and offering a "creel and shawl" to the best golfer of the fishermen's wives. The Edinburgh Burgess Golfing Society dates from 1735, but the efforts of its members were more convivial than sporting.

It is at about this time, shortly after the foundation of St. Andrews and Musselburgh, that we find the choicest bits of golfing literature, and these must have been the halcyon days of the old times. There was not that solemnity nor importance attached to play as to-day, and from all accounts the old fellows appear to have possessed a joyous golfing spirit that made a match the occasion for an outing, and the day's sport an excuse for a night of good cheer. But there was, none the less, form on the links, swallow-tail coats, knee-breeches, and tall hats being the vogue; the feather balls and play must have been far better than one would suppose, and the links harder than they are now, for 100 to 105 was the average winning score.

As usual, great tales come to us of the prowess of these players of the early days. It is altogether probable that the links were more difficult than now, since the whin has been worn away and the course widened, and some of the names given hazards, like Pandemonium (at Musselburgh) and Hell (at St. Andrews) substantiate the supposition. Unquestionably, more exact playing was required for a good score, and the narrower courses necessitated precise driving. The length of drive seems not to have been considered of such importance, placing being regarded the greater art; but the lies must have been better because the grounds were less worn.

It is true, however, that both amateur and professional playing is at a much higher standard to-day than ever it was; and while we are prone to exalt the skill of our younger days, and thus in history to credit the pioneers with exceptional powers, it is an undoubted fact that the general average of to-day is beyond what it was in those days of which we have been speaking. A few prominent names are chosen, whose prowess is enlarged upon regardless of their being exceptions; of the general players we hear nothing; while to-day, on the other side, there is quite a large class not very far from the exceptional.

BACK VIEW—BEGINNING OF FULL SWING
FOR DRIVING—INCORRECT POSITION

The Scotchman had always played the game he fondly fancies found its origin on his native heath; there was none of that overwhelming and popularizing wave which has spread over the country in the last dozen years; it went its way steadily and methodically, from the very day the St. Andrews club became a reality.

Blackheath survived the Scottish kings, but Englishmen seem to have ignored the game altogether, and there was scarcely any golfing until Westward Ho (the Royal North Devon Golf Club), located in one of the most picturesque and sporting sections of Great Britain, took it up in 1864. Wimbledon was founded in the following year, and the Hoylake links, of the Royal Liverpool Golf Club, laid out in 1869. Wimbledon added a woman's course to its links in 1872, and thereby was the first to recognize the gentle sex in golf.

Even so, golf was not booming; it was making its way only slowly. For at this time (say, in 1870) there were something like fifty clubs in Great Britain, and most of those in Scotland were very old, the little stir in England having had no effect whatever towards making new clubs across the Tweed. In 1880 this number had increased about twenty per cent. in England, but the great boom that set in along about 1886–88 multiplied clubs at an astonishing rate; at the time of my visit (February, 1894) there were about seven hundred and ninety-two in Great Britain, seventy-two of these being in Edinburgh alone, where nearly every mercantile house has a club formed of its employés.

It was, therefore, from about 1885 to 1890 that Englishmen suddenly awakened to the game they had ignored, and in quite an un-English-like manner took to it with a rush. Existing clubs were rapidly filled, professional ones grew in demand, club manufacturers sprang up, and golf links and clubs were started in every direction.

It was not long after golf began to take in England until the desirability of handicaps became apparent, and were speedily introduced, much to the disgust of the Scotch golfer.

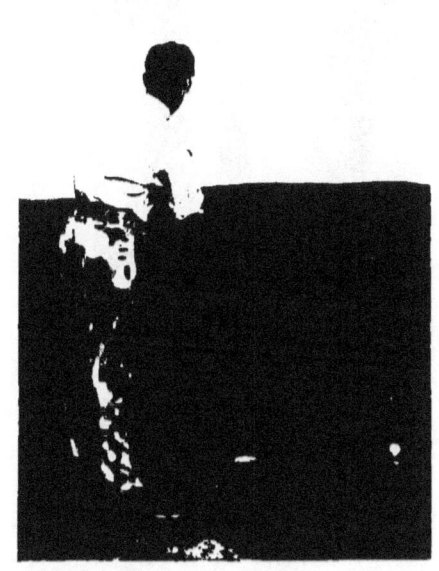

BACK VIEW—BEGINNING OF FULL SWING FOR DRIVING—CORRECT POSITION

For a long time such tournaments were scorned in the home of the ancient game; only recently have they been admitted, and even yet, every now and again, there is an outcry against them. There is no question that, for the large class of average players, they seem to have a mission, and to fill it well. All cannot be in the first class, and there must be some equalizer to create the rivalry that makes interest and increases the number of players.

Women are a very large factor in golf in the old country. Besides having their own clubs, they are admitted to membership in a large percentage of those which were once monopolized by the sterner sex, and which now, in nearly every instance, maintain a separate course for their exclusive use. A woman's championship was established in 1893, played at Lytham, St. Anne's, and won by Lady Margaret Scott, whose form is excellent, and whose quality of play may be judged from her having holed the full Westward Ho course in 96 strokes.

FRONT VIEW—BEGINNING OF FULL SWING FOR DRIVING—INCORRECT POSITION

The first championship in Great Britain was held by the Prestwick Golf Club, which offered a belt in 1860 that had to be won three times in succession before becoming personal property. After ten years' competition, it was finally captured, in 1870, by Tom Morris, Jr., son of the famous father who had himself won it four times, and who is to-day the revered care-taker of St. Andrews green.

A BIT OF HISTORY

WINNERS OF OPEN CHAMPIONSHIP BELT

Year.	Winner.	Club.	Score	Where played.
1860	Willie Park...............	Musselburgh..........	174	Prestwick.
1861	Tom Morris, Sr............	Prestwick............	163	Prestwick.
1862	Tom Morris, Sr............	Prestwick............	163	Prestwick.
1863	Willie Park...............	Musselburgh..........	168	Prestwick.
1864	Tom Morris, Sr............	Prestwick............	160	Prestwick.
1865	A. Strath.................	St. Andrews..........	162	Prestwick.
1866	Willie Park...............	Musselburgh..........	169	Prestwick.
1867	Tom Morris, Sr............	St. Andrews..........	170	Prestwick.
1868	Tom Morris, Jr............	St. Andrews..........	154	Prestwick.
1869	Tom Morris, Jr............	St. Andrews..........	157	Prestwick.
1870	Tom Morris, Jr............	St. Andrews..........	149	Prestwick.

There was no championship in 1871, but in 1872 the St. Andrews Honorable Company of Edinburgh Golfers and the Prestwick Club offered a championship cup worth one hundred pounds to replace the belt, and to be a perpetual challenge trophy played for at the respective grounds of the three clubs, open to both amateurs and professionals, as had been the belt, the winner to be determined by a score of 36 holes. Only two amateurs have been successful, namely, Mr. John Ball and Mr. H. H. Hilton, both Englishmen; and Mr. Ball bears the additional honor of having won the amateur championship four times. In the open championship, money is given winning professionals, and medals to the amateurs.

FRONT VIEW—BEGINNING OF FULL SWING FOR DRIVING—CORRECT POSITION

WINNERS OF OPEN CHAMPIONSHIP CUP

Year.	Winner.	Club.	Score.	Where played.
1872	Tom Morris, Jr.	St. Andrews	166	Prestwick.
1873	Tom Kidd	St. Andrews	179	St. Andrews.
1874	Mungo Park	Musselburgh	159	Musselburgh.
1875	Willie Park	Musselburgh	166	Prestwick.
1876	Bob Martin	St. Andrews	176	St. Andrews.
1877	Jamie Anderson	St. Andrews	160	Musselburgh.
1878	Jamie Anderson	St. Andrews	157	Prestwick.
1879	Jamie Anderson	St. Andrews	170	St. Andrews.
1880	Bob Fergusson	Musselburgh	162	Musselburgh.
1881	Bob Fergusson	Musselburgh	170	Prestwick.
1882	Bob Fergusson	Musselburgh	171	St. Andrews.
1883	Willie Fernie*	Dumfries	159	Musselburgh.
1884	Jack Simpson	Carnoustie	160	Musselburgh.
1885	Bob Martin	St. Andrews	171	St. Andrews.
1886	D. Brown	Musselburgh	157	Musselburgh.
1887	Willie Park, Jr.	Musselburgh	161	Prestwick.
1888	Jack Burns	Warwick	171	St. Andrews.
1889	Willie Park, Jr.‡	Musselburgh	155	Musselburgh.
1890	John Ball, Jr.	Hoylake	164	Prestwick.
1891	Hugh Kirkaldy	St. Andrews	166	St. Andrews.
1892	H. H. Hilton†	Hoylake	305	Muirfield.
1893	William Auchterlonie	St. Andrews	322	Prestwick.
1894	J. H. Taylor		326	Sandwich.

* After tie with Bob Fergusson.   † After tie with Andrew Kirkaldy.
‡ Course increased from 2 rounds of 18 holes to 4 rounds, or 72 holes.

AMATEUR CHAMPIONSHIP

The Royal Liverpool Club, held the first amateur tournament in 1885 on its links at Hoylake, following which the clubs of England and Scotland united in giving a challenge cup for annual play under tournament conditions.

Year.	Winner.	Where played.
1886	Horace G. Hutchinson	St. Andrews.
1887	Horace G. Hutchinson	Hoylake.
1888	John Ball, Jr.	Prestwick.
1889	J. E. Laidlay	St. Andrews.
1890	John Ball, Jr.	Hoylake.
1891	J. E. Laidley	St. Andrews.
1892	John Ball, Jr.	Sandwich.
1893	P. C. Anderson	Prestwick.
1894	John Ball, Jr.	Hoylake.

LEADING BRITISH CLUBS

Club	Established	Club	Established
Royal Blackheath Golf Club	1608	Prestwick Golf Club	1851
Edinburgh Burgess Golfing Society	1735	Prestwick St. Nicholas Golf Club	1851
Hon. Company of Edinburgh Golfers	1744	Tantallon Golf Club	1853
St. Andrews	1754	Cupar Golf Club	1855
Bruntsfield Links Golf Club	1761	Dunbar Golf Club	1856
Royal Musselburgh Golf Club	1774	Bruntsfield Allied Golf Club	1856
Crail Golfing Society	1786	Pau Golf Club	1856
Royal Albert Golf Club	1810	Earlsberry and Elie Golf Club	1858
Aberdeen Club	1815	Warrender Golf Club	1858
Old Manchester Golf Club	1818	King James VI. Golf Club	1859
Innerleven Golf Club	1820	Royal North Devon Golf Club, Westward Ho	1864
Royal Perth Golf Society and County and City Club	1824	London Scottish Golf Club	1865
Calcutta Golf Club	1829	Royal Wimbledon Golf Club	1865
Montrose Academy Golf Club	1832	Royal Liverpool Golf Club	1869
North Berwick Golf Club	1832	Montreal	1873
Carnoustie and Taymouth	1839	Great Yarmouth Golf Club	1882
Royal Bombay Gymkhana Golf Club	1842	Portobello Golf Club—instituted 1856—resuscitated	1893
Panmure Golf Club	1845	St. George's Golf Club, Sandwich	1887
Seven-Thistle Golf Club	1846	Ranelagh Golf Club	1890
Lanark Golf Club	1851		

LEADING CLUBS IN UNITED STATES

	Established		Established
St. Andrews, Yonkers	1888	Tuxedo	1893
Shinnecock Hills Golf Club	1890	Essex (Mass.)	1893
Brookline (Boston)	1892	Chicago	1893-4
Newport	1892-3		

RULES FOR THE GAME

1. The game of Golf is played by two or more sides, each playing its own ball. A side may consist of one or more persons.

2. The game consists in each side playing a ball from a tee into a hole by successive strokes, and the hole is won by the side holing its ball in the fewest strokes, except as otherwise provided for in the rules. If two sides hole out in the same number of strokes, the hole is halved.

3. The teeing ground shall be indicated by two marks placed in a line at right angles to the course, and the player shall not tee in front of, nor on either side of, these marks, nor more than two club lengths behind them. A ball played from outside the limits of the teeing ground, as thus defined, may be recalled by the opposite side.

The hole shall be 4¼ inches in diameter, and at least 4 inches deep.

4. The ball must be fairly struck at, and not pushed, scraped, or spooned, under penalty of the loss of the hole. Any movement of the club which is intended to strike the ball is a stroke.

5. The game commences by each side playing a ball from the first teeing ground. In a match with two or more on a side, the partners shall strike off alternately from the tees, and shall strike alternately during the play of the hole.

The players who are to strike against each other shall be named at starting, and shall continue in the same order during the match.

The player who shall play first on each side shall be named by his own side.

In case of failure to agree, it shall be settled by lot or toss which side shall have the option of leading.

6. If a player shall play when his partner should have done so, his side shall lose the hole, except in the case of the tee shot, when the stroke may be recalled at the option of the opponents.

7. The side winning a hole shall lead in starting for the next hole, and may recall the opponent's stroke should he play out of order. This privilege is called the "honor." On starting for a new match, the winner of the long match in the previous round is entitled to the "honor." Should the first match have been halved, the winner of the last hole gained is entitled to the "honor."

8. One round of the Links—generally 18 holes—is a match, unless otherwise agreed upon. The match is won by the side which gets more holes ahead than there remain holes to be played, or by the side winning the last hole when the match was all even at the second last hole. If both sides have won the same number, it is a halved match.

9. After the balls are struck from the tee, the ball farthest from the hole to which the parties are playing shall be played first, except as oth-

erwise provided for in the rules. Should the wrong side play first, the opponent may recall the stroke before his side has played.

10. Unless with the opponent's consent, a ball struck from the tee shall not be changed, touched, or moved before the hole is played out, under the penalty of one stroke, except as otherwise provided for in the rules.

11. In playing through the green, all *loose* impediments, within a club length of a ball which is not lying in or touching a hazard, may be removed, but loose impediments which are more than a club length from the ball shall not be removed under the penalty of one stroke.

12. Before striking at the ball, the player shall not move, bend, or break anything fixed or growing near the ball, except in the act of placing his feet on the ground for the purpose of addressing the ball, and in soling his club to address the ball, under the penalty of the loss of the hole, except as provided for in Rule 18.

13. A ball stuck fast in wet ground or sand may be taken out and replaced loosely in the hole which it has made.

14. When a ball lies in or touches a hazard, the club shall not touch the ground, nor shall anything be touched or moved before the player strikes at the ball, except that the player may place his feet firmly on the ground for the purpose of addressing the ball, under the penalty of the loss of the hole.

15. A "hazard" shall be any bunker of whatever nature—water, sand, loose earth, mole-hills, paths, roads or railways, whins, bushes, rushes, rabbit scrapes, fences, ditches, or anything which is not the ordinary green of the course, except sand blown on to the grass by wind, or sprinkled on grass for the preservation of the Links, or snow or ice, or bare patches on the course.

16. A player or a player's caddie shall not press down or remove any irregularities of surface near the ball, except at the Teeing Ground, under the penalty of the loss of the hole.

17. If any vessel, wheelbarrow, tool, roller, grass-cutter, box, or other similar obstruction has been placed upon the course, such obstruction may be removed. A ball lying on or touching such obstruction, or on clothes, or nets, or on ground under repair or temporarily covered up or opened, may be lifted and dropped at the nearest point of the course, but a ball lifted in a hazard shall be dropped in the hazard. A ball lying in a golf hole or flag hole may be lifted and dropped not more than a club length behind such hole.

18. When a ball is completely covered with fog, bent, whins, etc., only so much thereof shall be set aside as that the player shall have a view of his ball before he plays, whether in a line with the hole or otherwise.

19. When a ball is to be dropped, the player shall drop it. He shall front the hole, stand erect behind the hazard, keep the spot from which the ball was lifted (or, in the case of running water, the spot at which it entered) in a line between him and the hole, and drop the ball behind him from his head, standing as far behind the hazard as he may please.

20. When the balls in play lie within six inches of each other—measured from their nearest points—the ball nearer the hole shall be lifted until the other is played, and shall then be replaced as nearly as possible in its original position. Should the ball farther from the hole be accidentally moved in so doing, it shall be replaced. Should the lie of the lifted ball be altered by the opponent in playing, it may be placed in a lie near to, and as nearly as possible similar to, that from which it was lifted.

21. If the ball lie or be lost in water, the player may drop a ball, under the penalty of one stroke.

22. Whatever happens by accident to a ball *in motion*, such as its being deflected or stopped by any agency outside the match, or by the forecaddie, is a "rub of the green," and the ball shall be played from where it lies. Should a ball lodge in anything moving, such ball, or, if it cannot be recovered, another ball, shall be dropped as nearly as possible at the spot where the object was when the ball lodged in it. But if a ball *at rest* be displaced by any agency outside the match, the player shall drop it or another ball as nearly as possible at the spot where it lay. On the Putting Green the ball may be replaced by hand.

23. If the player's ball strike, or be accidentally moved by, an opponent or an opponent's caddie or clubs, the opponent loses the hole.

24. If the player's ball strike, or be stopped by, himself or his partner, or either of their caddies or clubs, or if, while in the act of playing, the player strike the ball twice, his side loses the hole.

25. If the player when not making a stroke, or his partner or either of their caddies, touch their side's ball, except at the tee, so as to move it, or by touching anything cause it to move, the penalty is one stroke.

26. A ball is considered to have been moved if it leave its original position in the least degree and stop in another; but if a player touch his ball and thereby cause it to oscillate, without causing it to leave its original position, it is not moved in the sense of Rule 25.

27. A player's side loses a stroke if he play the opponent's ball, unless (1) the opponent then play the player's ball, whereby the penalty is cancelled, and the hole must be played out with the balls thus exchanged, or (2) the mistake occur through wrong information given by the opponent, in which case the mistake, if discovered before the opponent has played, must be rectified by placing a ball as nearly as possible where the opponent's ball lay.

If it be discovered before either side has struck off at the tee that one side has played out the previous hole with the ball of a party not engaged in the match, that side loses that hole.

28. If a ball be lost, the player's side loses the hole. A ball shall be held as lost if it be not found within five minutes after the search is begun.

29. A ball must be played wherever it lies, or the hole be given up, except as otherwise provided for in the Rules.

30. The term "Putting Green" shall mean the ground within 20 yards of the hole, excepting hazards.

31. All loose impediments may be removed from the Putting Green, except the opponent's ball when at a greater distance from the player's than six inches.

32. In a match of three or more sides, a ball in any degree lying between the player and the hole must be lifted, or, if on the Putting Green, holed out.

33. When the ball is on the Putting Green, no mark shall be placed, nor line drawn as a guide. The line to the hole may be pointed out, but the person doing so may not touch the ground with the hand or club.

The player may have his own or his partner's caddie to stand at the hole, but none of the players or their caddies may move so as to shield the ball from, or expose it to, the wind.

The penalty for any breach of this rule is the loss of the hole.

34. The player or his caddie may remove (but not press down) sand, earth, worm casts, or snow lying around the hole or on the line of his put. This shall be done by brushing lightly with the hand only across the put and not along it. Dung may be removed to a side by an iron club, but the club must not be laid with more than its own weight upon the ground. The putting line must not be touched by club, hand, or foot, except as above authorized, or immediately in front of the ball in the act of addressing it, under the penalty of the loss of the hole.

35. Either side is entitled to have the flag-stick removed when approaching the hole. If the ball rest against the flag-stick when in the hole, the player shall be entitled to remove the stick, and, if the ball fall in, it shall be considered as holed out in the previous stroke.

36. A player shall not play until the opponent's ball shall have ceased to roll, under the penalty of one stroke. Should the player's ball knock in the opponent's ball, the latter shall be counted as holed out in the previous stroke. If, in playing, the player's ball displace the opponent's ball, the opponent shall have the option of replacing it.

37. A player shall not ask for advice, nor be knowingly advised about the game by word, look, or gesture from any one except his own caddie, or his partner or partner's caddie, under the penalty of the loss of the hole.

38. If a ball split into separate pieces, another ball may be put down where the largest portion lies, or if two pieces are apparently of equal size, it may be put where either piece lies, at the option of the player. If a ball crack or become unplayable, the player may change it, on intimating to his opponent his intention to do so.

39. A penalty stroke shall not be counted the stroke of a player, and shall not affect the rotation of play.

40. Should any dispute arise on any point, the players have the right of determining the party or parties to whom the dispute shall be referred, but should they not agree, either party may refer it to the Green Committee of the green where the dispute occurs, and their decision shall be final. Should the dispute not be covered by the Rules of Golf, the arbiters must decide it by equity.

SPECIAL RULES FOR MEDAL PLAY

1. In Club competitions, the competitor doing the stipulated course in fewest strokes shall be the winner.

2. If the lowest score be made by two or more competitors, the ties shall be decided by another round to be played either on the same or on any other day as the Captain, or, in his absence, the Secretary, shall direct.

3. New holes shall be made for the Medal Round, and thereafter no member shall play any stroke on a Putting Green before competing.

4. The scores shall be kept by a special marker, or by the competitors noting each other's scores. The scores marked shall be checked at the finish of each hole. On completion of the course, the score of the player shall be signed by the person keeping the score and handed to the Secretary.

5. If a ball be lost, the player shall return as nearly as possible to the spot where the ball was struck, tee another ball, and lose a stroke. If the lost ball be found before he has struck the other ball, the first shall continue in play.

6. If the player's ball strike himself, or his clubs, or caddie, or if, in the act of playing, the player strike the ball twice, the penalty shall be one stroke.

7. If a competitor's ball strike the other player, or his clubs or caddie, it is a "rub of the green," and the ball shall be played from where it lies.

8. A ball may, under a penalty of two strokes, be lifted out of a difficulty of any description, and be teed behind same.

9. All balls shall be holed out, and when play is on the Putting Green, the flag shall be removed, and the competitor whose ball is nearest the hole shall have the option of holing out first, or of lifting his ball, if it be in such a position that it might, if left, give an advantage to the other competitor. Throughout the green a competitor can have the other competitor's ball lifted, if he find that it interferes with his stroke.

10. A competitor may not play with a professional, and he may not receive advice from any one but his caddie.

A forecaddie may be employed.

11. Competitors may not discontinue play because of bad weather.

12. The penalty for a breach of any rule shall be disqualification.

13. Any dispute regarding the play shall be determined by the Green Committee.

14. The ordinary Rules of Golf, so far as they are not at variance with these special rules, shall apply to medal play.

LOCAL RULES FOR ST. ANDREWS LINKS

1. When the Green Committee consider it necessary, a telegraph-board shall be used to give the numbers for starting.

2. If the ball lie in any position in the Swilcan Burn, whether in water or not, the player may drop it, or if it cannot be recovered, another ball may be dropped on the line where it entered the burn, on the oppo-

site side to the hole to that to which he is playing, under the penalty of one stroke.

3. Should a ball be driven into the water of the Eden at the high hole, or into the Sea at the first hole, the ball, or, if it cannot be recovered, another ball, shall be teed a club length in front of either river or sea near the spot where it entered, under the penalty of one stroke.

4. A ball in the enclosure (between the road and dyke holes) called the Station-master's Garden shall be a lost ball.

5. If a ball lie within two yards of a fixed seat, it may be lifted and dropped two yards to the side of the seat farthest from the hole.

6. Any dispute respecting the play shall be determined by the Green Committee.

7. Competitions for the Spring and Autumn Medals of the Club (with the exception of the George Glennie Medal) shall be decided by playing one round of the Links, and the competitor doing it in fewest strokes shall be the winner.

8. The order of starting for the Spring and Autumn Medals will be balloted for on the previous evening, and intending competitors must give in their names to the Secretary not later than five o'clock on the previous evening. Any competitor not at the Teeing Ground when his number is called shall be disqualified, unless it be proved to the satisfaction of the Green Committee or Secretary that he has a valid excuse, such as serious temporary illness, a train late, or such like, in which case he may be allowed to compete, and, if allowed, shall be placed at the bottom of the list. The absent competitor's partner may start in his proper turn, provided he gets another player to play with him.

9. Competitors for medals or prizes are not allowed to delay starting on account of bad weather, but must strike off immediately after the preceding party has crossed the burn, and, after they have started, are not allowed to take shelter, but must complete their round in the order of their start. In cases of stoppage by accident, or severe temporary illness, the Green Committee may allow a competitor to resume play.

10. All private matches must be delayed till the last medal competitors have holed out at the first hole.

ETIQUETTE OF GOLF

The following customs belong to the Established Etiquette of Golf, and should be observed by all Golfers:

1. No player, caddie, or onlooker should move or talk during a stroke.

2. No player should play from the tee until the party in front have played their second strokes and are out of range, nor play to the Putting Green till the party in front have holed out and moved away.

3. The player who leads from the tee should be allowed to play before his opponent tees his ball.

4. Players who have holed out should not try their putts over again when other players are following them.

5. Players looking for a lost ball must allow any other match coming up to pass them.

6. A party playing three or more balls must allow a two-ball match to pass them.

7 A party playing a shorter round must allow a two-ball match playing the whole round to pass them.

8. A player should not putt at the hole when the flag is in it.

9. The reckoning of the strokes is kept by the terms "the odd," "two more," "three more," etc., and "one off three," "one off two," "the like." The reckoning of the holes is kept by the terms—so many "holes up "—or "all even "—and—so many " to play."

10. Turf cut or displaced by a stroke in playing should be at once replaced.

XVI

FIRST LESSONS

First of all let me say that no single chapter can give all the instruction necessary to cover the different strokes and situations arising in golf—pronounced g-o-f-f, by the way, not g-o-l-f. It was not my original intention to write this one, but so many inquiries have come to me about the game, I thought it might fill a place. This chapter is intended solely for beginners, whom I shall hope to give a few suggestions founded on sorrowful experience and a careful study of the game in its home. The illustrations of positions are from instantaneous photographs of Willie Dunn, son of the famous Willie Dunn, deceased, contemporary of "Old Tom" Morris, with whom he had many a golfing battle over Scotland's links. Dunn's form is said by those who know to be the very best, and we commend a study of the photographs to American golfers.

Probably there is no game, unless it be court-tennis, that requires so complete a mastery of first principles and such faithful practice in its rudimentary strokes. The elementary instruction of every game is of course most important, and its thorough adaptation by the pupil necessary to the development of highest skill. In golf, however, as well as in tennis, one may never acquire consistent form if he have not started off properly. He may ride a bicycle, play lawn-tennis, baseball, box, and even fence in a duffer sort of way, yet make a fair showing and have good sport, but he cannot play golf until he has mastered the very first strokes. Herein lies the fascination of the game, which, while appearing so simple to the on-looker, becomes most difficult when he takes a club and makes his first attempt at driving off the tee.

It is not that there are so many intricate rules in golf, but the few must be mastered thoroughly; and it is well for the beginner to remember that one of England's champions declares it takes six months, playing three times a week, before one may be said to have acquired consistent form.

CHOOSING CLUBS.—The golfer of to-day uses more iron clubs than formerly, probably because of the substitution of gutta-percha for feather-stuffed leather balls, but more likely on account of the ingenuity of manufacturers, that has provided different-shaped heads for different "lies"

THE WAGGLE

of the ball. Then, too, experience has taught that certain situations require heavier and stiffer clubs for the best work. Really good clubs are hard to get, and the beginner will do well to trust their purchase to some one who is experienced. They must not be too heavy, else they overbalance the player, but the shafts should be stiffish and of hickory, which is commonly used and is the best; orange wood and ash have been employed, but neither is so good as hickory. The heads of the wooden clubs should be of beech; other woods are harder, but it is not well to have it so, as the driving quality is lessened thereby. Remember, the more the face is laid back on all your clubs, the higher they will loft the ball. Straight-faced drivers and brassies drive farther and tend to more accurate play. Do not use extreme clubs of any kind; choose the one that experience has taught is the best for the play, and if you do your part properly the club will do the rest. There is somewhat of a fad among inexperienced players to buy, for large sums, clubs that professionals have used; but it is a futile extravagance; you may get just as good if only you use judgment in their selection.

FRONT VIEW—ENDING OF FULL SWING AFTER DRIVE—INCORRECT POSITION

The number of different clubs put on the market of late years is considerable, and new patents are constantly being taken out; but, as a matter of fact, seven are all any one needs—viz., driver, brassy, cleek, iron, lofter, mashie, putter.

Willie Dunn uses only six—driver, brassy, cleek, iron, lofter, niblick, and putts off the cleek. On the other side, as a rule, first-class golfers use seven—driver, brassy, cleek, iron, lofter, mashie, and wooden putter; they use the latter for ten-yard putts or over, and under that distance the cleek.

FIRST LESSONS

Driver.—Wooden club used off the tee, and thereafter whenever the lie is good enough. There are two kinds—straight-faced and bulgers; the latter, from the oval conformation of the head, are more difficult to handle, but, if you hit true, are better for straight driving. Beginners had best use straight-faced ones until they are absolutely certain of hitting where they aim. The bulger is only for the skilled player. Pick out a stiffish club, and execute the waggle to see how it feels in the hands: it should have a pronounced pliability down towards the head.

Brassy.—Wooden club, soled with iron, to be used where the lie of ball is not good enough for driver or the distance less than full drive. It should be shorter and stiffer of shaft, and more laid back in face to raise the ball.

Cleek.—Iron club used for worse lie than brassy and shorter distance. Beginners are apt to use it for driving, which is a mistake. If you cannot handle the regular driver (also a mistaken basis from which to start, because you should persevere until you can manage it), have one made with shorter and stiffer handle. It is bad to begin your driving off iron. The cleek should be shorter than brassy, and shaft stiffer.

FRONT VIEW—ENDING OF FULL SWING AFTER DRIVE—CORRECT POSITION

Choose thick heads, always remembering what is gained in loft is lost in distance. The blade is narrower than that of the lofter or iron; in fact, it has the straightest face next to putter.

BACK VIEW—ENDING OF FULL SWING AFTER DRIVE—CORRECT POSITION

Iron.—Shorter and stiffer shaft, and face more laid back than cleek. Is used for shorter distances than that club, and for playing out of long grass or what is called a bad lie. There are three kinds—driving, lofting, and heavy. Choose a medium one, with face neither too straight nor too laid back.

Mashie.—Compromise between iron and niblick, and has come to be used very generally now in place of the latter. Shorter and stiffer than iron, face laid farther back. Used for shorter strokes and for getting out of bunker, rut in road, long grass, or very bad lie. Beginners had better stick to iron, as the face of mashie, and especially of niblick, is so small as to require accuracy in hitting, though they pitch the ball deader.

Lofter.—Face most laid back of all the clubs. Used by experienced players with great skill in pitching ball dead on approach shot. Used largely for getting out of sand and over hazards, generally, where it is desired to raise the ball in its flight.

Putter.—There has always been considerable controversy over the relative merits of the iron and wooden putter, and some of the old Scotch school have never become reconciled to the more modern metal. It is very generally conceded, however, by first-class players that wood is best for long putts, and iron for short ones. The latter is a trifle laid back, and puts a drag on the ball, making it run off closer to the ground. When you become a veteran you can use metal for short putts, and add a wooden one to your clubs for long ones.

HOLDING CLUB.—Do not grip the club tightly, nor yet loosely; the dividing line is narrow but distinct. You should feel the shaft with fingers and palm, and more firmly with left than with right hand. Have the hands close together, the right in front of left; remember that every inch separating them means yards off the flight of ball. A loose grip argues uncertain driving; too tight with right hand, a tendency to slice the ball. Messrs. Hutchinson and Dunn advise both thumbs over the club, the left a trifle more than the right.

ADDRESSING THE BALL.—It would take a chapter alone to comment on the many different styles of addressing, and as it is not a matter of great importance it would be space wasted. There is altogether too much made of this incident to driving. A certain amount of it is good,

BACK VIEW—ENDING OF FULL SWING AFTER DRIVE—INCORRECT POSITION

FRONT VIEW OF FEET
FOR DRIVING—
CORRECT POSITION

FRONT VIEW OF FEET
FOR DRIVING—
INCORRECT POSITION

but too much is—not precisely bad, but rather fatiguing—to your opponent, for instance. The waggle is the beginning of the address, and betrays the player's temperament as no other feature of any game does. It may be menacing, solemnly warning, sanguine, nervous, phlegmatic—there is no end to individual manœuvre, which may promise much in preliminary flourish, but prove disappointing in the fulfilment. It has its usefulness, however. You begin your address by placing the club back of the ball and carrying it over and forward to take aim as it were; then you follow with the waggle proper (done by the wrists) as a sort of warming up, in which you feel the club with your fingers and palms, and the ground with the balls of your feet. It is well to remember about feeling the ground with your feet: the novice is apt to become lost amid the flourishes and forget to stand firmly on the ground, thus losing balance at the stroke. Always, after your flourish, place the club behind the ball, resting it an instant before the final sweep. Never swing at the ball from your flourish. In fact, beginners ought to make no flourishes; carry your club forward in the direction you intend driving, rest it back of the ball, and then swing. Flourishing is disconcerting to the tyro.

DRIVING. — Treatises go into mathematical niceties over the correct position in driving, such as to confuse the beginner. The chief thing for him to remember is to stand square to the ball; left eye, hands, club, and ball all in a vertical line, at right angles with proposed line of ball's flight; weight on left leg; feet 18 inches apart, and right one about two inches behind left; hands holding club just inside left knee (this is

ADDRESSING BALL FOR DRIVE — CORRECT POSITION

CORRECT POSITION OF FEET IN HIGH LOFTING

true of position in all strokes). Your distance from ball will be correct if, with the heel of club at ball, the end of shaft should touch left knee of player as he stands upright. Incidentally, remember, as distance for stroke decreases, have the ball nearer right toe.

The closer the feet the freer the swing, but if too close the driving is apt to be weakened and inaccurate; with feet far apart the player becomes stiffened, shortening the drive, though gaining great power. In the swing, bear in mind that as your club goes up so it will come down;

slow up swing, relatively speaking, is a *sine qua non* of fine driving. Regard the left arm as part of the club, and keep it taut. The greatest amount of practice is necessary to allow arms to swing well away, and yet bring them down and in, for the club must be travelling in the intended flight of ball when brought down. Mr. Horace Hutchinson, whose Badminton volume is far and away the most complete, instructive, and interesting of anything published on the game, explains this point clearly thus: Take a spot on the ground, and then draw away your club. You will find the only way to extend the proposed line of flight, *backward*, is to straighten out the arms well; if you bend them you find the head of club leaving the line. In the up swing, left arm should rest comfortably across chest, slightly bent at elbow; do not pause at top of swing; increase speed as you bring club downward, and get in your power when about 18 inches from the ball.

FRONT VIEW—BEGINNING OF HIGH-LOFTING STROKE

At the moment of hitting the ball you must be in precisely the same position as at the time of addressing it. This is the difficulty of golf, and can be acquired only by patient, persistent practice. There is no short-cut to golfing success. Remember to *sweep* away the ball—a sort of scythe motion; the beginner is likely to think only of hitting it. Never jerk your club except in bunker or similar hazard. Do not tighten up when you strike the ball, or try to knock it out of sight. Be easy, follow the ball with your club, and keep your feet on the ground. Hit fairly, clearly, firmly, not wildly.

Do not bother about too much detail at first. A beginner is likely to ask and be given no end of confusing and oftentimes worthless advice. He should seek counsel of one competent to give it, and then follow it, bearing in mind he must practise for weeks and months before he will have any form. He is apt to do better the first few times he plays, when he has no thought of style, and is intent only on whacking the ball, than a little later. Golf is learned by imitation, largely, and it is likewise, more than any other game, full of mimics. It is not good to become one of the latter, because mannerisms are not of the slightest value, and are to be avoided. Watch good form; try to attain a free style, and practise with that end constantly in view. It

FRONT VIEW—FINISH OF HIGH-LOFTING STROKE

is not possible, of course, for all men to have the same style. A very heavy man cannot expect to get the swing and freedom of a more athletically built one. Each player has a style that, starting (or at least it should start) from the one basis, is the reflection of the age at which he began, and of himself physically and mentally.

There is a great deal of buncombe about the waggle and style, the importance of both being greatly exaggerated. What the beginner need concern himself about is to get accuracy; keep the club travelling in the direction of the ball after the strike, and follow with the body; get the shoulders into the sweep—the entire body, in fact; bear weight on left leg at the address, transferring it to right on up swing, and again to the left as the ball is swept away. Let the lifting of knee and left heel on up swing be incidental to the swing—*i.e.*, you must not set out to do it, it will come in due course. Stand steady, feeling the ground with your feet; keep direction of swing right, and the eye *always* on the ball. Above all, keep your mind on the business of the moment; think of what you are trying to do; beginners are inclined to fancy golf so simple as to require no especial mental application. Never play weakly; remember the length of swing, and not strength of sweep, regulates carry of the ball. Use weaker clubs instead of making weaker effort. A full shot is the full swing; three-quarter shot, shoulders do not turn, work being done by arms, legs, and hips; half shot, use arms from elbow joints only;

FRONT VIEW—GETTING OUT OF A BUNKER

quarter shot is chiefly made by wrists.

Concentrate your efforts on learning to get the swing (no matter whether you hit the ball or not at first, hitting is of small importance compared with getting the swing properly), to drive straight; play out of a bad lie and loft out of a hole. When you can do these things in some degree of form you may call yourself a golfer. It is not enough to learn to drive. You must drive straight; that is important, else you get off the course, and lose considerably.

LOFTING A STIMIE

This is where the value of accuracy makes itself apparent. Remember the injunction not to use the cleek for driving, and remember also, if you do, that the "divots" (sods) you cut out should be replaced at once. Practise with the driver until you master it—in fact, make it a point to take that club which puzzles you and work with it until you control it.

Golf play is made up of driving, iron play, and putting, and of these driving is the most pleasing. Iron clubs are much the best for approaching the putting

FRONT VIEW—BEGINNING OF THREE-QUARTER SWING

FRONT VIEW—ENDING OF THREE-QUARTER SWING

green, and you should endeavor always to lay your ball dead.

An approach shot is one within sixty yards of the green, and it is difficult play. Only your instructor can give you the practical instruction that is needed here. But bear in mind that in all iron shots you play off your right foot—*i. e.*, right foot in advance (whereas in driving left foot is in advance), weight on left leg—ball distant the length of club to left knee, as in driving, and on a line that would run about midway between feet.

Putting is the least interesting and very important, though many ignore, or rather slight it, because of the difficulty, which is greater than in driving. Many a game has been won on the green. Practise long and carefully, but be sure you have a well-balanced club. Hit smoothly without jerk. Putt with the wrists. Let the club work from them, in fact, as a pendulum. Assume a position from which you can best send the putter straight as it meets the ball. Stand open, half facing hole, weight slightly on left leg, right foot in advance, ball equal distance between feet. In short putts of three or four yards and less, rest right elbow on thigh; be sure of the *exact* spot on putter that will hit the ball; hold club with both hands equally, and always "be up"—*i. e.*, putt strong enough to reach the hole. It is better to pass it than not strong enough to reach it.

The pleasure of golf depends very considerably on the quality of ground. Your links must not be too easy, nor yet too difficult, and the carries (distances from tee over bunker) should not be too long, so that the medium driver may have a chance. There should be plenty of hazards, so arranged that every hole is guarded. In fact, for good golf a difficulty should be put in the way of every shot. Putting-greens (and our American ones, generally speaking, are very poor) should be about thirty yards in diameter, and the hole ought to be moved when worn. Greens should be absolutely clear of obstruction and as smooth as possible. I mention this because so many that are planning home-made links seem to think the green

BEGINNING OF HALF IRON SHOT—
CORRECT POSITION

ENDING OF HALF IRON SHOT—
CORRECT POSITION

should have its share of trials. There is tribulation enough on the green without increasing it artificially. In building bunkers throw up the ground on the farther side, so the excavation becomes part of the hazard; the bunker should slant from the player (not straight-faced), and the bank be wide.

I follow with a few definitions in reply to the many letters received on the subject. The *Links* is the course of holes—18 being the regulation, but 12 is the largest number on any links in America, though Shinnecock intends lengthening its 12 to 18. *Tee*—starting-point. *Caddie*—generally speaking, the boy that carries your clubs; on the other side, however, he is often counsellor and father-confessor. To *foozle* or *duff* a shot means to bungle it. *Topping*—not hitting well behind the ball. *Slicing*—bringing club down with a cut instead of squarely. *Heeling*—hitting ball with heel of club. *Toeing*—hitting with toe. *Fore*—called at the time of driving to warn players in front of you.

Two holes up—means you are leading the opponent by two holes. *Dormie*—when you are leading your

FRONT VIEW—PUTTING—CORRECT POSITION

FRONT VIEW—PUTTING—INCORRECT POSITION

opponent by as many holes as there are left to play, so that were he to win all remaining, he could only tie you; for instance, if you were two up and two to play.

Stimie is the situation where your opponent's ball is between yours and the hole, and more than 6 inches separating the two balls. You are obliged to loft over it; if the balls were within 6 inches of each other you could remove opponent's while you played.

He whose ball is behind always plays first.

Those on putting-green are entitled to hole out before following ones play up to it.

Players in front are each entitled to second shot before following players tee off.

Do not talk while player is making his shot. Keep away 5 to 6 yards, and stand at side—never behind.

Never go on green while others are playing there.

A four-some (4 players) is entitled to pass two-some (2 players) on the links, and both to pass three-some. All of which must read ridiculously simple to golfers; but the newness of the game in this country warrants its publication for beginners.

Finally, get the St. Andrews (Scotland) club rules and abide by them. There is a tendency to petty infringement which should not be tolerated. To play three rounds a week is good; more than four is not advisable; but whenever you play, never fail to watch your swing: it is the most important; and always keep your eye on the ball once you start to play it.

THE END

www.ingramcontent.com/pod-product-compliance
Lightning Source LLC
Chambersburg PA
CBHW030604300426
44111CB00009B/1093